the Unofficial Guide™ to

Casino Gambling

Basil Nestor

WILEY

Wiley Publishing, Inc.

Library of Congress Cataloging-in-Publication Data:

ISBN: 0-02-862917-5

Manufactured in the United States of America

10 9 8 7

First edition

*This book is dedicated to Freddy Koenig.
Though I hardly knew you, our friendship was the
catalyst for most of the gambling and winning
I have accomplished in life.*

Acknowledgments

Thanks to Allen Brivic for his sports betting insights;
Bobbi Anderson for answering my endless questions;
Georgiana Nestor for her patience; A. James Lee for getting
me started in the gambling business; Ben Feiler for being a
nice guy; Frank Slinkman for checking my figures.

Special thanks to Fay Nestor for her loving support
and advice. Gratitude and appreciation to
Merv Griffin for teaching me how to win in a casino.

Contents

The *Unofficial Guide* Reader's Bill of Rights

We Give You More Than the Official Line

Welcome to the *Unofficial Guide* series of Lifestyles titles—books that deliver critical, unbiased information that other books can't or won't reveal—*the inside scoop*. Our goal is to provide you with the *most accessible, useful* information and advice possible. The recommendations we offer in these pages are not influenced by the corporate line of any organization or industry; we give you the hard facts, whether those institutions like them or not. If something is ill-advised or will cause a loss of time and/or money, we'll give you ample warning. And if it is a worthwhile option, we'll let you know that, too.

Armed and Ready

Our handpicked authors confidently and critically report on a wide range of topics that matter to smart readers like you. Our authors are passionate about their subjects, but have distanced themselves enough from them to help you be armed and protected, and help you make educated decisions as you go through your process. It is our intent that, from having read this book, you will avoid the pitfalls everyone else falls into and get it right the first time.

Don't be fooled by cheap imitations; this is the *genuine article Unofficial Guide* series from Wiley Publishing, Inc. You may be familiar with our proven track record of the travel *Unofficial Guides*, which have more than two million copies in print. Each year thousands of travelers—new and old—are armed with a brand new, fully updated edition of the flagship *Unofficial Guide to Walt Disney World*, by Bob Sehlinger. It is our intention here to provide you with the same level of objective authority that Mr. Sehlinger does in his brainchild.

The Unofficial Panel of Experts

Every work in the Lifestyle *Unofficial Guides* is intensively inspected by a team of three top professionals in their fields. These experts review the manuscript for factual accuracy, comprehensiveness, and an insider's determination as to whether the manuscript fulfills the credo in this Reader's Bill of Rights. In other words, our Panel ensures that you are, in fact, getting "the inside scoop."

Our Pledge

The authors, the editorial staff, and the Unofficial Panel of Experts assembled for *Unofficial Guides* are determined to lay out the most valuable alternatives available for our readers. This dictum means that our writers must be explicit, prescriptive, and above all, direct. We strive to be thorough and complete, but our goal is not necessarily to have the "most" or "all" of the information on a topic; this is not, after all, an encyclopedia. Our objective is to help you narrow down your options to the best of what is available, unbiased by affiliation with any industry or organization.

In each *Unofficial Guide* we give you:

- Comprehensive coverage of necessary and vital information
- Authoritative, rigidly fact-checked data
- The most up-to-date insights into trends
- Savvy, sophisticated writing that's also readable
- Sensible, applicable facts and secrets that only an insider knows

Special Features

Every book in our series offers the following six special sidebars in the margins that are devised to help you get things done cheaply, efficiently, and smartly.

1. "Timesaver"—tips and shortcuts that save you time.

2. "Moneysaver"—tips and shortcuts that save you money.

3. "Watch Out!"—more serious cautions and warnings.

4. "Bright Idea"—general tips and shortcuts to help you find an easier or smarter way to do something.

5. "Quote"—statements from real people that are intended to be prescriptive and valuable to you.

6. "Unofficially…"—an insider's fact or anecdote.

We also recognize your need to have quick information at your fingertips, and have thus provided the following comprehensive sections at the back of the book:

1. **Glossary**—definitions of complicated terminology and jargon

2. **Resource Guide**—lists of relevant agencies, associations, institutions, Web sites, etc.

3. **Recommended Reading List**—suggested titles that can help you get more in-depth information on related topics

4. **Important Documents**—"official" pieces of information you need to refer to, such as government forms

5. **Important Statistics**—facts and numbers presented at-a-glance for easy reference

6. **Index**

Letters, Comments, and Questions from Readers

We strive to continually improve the Unofficial series, and input from our readers is a valuable way for us to do that. Many of those who have used the *Unofficial Guide* travel books write to the authors to ask questions, make comments, or share their own discoveries and lessons. For lifestyle *Unofficial Guides*, we would also appreciate all such correspondence, both positive and critical, and we will make best efforts to incorporate appropriate readers' feedback and comments in revised editions of this work.

How to write to us:

Unofficial Guides
Attention: Reader's Comments
Wiley Publishing, Inc.
111 River St.
Hoboken, NJ 07030-5774

The *Unofficial Guide* Panel of Experts

The *Unofficial Guide* editorial team recognizes that you've purchased this book with the expectation of getting the most authoritative, carefully inspected information currently available. Toward that end, on each and every title in this series, we have selected a minimum of two "official" experts comprising the "Unofficial Panel" who painstakingly review the manuscripts to ensure: factual accuracy of all data; inclusion of the most up-to-date and relevant information; and that, from an insider's perspective, the authors have armed you with all the necessary facts you need—but the institutions don't want you to know.

For *The Unofficial Guide to Casino Gambling* we are proud to introduce the following panel of experts:

Doug Glass Doug Glass is originally from Overland Park, KS. He studied mathematics at the University of Kansas (BS) and New York University (MS). While at NYU, he was the instructor for the course Games of Chance, a math elective that covered probability and statistics focusing on casino games. He currently lives in

New York City working as an IT consultant. He is not a heavy gambler, but enjoys an occasional blackjack session, gaming mostly at the riverboat casinos in Kansas City when he returns home.

Bonnie Brunner After acquiring a B.A. in Mass Communications from Queens College in New York city, Bonnie Brunner made her way to Las Vegas, Nevada. Once there, she learned to deal blackjack and mini-baccarat, first at a small casino downtown and then on the strip. She also put in some time in the count room, counting money and documentation for markers dropped in the drop boxes on individual games.

Two and a half years later she traveled across country to help open one of the foremost casinos in Atlantic City. After seven years on the floor supervising high-limit blackjack games in the baccarat pit and dealing roulette, she married and moved to upstate New York, effectively ending her gaming career.

Now a mother with two sons, she still keeps her hand in gaming by occasionally teaching and dealing blackjack for charity.

Introduction

Las Vegas generates more than $6 billion a year in gambling revenue. Atlantic City earns nearly $3 billion. That's gambling *only*. Income from hotels, restaurants and peripheral business is not included in these totals. The gambling industry in the U.S. earns more than $50 billion every year. The amount handled is measured in hundreds of billions.

And it all starts with your $5 blackjack wager.

We certainly don't want to damage the national economy or depress the stock market, but we think it would be nice for you to win the bet. That's why we wrote this book. Glance through the pages and you'll see that we designed it with you in mind. This is essential information, whatever your level of gambling expertise. The guide covers all the major casino contests and most of the minor ones. It's more than just rules; you get proven strategies for winning and limiting loss, and we also show you how to calculate the cost of your gambling entertainment. That's always the bottom line. How much will the entertainment cost?

Along the way, we debunk many of the superstitions, misconceptions and downright strange notions surrounding gambling. You may be surprised how tough it is to jettison those old ideas. Gambling and its lore reach farther into our lives than most of us realize.

Thomas Jefferson gambled and so did Harry Truman. Richard Nixon financed his first political campaign with poker winnings. Julius Caesar used a gambling metaphor ("the die is cast") before crossing the Rubicon and changing the history of the world. Our language is filled with gambling terms. Among them are ubiquitous phrases like pressing your luck, odds on favorite, smart money, sure thing, going bust, sweeten the deal, fold under pressure, passing the buck, and the (eternally poetic) luck of the draw.

Gambling is part of our legends, past and present. Wild Bill Hickok, Bat Masterson, Wyatt Earp, Howard Hughes, Frank Sinatra and the Rat Pack, Steve Wynn, and Donald Trump are just a few of the personalities wrapped up in the story of American gambling.

Everyone has a gambling anecdote. Jokes about gambling filter into every corner of our culture. "This guy walks into a bar with a horse and a pack of cards..."

Gambling is (and always has been) all around us. And yet casinos were illegal everywhere in the U.S. except Nevada for most of the 20th century. That created an odd cultural contrast. Everyone knew about gambling, but few people actually did it. The average American played poker with friends and gambled in a casino once or twice in a lifetime. People learned about the games from watching movies.

Then came Atlantic City, riverboats, Native-American casinos, the Internet and now gambling seems to be everywhere, not just conceptually but physically. Most Americans have visited a casino at least once. More than 60% of the adults in the U.S. gamble in some way at least once a year.

Everyone is doing it. Unfortunately, most of them don't know what they're doing. It's not the players' fault. The public hasn't been allowed much practice for nearly a century. And of course casinos are happy to explain the rules, but they're less eager to explain odds and strategies. In some cases the casinos don't even know the optimal strategies. Why should they?

Gamblers are on their own and it shows.

Most casino games are designed to keep between 1% and 10% of a player's money. Yet players lose on average about 20% to 40% of every dollar they take into a casino.

Much of the loss can be attributed to the practice of repeatedly risking the same money (pressing bets), but some of it is simply the result of playing badly. It's amazing, but millions of players lose billions of dollars every year because they make mistakes. They use faulty strategy and flawed systems. They throw away the wrong cards, hit when they should stand, call when they should fold, bet when they should walk away, and otherwise stack the odds to their disfavor.

People could win more (or lose less), but they don't. This bizarre phenomenon is reflected in the latest generation of video poker games that have a certified player advantage. Casinos actually promote these games. Guess what? Players still lose!

It's obvious that some people don't even try. They've been thoroughly conditioned to believe that players should never win. When they do it's considered a freak aberration, a stroke of rare luck. Hey, that's gambling right?

No, that's losing. Gambling is a series of contests. It starts when you pick odds that are favorable (or at least not too unfavorable). The house has an advantage. Sometimes you win. More times they win. Strategy plays a role. This is true to varying degrees for all casino contests, even slot machines.

Of course, there is no amount of expertise or information that can make anyone a guaranteed winner. That wouldn't be gambling, and it wouldn't be fun. Guaranteed money comes from having a job, managing investments or being a wealthy scion. That's work. Gambling is entertainment. We pay for entertainment. The contest determines the price.

The standard and correct advice (usually offered by a sagely elder) is that you should "be prepared to lose it all." Yes, but we shouldn't be too willing. Let's play the games well, lose less, win more, and receive more entertainment for each dollar spent.

This book will help you do that. Sections are organized so that you can go directly to your favorite game or quickly find an answer to a question. Chapters can be read in any order, but we encourage you to start with Part One. The information there about budgeting, calculating costs, and analyzing probabilities applies to every contest covered in the book.

Do you like slots? Machine games are covered in Part Two. We tell you how to find loose slots and how to avoid the tightest ones. Chapters 4 busts machine game myths and gives you winning strategies for video poker. Yes there are machines that pay back more than you put in, but you've got to play them the right way.

Part Three is about table games. We cover the classics including blackjack, craps, roulette, baccarat and poker, but you'll also find an entire chapter on newer games like Caribbean Stud Poker, Let It Ride, and pai gow poker. Chapter 7 explains what experienced gamblers call the "best bet in the casino." It's true. The bet has no house advantage.

When the casino hubbub gets to be too much then you'll want to read Part Four. It's about waiting games. Keno and sports betting can be inexpensive and entertaining, or they can be the equivalent of attaching your wallet to a vacuum cleaner. It depends on how you play. We'll explain the strategies and give you tips for avoiding that sucking feeling.

Part Five is about casinos and how they operate. What is a pit boss? What is a marker? We also cover subjects like comps and handling money. Do you want free tickets to see Siegfried & Roy? Read Chapter 14.

The guide also has special sections about gambling on riverboats, cruise ships, Native American casinos, and the Internet. These venues are not clones of Las Vegas or Atlantic City. They operate under different rules that could affect your game.

We'll tell you what to expect. The Internet information is particularly important. Don't play online before you read it.

Lastly, you'll want a calculator and a deck of playing cards handy. We do the heavy math, but you'll find it enlightening to occasionally crunch some of these numbers yourself. The playing cards are an excellent tool for demonstrating how the crunched numbers and the real world always agree. The congruity is sometime scary.

Remember, clutching a lucky rabbit's foot is fine, but using a good strategy is a better way to win.

Have a good time!

The Truth About Winning And Losing

GET THE SCOOP ON...
What makes a winner and a loser ▪ A simple
price-for-fun formula ▪ Dangerous gambling
mistakes ▪ Using a "bankroll"

PART 1

Simple Arithmetic: Fun Has a Price

A few years ago I produced a casino commercial called "Simple Arithmetic." It was a cute little spot that featured Merv Griffin and looked like a Loony Toons cartoon. The concept involved distance; Las Vegas was far away and Merv's casino in Louisiana was closer and cheaper to visit. So a win in Louisiana was (presumably) worth more than a win in Las Vegas. To demonstrate this I made Merv very small (as if he were far away) and I had him shout the lines "from Las Vegas." It was "Simple Arithmetic."

Bang! The casino was filled with patrons. The 800 number for reservations was swamped.

Why the big response? Well the commercial was charming, but the true power was in the premise. We were offering people an advantage, an edge. Everyone, and I mean everyone, wants an edge. Everyone wants to win.

Chapter 1

3

In fact, deep down everyone expects to win. The grownup side of us preaches caution, but the kid inside believes we're special. Did we lose? Let's make an adjustment and try it again. The wheel should spin in our favor this time. Our quarter should win the jackpot. Losing is only temporary. Winning is our nature. Right?

It's one of our finest human qualities. We call it optimism. It's a basic requirement (in proper amounts) for all successful people and all good gamblers. The fact that you're reading this book means you have optimism. And guess what? The kid inside you isn't wrong. There is a way to win more. But the adult is right too. You must understand the odds and know the real price you're paying for the contest. You must understanding the true nature of the edge that Merv was shouting about.

The nature of a gamble

Ignore the photographs of smiling winners receiving gigantic checks. Ignore the flashing signs, the dancing dollar symbols, and the ringing bells. Casinos are *not* designed to give you money. Not at all. We'll give you a detailed explanation as to why in Chapter 2, but the important thing to remember right now is that casinos *are* designed to sell you a contest. It's entertainment, a thrill, typical good-old-fashioned fun. The excitement is enhanced because something that reflects you (your money) is riding on the outcome.

Why is a home-team game more interesting? It's about you. An adventure movie is more exciting when you are emotionally invested in the hero. The perils and progress of a company like IBM or Microsoft matter more when you own the stock.

> " This guy is going to offer you a bet that he can make the jack of spades jump out of this brand-new deck of cards and squirt cider in your ear. But son, do not accept this bet, because as sure as you stand there, you're going to wind up with an ear full of cider.
> —Sky Masterson (Marlon Brando) in the movie *Guys and Dolls* "

You'll notice the last situation is an example of excitement generated from a contest than can materially affect you. Let's consider another such contest. This one is unfortunate (I would say insane): racing a train to a railroad crossing. The wager is the driver's life. The winning payoff is strictly a bit of excitement. This is how it looks as a mathematical formula. Don't be put off by the equation. The math is simple. Any bet can be analyzed this way.

Wager = desired outcome/all possibilities × payoff

Here is the same formula with the contest values in place.

Driver's Life = $^1/_2$ × excitement

There are two possibilities and one desired outcome. We are assuming that both possibilities have an equal chance of happening, so the foolish driver has a 50 percent ($^1/_2$) chance of getting across. Some people might express this formula differently, with additional fractions, or they might use other terms (like risk, reward, or odds), but I've written the formula this way to make a point. We set a value on a wager when we bet. We are purchasing an opportunity for a desired outcome. Wagering more than we can ever expect to receive is the same as devaluing our bet. This formula shows the driver's life as equal to twice the pleasure of beating a train. Is that a smart bet? Of course it isn't. The driver is throwing his wager (his life) away.

The decision is easy (for most of us) when the bet grossly outweighs the payoff, but it's tougher when the two sides are closer to being equal. Remember, payoff isn't just money. It's the pleasure of a contest, the satisfaction of making the correct choice, the enjoyment of tangible and intangible rewards.

Unofficially...
American statesman Henry Clay was an avid gambler and once wagered his life when he challenged John Randolph of Virginia to a duel. Both men missed. President John Quincy Adams said of Clay's passion for gambling, "In politics as in private life, Clay is essentially a gamester."

Gambling at the movies

Going to the movies is a common gamble. The typical cost for two people to see a first-run movie (including popcorn, soda, and candy) is $25. It's a wager that the movie will be good, the popcorn fresh, the soda bubbly and the theater clean.

Unofficially...
An average Hollywood movie must earn twice as much as its cost to turn a profit. That's identical to a blackjack payoff, and the casino bet is more likely to win. It's the occasional megahit that keeps Hollywood studios in business.

Sometimes the bet wins and sometimes it does not. Discriminating patrons choose a theater and movie carefully, but nothing guarantees the latest Hollywood blockbuster won't be a stinker. Yet we continue going to the movies.

What if the evening is an important one for you and your honey? A regular movie may not provide a big enough payoff. Perhaps a live performance and a fancy restaurant would be more appropriate. Bigger wager, higher opportunity, lower risk, bigger reward. A hit musical and a four-star dinner may be a good bet, but even that isn't a sure thing. What if the Broadway star is sick? What if the chef spoils the soup? On the other hand, what if everything goes right? The gamble paid off and romance is in the air.

A bet is a bet even in a casino

This is where most people get lost. They spend every day reasonably calculating cost, odds, and payoffs of normal activities like buying groceries, going to college, and scuba-diving. Everything in life is a gamble. Crossing the street involves risk.

Yet those same people check their brains at the door when they walk into a casino. They forget that a bet is a bet. Mathematical rules don't change when bells are ringing or wheels are spinning.

Price-for-fun—a formula for winning

It's sad to imagine how many people will skip this chapter and rush ahead to sections like "Beating the Wheel" in the vain hope of finding the winning formula. They may never get back to these words. They'll never know that the focus of the whole book, the formula that separates winning from losing, is right here:

Wager = (desired outcome/all possibilities × monetary payoff) + fun

This also happens to be a formula for calculating the casino's expected profit (commonly known as the house edge and covered in Chapter 2), but I'm going to call it the price-for-fun formula in this chapter. The casino is selling and you're buying. The more fun you get, and the less you pay for it, the more you win.

The methods explained in this book make it possible to sometimes pay zero dollars for fun, and even when you do pay you can still be winning. How can paying and winning happen simultaneously? We'll demonstrate in the next few sections. Right now, just remember this: paying too much for fun is losing; getting fun at a discount or at no cost is winning. Your goal is to establish a maximum price for fun and then pay less whenever possible.

A price-for-fun example

When playing $5 per spin roulette and betting red, our price-for-fun formula looks like this:

$$\$5 = (^{18}/_{38} \times \$10) + \$.26$$

$5 is the wager. You have 18 chances (desired outcome) out of 38 (all possibilities) to win $5, for a total of $10. Every possible outcome has an equal chance of happening. Assuming average luck (we'll cover that assumption in Chapter 2), you should get at least $.26 worth of fun from every spin. That's the casino's expected profit, the house edge. If you're not receiving at least that amount of fun on average per spin, then you're paying too much and losing money. It's that simple.

Timesaver
It's easier for you to calculate the value of a gambling purchase when all the positive results are grouped together. We're using the word fun to describe drinks, meals, shows, laughter, excitement, thrills, and everything else. Fun has value. Not having fun (a bad time) is actually an expense.

Watch Out!
Gambling is about numbers, and casinos are hoping you won't do the math. Don't oblige them. Our $5 roulette bet works this way: 18 divided by 38 equals .474 (rounded). Multiply it by 10 and you get $4.74. Add $.26 to get $5. Appendix D has prices for all the major games.

Of course, you don't give the dealer a quarter and a penny. You either get $5 or the dealer takes $5. As the decisions multiply you'll either pull ahead or (more likely) fall behind. It's up to you to watch the chips and do the arithmetic over time to determine if your fun is worth the price. Let's say you play three hours at fifty spins per hour and your luck is absolutely average (you win 18 times in 38 spins). Here are the numbers for our hypothetical low-stakes roulette play.

$.26 × 50 decisions per hour × 3 hours = $39

The average player will be down $39. Now consider what you have received in that three hours. Remember to include the thrill of the contest, the free drinks, and the pleasure of flirting with the player next to you. If it wasn't worth at least $39 then you need to lower your bets. Was it worth more? Then you're winning!

As we said previously, casinos use this formula to calculate how much they expect to earn. The beauty of using the same formula for our purposes is that upping the bets corresponds to a sobering (or perhaps stimulating) requirement of upping the fun. $50 bets require the value of your fun to be $2.60 per spin, $390 for three hours. Are $50 bets that much fun? You now have a sure-fire way of figuring it out.

The money is not funny

Don't make the mistake of thinking our calculated price for fun is hypothetical. It's not like putting money in your shoe or your back pocket and forgetting about it. The house edge is real. All those giant hotels, waterfalls, and riverboats were built with it. Every spin of the wheel and turn of the cards puts that money in a casino pocket. It's up to you to be sure you are getting your money's worth.

What it takes to be a winner

Jo is a silver-haired slot player who thoroughly understands the concept of price for fun. This is what she told me when I asked her why she traveled hundreds of miles from Indiana to gamble on an Illinois riverboat:

"My children and I, they're all in their thirties; we come here on a bus, get our friends together, and always have a fantastic time. The facilities are absolutely fantastic. The people couldn't be better. It's extremely elegant, clean, a clean form of entertainment. I bring my family and friends and we have a nice day together."

Sounds like mom and apple pie, right? You might say Jo was rationalizing her loss (down $75 at that moment), but believe me, this woman was grinning ear to ear. She wasn't losing; she was winning. Every quarter was purchasing much more than $.25 worth of enjoyment. For Jo it was a fire-sale of fun!

Us versus them?

Contests are adversarial by nature, so the natural inclination is to pit yourself mentally against the casino. Big mistake. It's true they want your money, but so what? You own the wallet. Their job is to deliver fun. You only need to receive and evaluate it. Negative energy will cloud your thinking. This is especially true when playing games you can win, like blackjack and poker. A grudge can make you deviate from optimal strategy. You'll lose and the adversary won't be the casino. It will be *you!*

On the flip side, it's important not to go all weak in the knees and throw money at your seemingly benevolent hosts. Casinos are not your friends. It doesn't matter what they advertise or what they give you for "free." They are businesses. Treat them like

Timesaver
There is no need to guess how many games per hour when calculating a price-for-fun. Use the following numbers as an average: baccarat—80, blackjack—60, craps—30, keno—7, roulette—50, slots—400, and video poker—400. Remember, the speed of play can vary significantly depending on the time of day and number of players.

any hotel, restaurant, or theater. Hold them to the same standards. It should always come down to one question: Are you receiving fun? How much are you paying for it? Do the arithmetic.

Losing is not OK

Take another look at our price-for-fun formula. This time I plugged in the numbers for blackjack when playing perfect basic strategy against a single deck with favorable rules. Each hand is $10. There is one desired outcome (winning), and two possibilities (winning or losing) that have an equal chance of happening.

$$\$10 = (^1/_2 \times \$20) + \$0$$

It's a *push* (a tie). Fun is costing nothing. If our player (let's call him Steamer) is having fun then he's winning. But let's say he's not having fun. Steamer has been playing for a while and he has blown a big money lead. He's back to square one and frustrated. Money that would have paid for a gourmet restaurant meal has disappeared in the last five hands. Should he try to win it back with one bet all or nothing? Let's look at the formula for one hand.

$$\$0 = (^1/_2 \times \$100) - \$50$$

$50 is the cost of the dinner, a price in negative dollars for entertainment. Steamer set the price because he's frustrated and he won't be happy unless he wins that amount. Steamer isn't willing to pay for fun. In fact he wants someone to pay HIM! Look at the left side of the formula. Zero is the only number that will work. If $50 is what Steamer is after, he already has it. He should cash in his chips.

Of course anything can happen in the short run, but in the long run Steamer would consistently lose this bet because he would be risking more than he could reasonably expect to receive. That's a guaranteed loss and it's not OK.

Repeatedly wagering in this way is an indication that the focus of the game has shifted away from purchasing fun. It's a dangerous approach to gambling that can cause serious problems, so before we talk more about winning, let's take a closer look at losing.

Dangerous gambling mistakes

The fact that you're reading this book means you're probably not the type of person who is likely to gamble in an unhealthy way. That's great, but you should always take periodic gut-checks anyway, especially if you're spending a lot of money. Consistent losing can usually be traced to one of the following mistakes.

Trying to prove something

Gambling to prove that you're rich, sexy, powerful, or anything else will negatively influence your ability to have fun and to win. You are not James Bond or Mrs. Peel from *The Avengers*. You are not the Sultan of Brunei. You are you and that is far better; no extra wagering or risk-taking is required.

Drinking excessively while gambling

Alcohol is free in many casinos when gambling at the tables or playing the machines. Smart gamblers stick to soft drinks. If your idea of fun includes wine or liquor, remember to factor it into your formula. If you can't do the math, then it's time to stop drinking.

Ignoring the odds

This will sink you every time. One minute you're up and the next minute you're flat broke. Why? You blew your bankroll on a series of risky bets. That's the price of ignoring the numbers. We'll give you accurate odds in this book on all the major games. Read them. Use them. Protect your bankroll.

Bright Idea
Remember, a wager is a wager. The price-for-fun formula works with any bet inside or outside a casino. Pull out a calculator and try it the next time you're at a fork in the road of life. The results will surprise you.

Playing when you're tired, angry, or hungry

It's easy to slip into a bad mood or fatigue without realizing it, especially when you're concentrating on a game. Stop when you're tired. Stop when you're hungry. Stop when you're frustrated. Each of these conditions is an indication of plummeting fun. As we said before, it usually happens when you've been playing for a while and you've blown a big money lead. Can you win it back? Don't even think about it. Pressing ahead will only make it worse.

Playing unfamiliar games for high stakes

It's fun to try something new. We encourage it. But don't risk your bankroll on a game you don't understand. Take the time to learn the game and learn the odds. Yes, it's fun to take a wild shot, but don't do it with big money unless throwing away cash is part of your formula for fun. Betting intelligently requires you to understand the odds.

Going over or under your limits

We'll talk about setting limits later in this chapter and again in Chapter 2. The important thing to remember here is that limits are established in advance when your mind is clear precisely because casinos can be confusing. You will be constantly tempted to bet more, play more, or wager in ways that are unwise. Never give in to the temptation.

Betting for the sole purpose of winning money

We've said it before and Chapter 2 is all about this. Casinos are not designed to give gamblers money. Betting with the expectation of coming out financially ahead in the long run (with very few exceptions) simply flies in the face of the facts. It's not rational. Gambling with this mentality almost guarantees that you will lose.

> **"**
> Some people gamble to be big shots. They're trying to prove something so they bet big and take major action. It's all a show to say 'I'm rich. I'm powerful. I'm successful.' There is no way a person like this can win because when they do they turn right around and bet even more.
> —Don, recovering compulsive gambler
> **"**

Borrowing money to gamble

This is a particularly sticky issue. It's not about cash management. It's about borrowing money that would otherwise be unavailable. Most of us think nothing of paying with a credit card for a movie, dinner, or a vacation. That's entertainment, and so is gambling. Right? That's true, and the world won't end if you take a small advance on a credit card or borrow a few bucks from a friend, but before you bet that money be sure you figure it and the interest into your formula. You may get lucky, you may be a blackjack or poker wizard, but on the whole there isn't a single game in a casino that will return the cost of borrowed money. Gambling with borrowed money ruins the odds, ruins your fun, and may ruin your business relationships and friendships too. Don't do it, even in small amounts. People who are tempted to borrow large amounts should see "Playing with 'scared money'" below.

Increasing bets to cover losses

Gamblers call it *chasing losses*. It's mathematically unsound. We'll show you why in Chapter 2. Increasing bets when you're losing is also not fun. That means you'll be losing in two ways.

Playing with "scared money"

This is the biggest taboo of them all. Betting rent money, betting food money, betting any funds that are not purely discretionary is a *big* mistake. It's more than that, it's a sickness. Estimates vary about the number of people in the United States who are problem gamblers, but one Harvard analysis put the figure at 3.8 percent of the U.S. population. The rate for adolescents was a shocking 9.4 percent.

Timesaver
The outcome of a single turn of the wheel, roll of the dice, or flip of the cards cannot make you lose in the long run unless you are wagering above the level determined by the price-for-fun formula.

Watch Out!
Gamblers Anonymous has chapters throughout the United States and the world. You can contact them in Las Vegas at (702) 385-7732, in Los Angeles at (323) 386-8789, or write to Gamblers Anonymous, P.O. Box 17173, Los Angeles, CA 90017. The Web address for Gamblers Anonymous is www.gamblers anonymous.org.

Don, a recovering compulsive gambler, describes it this way:

"There's a certain mentality. It consumes your entire life. You can always find a game somewhere. The goal is to get rich, make that one big killing, so you play $5,000 here, $10,000 there. You take one credit card advance, then you take another. You make a sports bet on Sunday afternoon to cover a loss the day before. Then you make a bigger bet on Sunday night to cover the loss Sunday afternoon. It was my wife's birthday, but I didn't buy her a present. I spent the money gambling."

Fortunately Don recognized his problem and got help from Gamblers Anonymous (see the sidebar on this page).

Gambling and other high-risk sports

One final thought and then we'll get back to the subject of entertainment.

A person doesn't have to be a compulsive gambler to lose his head and lose his money. It can happen to anyone who ignores the rules. Countless people have found themselves flat broke on the Strip in Las Vegas or the Boardwalk in Atlantic City. Not one of them expected to be there.

Gambling gives pleasure but it requires personal responsibility. It's a lot like scuba-diving or mountain climbing. One or two wrong moves can be disastrous. Remember that and take appropriate precautions.

The size of your bankroll

Gamblers use the word *bankroll* to describe money earmarked for gambling, funds to be put at risk. A bankroll does not necessarily include winnings, although winnings can be added to your bankroll. The purpose of a bankroll is to establish a finite amount of money that will be wagered. When you finish the bankroll, then you stop gambling. Period.

The following worksheet is designed to help you figure how much to bankroll. On the opposite page, you'll see how we filled in the amounts for a hypothetical trip to Las Vegas.

Unofficially...
Edgar Allen Poe gambled in college with the intention of increasing his meager allowance. The opposite happened (as it usually does) and Poe lost thousands of dollars. Those losses contributed to his eventual withdrawal from the University of Virginia.

WORKSHEET 1.1: BANKROLL

Discretionary funds	1	_____
Travel	2	_____
Lodging	3	_____
Food	4	_____
Non-gambling entertainment	5	_____
Ready cash	6	_____
Total non-gambling expenses	7	_____
Total bankroll (Line 1 – Line 7)	8	_____
Number of Sessions (? @ ? hours each)	9	_____
Session bankrolls (Line 8 ÷ Line 9)	10	_____

Treat a gambling getaway like any vacation or excursion. How much is the total experience worth? Some people start with a predetermined amount of money and work down the columns to arrive at a bankroll. Others prefer to start with a bankroll and work their way up to a proposed cost. Both ways work well.

Our hypothetical gambler, Lois Maven, is a Las Vegas enthusiast. She flies to the desert twice a year and typically stays for a weekend. Lois wrote $1,500 on Line 1 of her bankroll worksheet (see Worksheet 1.2) as her total discretionary funds for this trip. She purchased a discount airline ticket for $300 and has a rental car reserved that will cost $100, so her total travel expenses are $400. The hotel will cost $200. Meals will be about $50 per day. Lois will visit a few attractions and maybe buy a souvenir or two. Item 6, ready cash, is money for unexpected expenses. I don't call it emergency cash because you really should have much more money available for an emergency. One credit card with a low outstanding balance is usually enough. We'll talk about that and other matters related to handling your money in Chapter 14. Comps are not included on this worksheet and they shouldn't be unless you have a confirmed arrangement with a casino.

Lois' non-gambling expenses will be $875. She's an enthusiast so every dollar that remains will go to gambling. That's $625, her bankroll for the trip.

WORKSHEET 1.2: BANKROLL WORKSHEET FOR LOIS MAVEN

Discretionary funds	1		$1,500
Travel	2	$400	
Lodging	3	$200	
Food	4	$100	
Non-gambling entertainment	5	$75	
Ready cash	6	$100	
Total non-gambling expenses	7	$875	
Total bankroll (Line 1 – Line 7)	8		$625
Number of Sessions (4 @ 3 hours each)	9		4
Session bankrolls (Line 8 ÷ Line 9)	10		$156.25

The session bankroll

Lois is arriving Friday night and leaving on Sunday night. She has decided to play four gambling sessions. Each session will last about three hours. $625 divided by 4 is $156.25 per session. Lois has this down to a science. She likes to play quarter slots. When she finds a machine that pays well the money can easily last three hours, usually more. Occasionally she'll hit a jackpot and end the session a winner, but if her luck is bad the machine will quickly gobble her quarters. When that happens Lois will stop when her losses are exactly $156.25. Lois will play that last quarter (because she's an enthusiast), but she won't play a quarter more in that session because she is there to have fun. There are more sessions to come, and she doesn't want to sacrifice any spins from those future sessions on the current losing streak.

Just say, "Whoa"

Of course, there are times when things really go wrong. That's when having a bankroll is essential.

I met Hal, a day-tripper, on the deck of a riverboat a few years ago. Hal was affably munching a salami sandwich, but he would have much preferred to have been playing $10 per hand blackjack. Unfortunately, the cards did not fall his way that day. His bankroll was $100 and it disappeared in this way: four losses, one win, three losses, two wins, and six losses. Sixteen hands took about fifteen minutes. Hal spent the rest of the trip watching the sun set on the horizon.

Watch Out!
Deciding how much to bankroll can be a sobering process because sometimes the correct answer is zero. If this happens, don't jigger the numbers to create money for gambling. Accept the truth that now is not the best time to be purchasing fun.

Maybe Hal should have been playing $5 hands. Maybe he should have had a bigger bankroll. Maybe he should have played the quarter slots. The fact is Hal stopped gambling when his bankroll was gone. Hal was smart. He had money left for the trip home and for all the food he could eat on the boat.

Price-for-fun can save your bankroll

Of course, if Hal had seen our price-for-fun formula, he might have been even smarter. He would have bet less or quit sooner. Here is the optimum formula for the game Hal was playing.

$$\$10 = (^{49}/_{100} \times \$20) + \$.20$$
$$\$.20 \times 16 \text{ decisions} = \$3.20$$

Assuming that he was prepared to pay only $.20 per hand for fun, Hal overpaid $96.80. A person who used the price-for-fun formula would have quit or reduced the bets seven or eleven hands into the streak. Why? Because he would not have been getting his money's worth. A very conservative player would have walked away after four hands.

The bottom line is that Hal's luck was horrible and at the same time he was probably betting too much. $5 bets wouldn't have finished his bankroll after 16 hands. Here's an example of what might have happened if Hal's luck had returned to average (around 49 percent win rate) on hands 17 through 41:

Moneysaver
Want to minimize the possibility of losing your entire bankroll? Try the ultra-conservative once-through method. Each dollar (or group of dollars) is wagered once and then set aside. $100 would get you exactly 100 $1 slot spins. The odds of ending the session with some money will be astronomically in your favor.

17—win, 18—loss, 19—win, 20—win, 21—loss, 22—loss, 23—loss, 24—win, 25—loss, 26—win, 27—loss, 28—win, 29—win, 30—loss, 31—loss, 32—loss, 33—win, 34—win, 35—loss, 36—win, 37—win, 38—loss, 39—loss, 40—win, 41—loss

12 wins	13 losses
Hands 17 through 41 = -$5.00	
$.20 * 25 decisions = $5.00	

The price for fun would have been right on target (equal to the house edge) for hands 17 through 41. At $5 per hand Hal's total losses including the losing streak would have been $55. The per decision price for fun after 41 decisions would have been:

$55 ÷ 41 = $1.34 (or $1.34 × 41 decisions = $55)

Betting $5 per hand would have allowed Hal to decide for himself when to quit.

It's amazing how a seemingly minor adjustment like changing your bet from $5 to $10 can decimate your bankroll. It's also amazing how unpredictable a series of supposedly predictable decisions can be. What are the chances of losing six consecutive hands of blackjack? Should you bet on it? Should you bet against it?

In the next chapter we're going to answer those questions and also give you the good news and bad news about odds and the house edge.

Just the facts

- Casinos sell entertainment. Smart gamblers focus on buying entertainment.

- You can use a simple formula (price-for-fun) to calculate an optimum price for casino entertainment. Paying more than the optimum price is an automatic loss.

- Gambling with "scared money" can be emotionally and financially devastating. Gambling for any reason besides having fun is never a good idea.

- You should establish a bankroll before gambling. That money is the absolute most you will spend. No exceptions.

Moneysaver
When a losing streak materializes and your bankroll is evaporating, take a break; just stop. You may be down, but you won't be out. Change tables or machines. Wait a while. A pause in the action won't necessarily improve your luck, but it will guarantee you a longer run for your money.

GET THE SCOOP ON...
Probability and predicting the future ▪ Dangerous betting systems ▪ The real way
casinos earn money ▪ Games you can win
and games you can't

Probability and the House Edge

You've probably heard the story of the woman who came home and found her husband on his hands and knees on the front lawn. He was frantically searching for a set of keys that had dropped from a hole in his pocket. She knelt down to help in the search. After ten minutes with no luck the woman asked her husband to stand exactly in the spot where he dropped his keys. He inexplicably walked to the back of the house.

"This is where I was standing."

"Then why were we looking on the front lawn?" she asked.

"The light is better out there."

It sounds silly, but that is exactly what many people do when they walk into a casino. They look for a situation that doesn't exist, and they bet that it does. This inevitably leads to losses; hence the term loser. Losers make sucker bets. They use dangerous wagering systems. They have absolutely no idea what is happening or why the chips are disappearing so

21

quickly. Losers have holes in their pockets, and they spend time and money wishing the keys were on the front lawn.

It's amazing when you consider that winners and losers have the same luck. Yes! A winner's normal luck seems positively charmed when the bets aren't reckless. Winners understand the odds. They use mathematically sound strategies. Winners accept the truth and act on it. Do you want to win? Good! Let's get to some truths.

Casinos win in all probability

Flip a coin three or four times. Heads will probably come up at least once.

The concept of *probably* is a strange one because there is no rule in the universe that requires a probable event to actually happen. It usually does. Sometimes it doesn't. Attempts to refine the measurement and further predict the outcome will result in more forecasts that use the word probably. Ignoring probability is foolish, but expecting probability to absolutely foretell any single win/lose decision is equally unwise. Even groups of outcomes are not absolutely predictable.

For example, flip a coin 1 million times. Heads and tails have an equal chance, but one side will probably pull ahead of the other by thousands of decisions. Flip the coin a trillion times and the percent difference between heads and tails will likely go down, but the actual number of decisions that vary from exactly one-half will probably go up. There is no guarantee either side will overtake the other or that they'll ever be exactly even.

Here's the kicker. You're not flipping the coin 1 trillion times, but the casino is. Their aggregate

Watch Out!
The word *win* is commonly used to describe a favorable decision. It also means receiving more money than you are paying out. Don't confuse the two meanings. If you bet poorly you can win decisions and still lose money.

numbers are always closer to the norm and yours in comparison are forever fluctuating.

Probably is not definitely

When you flip a coin there is a 1 in 4 chance of seeing heads two consecutive times, 1 in 8 for heads three times in a row, and 1 in 16 for heads four times in a row.

Here's where it gets crazy. Flip the coin 64 times (sixteen sets of four trials) and the probability is you'll see four consecutive heads once, 1 in 16. But you may not. It may happen zero times, two times, seven times, or all sixteen times. They're all mathematically possible. And it gets worse. When can you *expect* four heads in a row? What if it doesn't come in the first fifteen sets? Is it due in the sixteenth? The inscrutable answer is that four heads in a row have a 1 in 16 chance in each of the next sixteen trials. What happened before is history and the next contest is the first in a new line.

Probability is like a mirage. It's always ahead of you. You could flip another 64 times (128 times in all) and never see four consecutive heads, but you probably will. Is your head spinning? Most people want to throw the coin away at this point, but stick with it. We're on our way to the single most important truth in gambling.

History does not necessarily affect the future

The following figure shows how our coin flips look as a graph. The probability of seeing heads or tails just once is highest. The chances of having repeated heads extend to the right. Tails extend to the left. You can see that the probability of repeats drops off quickly. Just one repeat is halfway down the curve.

Unofficially...
The principles of probability were developed in the 17th century by Blaise Pascal and Pierre de Fermat. Pascal had a lot of friends who gambled and he wanted to help them win. Probability is used today for many important purposes, such as insurance actuarials and weather forecasting, and we owe it all to gambling.

Timesaver
Multiple proba-
bilities are easy
to calculate. Just
multiply the
individual num-
bers. For exam-
ple, the chance
of winning two
decisions that
each have a 50
percent probabil-
ity is .50 × .50 =
.25, or 25 per-
cent. Pulling a
blackjack (ace
first then ten)
from the first
two cards of a
deck is $4/_{52}$
(.077) × $16/_{51}$
(.313) = .024, or
2.4 percent.

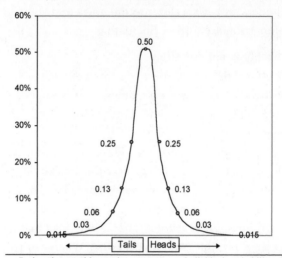

Each point on this graph represents an individual probability of
seeing heads or tails flipped a specific number of multiple times.

Does that mean we should switch our bet to tails
after one win or perhaps two consecutive wins? The
chance of seeing heads is dropping, right? Unfortunately, no. Take a closer look at the line. There's a
long gap between one flip and two consecutive flips,
then the rest of the numbers bunch up. That's
because each point is always half the amount (50
percent) of the previous point. Sound familiar?

As each point becomes history the next point
becomes a 50 percent possibility. Now look at the
left side of the graph. The probability for seeing tails
once in one flip is 50 percent. That's as high as it
goes.

So heads and tails always have an equal chance,
and you have the same chance of flipping heads two
consecutive times as you do flipping heads once and
then flipping tails. The odds are 1 in 4 both ways.
The result of one flip has absolutely no effect on
subsequent decisions. None. No exceptions.

Dice, decks, and wheels have no memory

There are situations when one decision will affect another, but in most casino games this is not the case. Here's why:

Draw one card from a deck of cards. You have a 1 in 2 (26 in 52) chance of drawing red and a 1 in 52 chance of drawing any particular card. Let's say you drew the five of diamonds. The chance of someone else drawing the five of diamonds has dropped to zero. In addition, the chance of drawing any red card has dropped to 25 in 51 and drawing black has increased to 26 in 51. In this situation the first decision will affect subsequent decisions.

Now put the five back and shuffle the deck. The chance of drawing the five of diamonds is back to 1 in 52. The deck doesn't remember your previous draw.

Spin a roulette ball. Let's say it hits black three consecutive times. Is black now less likely to hit? No. The wheel has no memory.

Dice are the same. Inanimate objects don't respond to history.

Misunderstanding this one truth has cost gamblers more money than all the unfavorable games and poor odds in the entire history of gambling. In the next few pages I will show you why, but before I do, please heed the warning in the following section.

Dangerous betting systems

Negative betting progressions (systematically increasing bets after losses) can be extremely dangerous. I am explaining them so that you may better understand why they are to be avoided. Play with negative betting progressions on paper or in a computer simulation if you must, but *don't use these systems in a casino!*

Moneysaver
Card games are by nature somewhat more predictable than dice or wheel games. Choose the right card game, play it well, and it could be the best bet in the house. See Chapter 4 on video poker, Chapter 5 on blackjack, and Chapter 9 on poker for more information on finding the right card games.

Watch Out!
Have you discovered an "unbeatable" betting system? It's almost certainly a mistake in your math. Don't risk money in a casino. Play the game with a reliable computer simulation. Your betting system will probably fail. If it doesn't, the next step is to find a mathematician, not a casino.

The martingale

Early in my career I produced a program that featured a roulette wheel in one key scene. The last night after the shoot, I was in my hotel room falling asleep. A little roulette ball was bouncing around in my dreams. I heard my own voice say, "How long will I wait for seven reds?"

My eyes popped open and I grabbed a pen. Roulette has eighteen black numbers, eighteen red numbers, and (on an American wheel) two green numbers. I ignored the green ones to simplify my calculations. What was the probability of red coming up seven times in a row? On a fifty-fifty proposition it was 1 in 128. Seven reds were possible, but one black in seven spins was much more likely. My heart was beating fast. Roulette suddenly seemed predictable. I would bet against seven consecutive red decisions; in other words I would bet black would come up at least once.

But how? Betting a fixed amount on every decision wasn't good enough. Let's say my luck after six spins was only average. Three red losses and three black wins would leave me even. I needed to bet less on the red losses and more on the (seemingly) inevitable black wins. The only way to be sure that I would bet more on a winning spin than a losing spin would be to increase my bet every spin until I won.

It seemed so simple, so obvious. I was young, inexperienced, and slipping down a perilous slope of wishful thinking.

How a martingale progression works

The progression I "developed" was simple. Begin with one unit. Double the bet after a loss and continue doubling until a win. Then return to the one unit bet. A win at any time would leave me ahead by one unit. I had unknowingly stumbled upon a centuries-old system known as the *martingale*.

TABLE 2.1: MARTINGALE

Black in 1

Wager		Total
10	Black	+10

Black in 2

Wager		Total
10	Red	-10
20	Black	+10

Black in 3

Wager		Total
10	Red	-10
20	Red	-30
40	Black	+10

Black in 4

Wager		Total
10	Red	-10
20	Red	-30
40	Red	-70
80	Black	+10

Black in 5

Wager		Total
10	Red	-10
20	Red	-30
40	Red	-70
80	Red	-150
160	Black	+10

Black in 6

Wager		Total
10	Red	-10
20	Red	-30
40	Red	-70
80	Red	-150
160	Red	-310
320	Black	+10

Black in 7

Wager		Total
10	Red	-10
20	Red	-30
40	Red	-70
80	Red	-150
160	Red	-310
320	Red	-630
640	Black	+10

This dangerous negative betting progression is commonly known as the martingale. It begins with a one unit bet (adjusted here to reflect a $10 table minimum). A bet after a loss is double the previous bet. Doubling continues until a win. A win at any time in the progression leaves the bettor ahead by one unit.

Yes, it was simple, and dangerous. I was so naïve. The big numbers at the bottom of the progression didn't scare me. What was the chance that I would see seven reds in a row? Only 1 in 128. That many spins would take hours. Seven reds might never happen. In the meantime every black win would pay me $10 and red losses (after a black win) would cost nothing!

Results of using the martingale

Down to the casino I went. I bought in for $700 and began betting. The progression worked perfectly for a couple hours. I was up $380. Runs of red didn't scare me. One time I saw four reds in a row. No sweat because black, according to the calculations in my deluded mind, had a 97 percent chance of winning on the next spin. I bet $160 and sure enough the ball fell black.

Thank goodness reality kicked in before I sold the farm to play roulette. The smart side of my brain finally began watching the numbers. Doubles and triples came more often than my crude figures had predicted. There was even one run of eight blacks! What if that had been red?

All this was happening as the wheel was spinning and I was betting. The truth hit me like it hits Wile E. Coyote when he chases the Roadrunner off a cliff. The smoke cleared, and I was standing on thin air. For a moment I hung suspended. Then I fell.

I looked down and there were no more chips. $640 was sitting on the black square and the dealer had stopped bets. The ball went round and round. It didn't even give me the dignity of hitting red. It hit green. I was down $1,270!

I could hear the Roadrunner laughing all the way back to my hotel room.

Martingale mistakes

That was years ago. Since then I've learned the truth, seen the scams, and run millions of simulation games to prove the figures. My stunning roulette loss wasn't bad luck; it was bad math. The first mistake was ignoring the green roulette numbers. The probability of hitting black in one spin is 47 percent, not 50 percent.

The second mistake was misunderstanding probability. There is no law that says seven reds have to wait 128 spins, 64 spins, or one spin before they appear. I could have lost my entire bankroll on the first seven decisions.

The third and most grievous mistake was that I bet my $1,270 against the casino's $10 that red wouldn't come up seven times. What a stupid bet!

Labouchère—the cancellation system

Another well-known and equally dangerous betting system is *labouchère*, or the cancellation system. In this negative progression a series of numbers like 1-2-3 or 1-2-3-4 are used, the sum of which is the final desired win: $1 + 2 + 3 + 4 = 10$.

The labouchère gambler begins by wagering the sum of the two outside numbers in the progression. If that bet wins, the outside numbers are crossed off and the next two inside numbers are wagered. When a bet loses, the amount of the loss is added to the end of the list and the progression continues. As in the martingale, the early stages are small, but the following table shows what happens when losses multiply. A straight $5-per-hand gambler would be down only $30. The system gambler loses nearly three times that amount.

Table limits

Some ignorant pit bosses and dealers joke about how much they like to see people using negative betting progressions because it's great for the casino's bottom line. Casino executives have a more pragmatic view. Bets escalating to ruinous levels are bad for business.

The solution is table limits. Every table has a minimum and maximum allowable bet. Most progressions can't get past seven or eight levels before

Moneysaver
It's possible to "win" more frequently at some games by simply placing more bets, but it costs money. Thirty-four simultaneous $1 roulette bets on the numbers will win one dollar 89 percent of the time. Unfortunately the bets lose thirty-four dollars the other 11 percent of the time. One hundred spins costs $285.

TABLE 2.2: LABOUCHÈRE

		Wager		Total
Begin	1 2 3 4	5	loss	-5
	1 2 3 4 5	6	win	+1
	2 3 4	6	win	+7
	3	3	loss	+4
	3 3	6	loss	-2
	3 3 6	9	loss	-11
	3 3 6 9	12	loss	-23
	3 3 6 9 12	15	loss	-38
	3 3 6 9 12 15	18	win	-20
	3 6 9 12	15	loss	-35
	3 6 9 12 15	18	loss	-53
	3 6 9 12 15 18	21	win	-32
	6 9 12 15	21	loss	-53
	6 9 12 15 21	27	win	-26
	9 12 15	24	loss	-50
	9 12 15 24	33	win	-17
	12 15	27	loss	-44
	12 15 27	39	loss	-83

The labouchère system is even more insidious than the martingale (if that's possible) because it has a tendency to bounce you up and down as it drags you further into negative territory. Look at all the action in pursuit of a paltry $10 profit.

Moneysaver
Table limits discourage progressions, but they also have other functions. Minimum limits are raised during busy periods to dissuade low rollers from taking seats that would otherwise be filled by higher rollers. If you can't find a table that suits your minimum, take it as a sign that you're in the wrong casino! Don't gamble.

hitting the table limit. In some cases there is a table payout limit also. The negative progression gambler can make the bet, but the casino won't pay all the money on a win.

Systems for sale

Betting systems for sale litter the Internet and back pages of magazines. Some cost as little as $10, but many are sold for hundreds of dollars. The pitch often includes a clever requirement that you sign an agreement to pay the seller a portion of your profits. Isn't that precious? They all come "guaranteed." They have been "developed over thousands of hours." Some have been "tested and proven by mathematicians." For a couple hundred dollars you can buy one that has "linked consistency with other key factors to produce a devastating winning combination."

Most betting systems are negative progressions. Many are based on the premise that cards, dice, and wheels have memory. Systems like that don't work. Think about it. If the system were yours and it were genuine, would you sell it on a personal Web page?

Positive betting progressions

The thinking behind a positive progression is to bet more when you're winning and less when you're losing. That sounds like a good strategy, but the unexpected problem is to identify when you're winning. Take a look at the following table.

TABLE 2.3: POSITIVE PROGRESSION

Wager		Progressive Total	Straight Bets (1 unit) Total
1	win	+1	+1
2	win	+3	+2
3	win	+6	+3
4	win	+10	+4
5	loss	+5	+3
1	loss	+4	+2
1	loss	+3	+1
1	win	+4	+2
2	win	+6	+3
3	loss	+3	+2
1	loss	+2	+1
1	loss	+1	0
1	win	+2	+1
2	loss	0	0
1	win	+1	+1
2	loss	-1	0
1	win	0	+1
2	loss	-2	0
1	win	-1	+1
2	loss	-3	0

This is a basic 1-2-3 positive progression. The bettor increases one unit after a win and drops back to a one unit bet after a loss. Consecutive wins bring profit even if there are consecutive losses. The problem with most positive progressions is that they're not very positive if the table goes choppy (wins and losses alternate).

I have mixed feelings about positive betting progressions. They tend to make you win more on a streak and win less (or lose money) when your luck is only average. In Table 2.3 the straight bettor remains even when the table goes choppy, but the positive progression bettor is losing one-half unit per hand. Remember, a long string of alternating decisions is just as likely as consecutive wins or losses. You've probably noticed that unfavorable table conditions for positive progressions are ideal for the martingale. The reverse can also be true. You might even wonder if there is a way to combine the two systems. There is. It doesn't work.

How casinos make money

You can take comfort in the fact that runs of red and other deviations from the norm can be as troublesome for casinos as they are for players. If you win quickly and stop playing, the casino has lost money. If you lose quickly and stop playing, the casino stops earning money. The ideal situation from the casino's perspective is for you to win a little or lose a little but to keep playing because the casino is selling you the game. That's what it's all about, to keep you playing.

Watch Out!
One of the dangers of betting systems is that they tend to get you thinking about money in an abstract way. It's easy to double a number and imagine a positive result. Don't do it. Figure your maximum price for fun and never exceed that amount.

You'll remember in the last chapter that we discussed price-for-fun. Casinos call it the *house edge*. It's their profit for providing entertainment. They collect it in one of three ways:

House-edge game 1: Reduce the payout

Let's say I have two inverted coffee cups. A silver dollar is hidden under one of them. You bet $1.00 for an opportunity to guess which cup covers my dollar. If you're wrong I get your money. If you're right I pay you $.96. That's right. Four cents short. Play the game 50 times and on average you'll be down one dollar.

House-edge game 2: Charge a fee for winning

OK, the first contest wasn't exactly fair. You can have the whole dollar this time. Did I mention the fee for winners? It's 5 percent. Play the game 40 times and on average you'll be down one dollar.

House-edge game 3: Obscure the odds

OK, OK... You want a better game? This time there is no percentage fee. I'll pay you the full dollar and only charge you 33 cents to play. Did I mention there will be four cups? Play the game 12 times and on average you'll be down about one dollar.

All the games are fair in the sense that cheating is not possible and you have a measurable chance of winning in the short run. The payouts in Game 1 are comparable to those of video poker. Game 2 is a rough approximation of baccarat. Game 3 resembles keno. That's right. We've been playing with actual casino odds.

The house edge: Now you see it, now you don't

If the coffee-cups game doesn't seem tempting, that's because we haven't dressed it up like a casino would. How about Mega-Jackpot Coffee Cups with a chance to win $100,000? Imagine eighty giant coffee cups and a man in a tuxedo who turns them over. Twenty of the cups will be winners. Players bet a dollar and can choose as few as one cup or as many as fifteen. One catch out of twenty pays $3. If fifteen catch out of twenty the player receives $100,000. Our slick brochure would begin with the giant head-line, "Coffee Cups! More choices and more ways to win!"

That's keno (covered in Chapter 11) and it's basically the third version of our coffee-cups game.

Moneysaver
Gambling is a series of purchases. This is true even when you're winning money, because every bet has a potential to lose, and winning bets are usually paid at house odds which are less than a true reflection of the risk. The only way to stop the purchases is to stop gambling.

True odds and house odds

True odds are mathematical ratios that describe what will probably happen. House odds are how much a casino will pay you for winning a contest. For example, the true odds of one number winning a roulette spin are 1 in 38. House odds are 35 to 1. Casinos pay $35 for every $1 wagered, so a $10 bet wins $350.

Casinos often talk about house odds, but they rarely mention true odds except in ultra-rare circumstances when they offer a player edge as a promotion. As we said in Chapter 1, it's up to you to figure the house edge (price-for-fun) and decide if your fun is worth it.

Here is the house edge (price-for-fun) formula for the bet in coffee-cups game 1.

$$1 = (1/_2 \times 1.96) + .02$$

True odds are 1 in 2. This can also be expressed as one for and one against, or 1:1. House odds are 96:100. As you can see the house edge sticks out like a sore thumb. A savvy casino executive would change the game, slightly lower the odds of winning and offer house odds of even money 1:1.

You'll also notice that the game 1 payout is $.96 on winning bets but the house edge is only $.02. That's because winning bets only come on average every other time in this game, and the house figures its edge as working on every decision.

Negative expectation versus positive expectation

Positive expectation has nothing to do with your attitude and everything to do with the probability that you'll win. Most games in a casino are negative expectation games. That means if your luck is exactly average you may win or lose individual decisions, but over time you will lose money. There are no exceptions.

Positive expectation games are different. They pay out more on average than they take. It's true! Many casinos offer positive expectation games. They are most commonly poker, video poker, blackjack, and sports betting. But don't quit your day job just yet. These games only offer positive returns under two strict conditions. The first condition is that you must play the game perfectly. No mistakes ever. In the case of video poker that means you must play perfect strategy, no hunches, and maximum coins on every hand. In blackjack you must count cards accurately and effortlessly. Poker and sports betting require comparable expertise.

The second condition is finding the right game. Some video poker machines are positive expectation and some are negative expectation (see Chapter 4 for information on finding positive video poker machines). All blackjack games are not created equal (see Chapter 5). The same is true for poker (Chapter 9) and sports events (Chapter 12). This book will tell you when and how a game is beatable, but be forewarned, just because a game can be beaten doesn't mean it will be.

Feeling lucky?

I have a friend who is psychic. One day Connie and I were walking through a casino and she told me to play a particular slot machine because she had "a feeling." I was busy and the whole thing sounded impractical, but I played one quarter just to please her. Nothing happened so I went about my business. Connie played two more quarters and hit the jackpot.

Ouch!

Moneysaver
Negative expectation games always take more than they pay back over time. Frequency of wins has no effect on this. If you're lucky and find yourself significantly ahead in a negative expectation game, don't wait for the numbers to turn against you. Take the money and run.

If you're one of those exceptional people who derive great pleasure and satisfaction from plugging into the universe, don't let the strategies in this book stop you from playing hunches. It's your money. Spend it in a way that will bring you pleasure, but please be honest with yourself. Do the arithmetic and know your price-for-fun. Don't overpay.

Win limits: walk away a winner

The house edge nibbles away at your bankroll with every turn of the cards and toss of the dice. If you win a lot and keep playing, the house eventually wins it back and sometimes more. Remember, money you have won is not casino money, it's yours. How are you spending it? Is it buying you enough fun?

In the previous chapter we discussed your bankroll and setting a limit for losses. Now we're going to talk about a win limit. That's right. You should set a limit for how much you will win.

One common win limit is doubling your bankroll. If you start with $100 and get to $200, then you stop for the day. Too abrupt? Here's another popular method: Some players adjust the win limit and reduce the bankroll to allow for additional play. For example, if you start with $100 and get to $200, you reset your bankroll to $50 and put away the extra $150. Don't touch that money. Your new win limit is $100. When you reach $100 another $50 is put away.

Some people don't make a big deal of the arithmetic; they just keep stuffing chips in their pockets or their purses. The key is to stop when you're ahead. It's easy and it makes you feel great. Pick up your chips or push the cash out button on the machine. Savor your victory. Walk to the cage and watch with pleasure as your money is counted. You're a winner!

Just the facts

- The results of previous contests do not affect the outcome of identical future contests. Dice, decks, and wheels have no memory.

- Negative betting progressions are destructive. Never use them. Positive betting progressions are less dangerous, but should be used with caution.

- True odds are a measure of probability. House odds are a measure of how much a casino will pay on your winning bet. The difference between true odds and house odds is the house edge, or profit for the casino.

- Negative expectation games on average take more money than they pay. You can win money playing them in the short run but never in the long run.

- Positive expectation games on average pay more than they take. Finding such games can be difficult, and playing them properly is not always fun.

- The house edge in negative expectation games is relentless. The only way to avoid losing short-term winnings is to stop gambling when you're ahead. Setting a win limit helps you do that.

Bright Idea
Cashing out (exchanging chips or coins for bills) is a good way to mentally break from the game. Folding money is more tangible for some people and see-ing it gives them perspective on the action. You should cash out often, even when you take a short break. It's fun. It helps you refo-cus, and the process makes you feel like a winner.

Machine Games

GET THE SCOOP ON...
How a slot machine works ▪ Finding loose
slots ▪ Money management strategies that
preserve your slot winnings ▪ Slot machines
you should avoid ▪ Slot tournaments

PART II

Slot Machines

Chapter 3

Centuries of domination by cards, dice, and
wheels were swept away in the late 20th century when the humble slot machine turned
the world of gambling on its ear. Table games were
removed from their preeminent positions, squeezed
into small areas, and the lion's share of casino real
estate was set aside for the more profitable coin-
operated slots and their cousins video poker. Maximum payouts increased exponentially, and now a
few quarters will buy you a chance for millions. No
tuxedo required.

Such a game could only have been invented in
America. Like most things that are thoroughly
American, slot machines are a combination of
straightforward and easy-to-use features wrapped in
a loud but lovable exterior. They are not genteel;
they have a rough-and-tumble history, and they're a
lot more complicated on the inside than they
appear on the outside.

Playing a slot machine is like having your own
personal gambling party. No impatient dealers or
unhappy players to mess up your good time. It's just

you, your luck, and the cheerful machine. Unfortunately, some machines are more cheerful with their payouts than others. Choosing a slot that gives you the biggest opportunity for winning requires a look past the bright and easy exterior into the heart of the mechanism.

How slot machines work

Modern slot machines have more lights and gadgets than slots from previous eras, but from a player's perspective the operation of the game hasn't changed much. This appearance is intentional and thoroughly misleading. What you see does not represent what is actually happening. The reels and the handle are only props in an elaborate show that simulates the experience of a classic mechanical slot. Disappointed? Don't be. Modern slots can be much more generous than their venerable predecessors. You just have to understand where the show stops and the truth starts. That requires letting go of a lot of old notions. Let's take a brief look at the history of the slot machine to see what those notions are.

The way it used to be

The earliest "nickel in the slots" were built in America during the 1880s and were common by the turn of the century. They featured many designs, but the most popular was a machine created by Charles August Fey in San Francisco. It was called Liberty Bell, and it had three reels. Each reel had ten sections, or stops, with a symbol at each stop. The symbols included horseshoes, card suits, and bells. A player put a coin into the slot, pulled the handle, and the reels spun. If the reels stopped with identical symbols in a line, the player would win. The operation was strictly mechanical and (assuming the

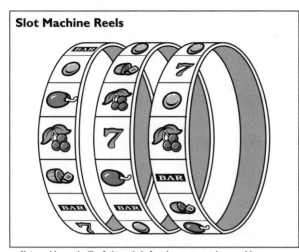

Slot Machine Reels

Slot machine reels. The fruit symbols found on many modern machines are a holdover from earlier times when slots dispensed gum. Image courtesy of the *Unofficial Guide to Las Vegas* by Bob Sehlinger.

Unofficially...
Have you ever wondered why some slots have "bar" symbols on the reels? They're a holdover from the early 1900s when slot machines delivered gum in their jackpots. Look at an old-style pad of Bazooka bubble gum (if you can find one), and you'll see the resemblance.

machine wasn't rigged) the probability of hitting any single three-symbol combination was $10 \times 10 \times 10 = 1,000$, or 1 in 1,000.

The machine payout was a paltry twenty-two coins. Many gamblers didn't understand the odds and were surprised when they lost money. That's how slots developed the nickname *one-armed bandits.*

Yet it was all exactly as it appeared. The handle was directly connected to the mechanism, so pulling it in different ways could affect the spin of the reels. By the 1960s the handle had been separated from direct contact with the rest of the mechanism and the average reel size had been expanded to twenty or more symbols, but the mechanics of winning were basically the same. The reels spun and they stopped where they stopped. You could figure your chances of winning simply by knowing how many symbols appeared on each reel. The reels decided everything.

Bright Idea
Want to play an
antique slot
machine in a real
gaming estab-
lishment? Try
Fremont Street in
Las Vegas. Sand-
wiched in
between the big
casinos will be a
few small places
with old carpet
and even older
machines. Don't
expect them to
be loose. Do
expect a lot of
attention and
high-pressure
promotions.

That was the old way. You can take all the truths connected to that and put them on the shelf. Absolutely none of it applies to modern slot machines.

The way it is now

The heart of a modern slot machine is a computer device called a *Random Number Generator,* or *RNG.* The RNG randomly selects numbers in a particular range, usually zero to a few billion. Each number in the range corresponds to a unique combination of symbols on the slot's reels. The RNG never stops working. Every millisecond a new number is select-ed, one after another, as long as electricity is sup-plied to the machine.

When you put a coin in the slot and push the spin button (or pull the handle), the number that happens to be on the RNG at that particular moment is delivered to a mechanism that controls the reels. They spin and give the impression that the contest has yet to be decided, but in fact it's all over. The symbols that appear simply reflect the number selected by the RNG. The handle, the reels, and everything else is just for show.

Not very romantic, huh?

Here's the good news. This advanced technology makes it possible to have identical machines with different rates of return. Casinos use *loose* and *tight* machines in complex placement strategies to maxi-mize profits. You can take advantage of those strate-gies to win more money. It's a lot like buying a cheap airline seat that was sold as a promotion. We'll tell you how to find loose machines later in this chapter.

Button and jackpot basics

The outside of a slot totally belies its complex inte-rior. Most slots still come with a handle. Pulling it will deliver a wonderfully visceral drag that approxi-

Slots feature different designs, but they all have layouts similar to this. Note the payout schedule (pay table) on the upper portion of the machine. Image courtesy of the *Unofficial Guide to Las Vegas* by Bob Sehlinger.

mates some designer's idea of how moving gears should feel. If you like a workout, use the handle. The alternative is pressing the spin button. It doesn't matter which method you use. The results will be the same.

The rest of the machine is very straightforward. The *Change* button is used to summon a slot attendant. *Cash/Credit* is used to cash out or switch from machine credits to receiving coins. *Bet One* will wager one credit. *Bet Max* wagers multiple credits when the machine has multiple paylines. A *payline* is where winning symbols must line up. There's a slot for coins and a bill receptacle for paper money. A meter records your play credits and wins. There's also a receptacle for your slot club card (more on slot clubs in Chapter 14). At the bottom or the side of the machine is a tray for holding coins. The rest of the machine is usually dominated by the *pay table*, a bright and happy list of what you might win.

Unofficially...
New York City mayor Fiorello La Guardia once personally supervised the dumping of more than 1,000 slot machines into the Atlantic Ocean. They were probably tight.

Read the table carefully. Some jackpots will not be available unless you bet maximum coins. We'll discuss jackpots later in this chapter. The important thing to remember here is that the symbols (cherries, pots of gold, flaming 7s, and such) have no importance beyond what is posted on that specific table. Machines and pay tables vary. Sevens may win you a jackpot on one slot, but may have less or no importance on another. The critical information is always on the pay table.

The odds: loose, tight, and progressive

Slots are negative expectation games. Over time you will lose money. It's inevitable. The good news is that some slots keep less coins on average than others. Those that do are called *loose*. Slots that keep more coins and pay less are called *tight*. Both terms are relative. A tight slot in Las Vegas might pay back like a loose slot on a riverboat.

Slots in Nevada must by law pay back on average at least 75 percent of the money played into them. New Jersey requires Atlantic City slots to pay back at least 83 percent. Other jurisdictions have different requirements, but markets with competition (like Las Vegas) often have slots that pay better than 90 percent. Some casinos even advertise their slot paybacks. Just be sure to read the fine print. "Up to 98 percent" is not the same as "98 percent payback on all slots."

What you will "probably" win

Unless the machine has a sign on it (which is rare) there is no way for a player to absolutely tell if a slot is loose or tight without playing it or watching someone else play it. Sometimes even that isn't a sure indicator because (as we saw in Chapter 2) limited streaks of wins or losses frequently defy probability.

And there's another consideration. A machine set to pay back 90 percent will almost certainly not return exactly $90 for every $100 played. If the top payout is $1,000 with many smaller jackpots, some $100 players might only see $75 returned. Some might see $85. And a lucky few will win $250, $500, $1,000, or more.

This situation is magnified when playing a slot machine that has a growing *progressive* jackpot shared with other machines. A portion of every wager feeds the jackpot. That lowers the overall payback percentage when you exclude the lottery-like probability of winning the single biggest prize. Some progressive systems are just a few linked machines; others contain hundreds of slots. If you don't want to sacrifice small jackpots for a chance at millions, don't play a progressive. Choose instead a *flat top,* a slot with a fixed top payment.

The yin and yang of dollars versus quarters

The size of your bet has absolutely no effect on your chance of winning in most casino games. But this is *not* true when playing slots. Quarter slots are generally looser than identical nickel machines; dollar slots are looser than their quarter counterparts, and so on. The reasoning behind this is simple. A slot machine requires a fixed amount of electricity, floor-space, and maintenance regardless of its denomination. Even if lower-coin machines receive more play, they need to be tighter to earn back their costs.

On the other hand, most slot machines, especially progressives, have multiple paylines and require multiple coins to be eligible for the largest jackpots. So should you play one coin in a looser dollar machine or five coins in a tighter quarter

Timesaver
Which casinos have the loosest slots? No need to guess. *Casino Player* magazine will tell you. Every month the magazine publishes a list of slot payouts for casinos around the U.S. For more information visit the publisher's Web site at www.casinocenter.com or call (800) 969-0711.

Watch Out!
Flat top machines are sometimes mistaken for progressive slots (and vice-versa) in the sea of blinking casino lights. The top amount on a *progressive* pay table is usually the word progressive instead of a printed number. An LED counter that shows the current (and growing) jackpot amount will be on or near the machine.

machine? The key is to check out the pay table on the front of the slot. If the jackpot for maximum coins is only proportionally larger (five times larger for five coins), then play one coin. If the biggest jackpot is exponentially larger or if it's a progressive, you should play maximum coins or find a lower denomination machine.

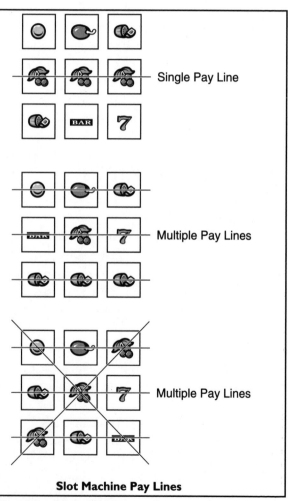

Slot Machine Pay Lines

Image courtesy of the *Unofficial Guide to Las Vegas* by Bob Sehlinger.

Multiple paylines require more quarters and offer more ways to win. The actual probability of winning per quarter is unchanged, although additional quarters can make you eligible for larger jackpots.

Finding the holy grail, a loose slot machine

Casinos use loose slot machines to stimulate play. When a machine is paying like crazy, other slot players want to get in on the action. The loose machine is occupied, so excited players choose nearby machines that are invariably tighter. Other eager players already at machines often play faster. There is more spending, but also more winning, more bells ringing. The whole experience feeds on itself. That's great for the casino, but bad news for the poor slot players who choose tight machines.

Unofficially...
The opening of the MGM Grand in Las Vegas was a grand example of how slots dominate gambling. Thirty-nine armored cars took two nights to deliver the millions of coins necessary for slot operations.

Think like a casino executive

The key to finding a loose slot is evaluating the entire layout of the particular casino where you're playing. That means letting go of rigid popular wisdom that says (among other things) that loose slots are always near entrances and high traffic areas. Maybe they are; maybe they're not. The casino executive who supervised slot placement was not following rigid popular wisdom. The executive was making a unique plan for that unique casino. Here is an example of what that person was probably thinking:

- Table players don't like ringing bells and other distracting slot noise. Distractions tend to slow table games, and that's bad for the casino.

- Table players who pass by or through a row of slots sometimes play a few coins. But they rarely spend more. Table players prefer tables.

- Slot players are more eager to play when they see other people win.

Bright Idea
The exact locations of loose slots are closely guarded casino secrets. Slot hosts, attendants, and slot supervisors are not officially privy to this information, but some are more "aware" than others. Cultivate friendships, listen, and evaluate. Don't forget to tip if you win.

- It's easier to influence slot players just before, during, or just after a session than when they're focused on another activity like checking in or waiting in line for a show.

- Loose slots are a promotion. They are placed in ways that stimulate the maximum amount of play.

- Medium or mid-range slots are the bread and butter. They're neither loose nor tight relative to the extremes. An average slot player will usually be satisfied with a mid-range machine.

- Tight slots are most profitable when players are so eager or so casual that they won't be disappointed when the wins are less frequent.

- The range from loose to tight is relative. It varies from casino to casino, and it covers many different payout percentages.

- There is no switch or button that can instantly make a slot tighter or looser. Each machine is set to pay back at one particular level. Any change would require the machine to be removed and reprogrammed.

Evaluating the casino layout

Now let's walk through a casino thinking like an executive and see if we can find the loose slots.

Any machines at the end of a row next to a table should be tight. That's probably true for the second, third, and fourth machine into that row. The fifth or sixth machine may be looser, but look around. Is the aisle frequently used by people who don't play slots? If it is, then most of these machines will be tight or in the mid-range. The really loose machines will be away from the tables and the table players.

Will slot players be influenced by slots they can't see? No. Loose slots should be in high visibility areas surrounded by other slots. Crosswalks (where multiple rows converge) are ideal. So is an elevated carousel. Another good place is near a change booth or the exit from a buffet area. Loose slots won't be in corners and isolated areas.

Do you see the waiting area for the fancy bistro? Are there slots nearby? They're probably tight. Now check out the sandwich shop. Can you see the machines from the dining area? A large bank of visible slots there might have one or two loose machines to keep people excited and draw them back into the slot area after the meal.

Should two loose slots be together? No, loose slots should be surrounded by tighter slots, but not necessarily the tightest.

That's how casino executives think, and that's how you should think, too.

The tightest of the tight slots

Slots in non-gaming venues such as airports, gas stations, and convenience stores are notoriously tight. That's because Brake-n-Buy is not competing with a casino and doesn't care about generating slot excitement. A few occasional quarters from bored patrons is fine with them. Of course, tight does not mean "impossible." Any slot anywhere that is operating within legal specifications can and will provide some wins. During a recent trip to Las Vegas I was waiting for baggage at the airport, so I bought a five-dollar roll of quarters. I played seven spins and won an eighty-coin jackpot. The silver immediately went into a pocket of my travel bag, and I stopped playing. Yes, it's possible to win; just don't expect the airport or a gas station to be as generous as a casino.

Timesaver
Five-dollar, twenty-five-dollar, and higher slot machines tend to be looser than their nickel, quarter, and dollar counterparts. This makes loose machine placement less of an issue in the high-roller area. Don't bother looking for a high visibility machine next to the dessert cart.

Bright Idea
Have you found a loose slot? Don't lose it. Casinos move machines around from time to time, but you can follow your favorites. Each machine has a unique number. Write it down. If the slot machine is gone on your next visit you can find it with the number.

Slot machine strategy

Add up all the variables about slots and you get one of those jokes of the universe. Games that seem complicated, like craps and roulette, have odds that are absurdly easy to calculate. Slots are easy to play, but true odds and the house edge (which are identical in this situation) seem impossible to accurately determine. That's why casinos love slots. Most people just give up, plunk their money into the machine, and hope for the best.

Here's the bad news for the casino. We have a slot strategy that accounts for the mysterious house edge. The first part of the strategy is a series of decisions and the second part includes three playing options to correspond with different-sized bankrolls. Ready?

Decision 1: progressive or nonprogressive?

Do you like many small jackpots or do you want to give up some smaller wins to shoot for the big enchilada? Either choice is fine. Just be sure you understand the implications. You'll lose more in the long run playing a progressive. That is guaranteed.

Decision 2: maximum coins or maximum edge?

We've covered this previously. If you're playing a progressive, choose a lower denomination and play maximum coins. Reverse that if you're playing a nonprogressive that doesn't pay a bonus for maximum coins.

Decision 3: crowded or empty casino?

How desperate are you to play immediately? Are you willing to play a tight machine? A crowded casino means you'll need to wait for a hot slot or play one in the corner that is probably tighter than the airlock on the space shuttle. The decision is yours. Wait or play?

Slots money management strategy: level 1

If you're playing a very short session of twenty to forty coins (typically one-half or one roll of quarters), the machine may gobble them all, give a few back, or deliver a jackpot. There is simply no way to predict. The most practical strategy for a very short session player is to play once through with your bankroll and expect zero percent back. Your price for fun is one coin per pull. The probability of winning something and paying less than the full price using this strategy is extremely high. If this strategy sounds too conservative consider the alternative. Putting forty coins into a machine and only getting twelve back is a drag unless you were prepared to spend the money.

Slots money management strategy: level 2

Longer session players with bigger bankrolls are more likely to experience payouts closer to the average, so they can reasonably include some of the value of those expected payouts in the price-for-fun calculation. Let's say the session bankroll is $100. You're playing single coins on a quarter machine. $100 will buy you 400 spins. How much should you expect to win back? Anything can happen, but remember that you're setting a maximum price for fun. My personal favorite is an ultra-conservative and easy-to-figure 50 percent. That means when the original $100 is gone and the 400 spins are over you intend to have at least $50 in winnings. You're willing to pay up to $50 for the pleasure of 400 spins. I've never personally had a run as bad as 50 percent, but I've seen other people who have. The key to avoiding such a catastrophe is monitoring your winnings. One quarter of the way through your bankroll (100 spins) you should be down a maxi-

Watch Out!
If you load maximum coins and the machine registers anything less then don't spin. Call an attendant. If you spin and win, the machine won't pay the top prize. You could lose millions.

mum of $12.50. Anything more and you're paying more than 50 percent, way too much for fun. Find a looser machine.

Slots money management strategy: level 3

You're in for the long haul and playing for multiple hours. It's possible to see returns approximating the actual house edge at this level of play, but don't count on it. Set your overall price for fun at 25 percent of your bankroll (75 percent return) and play the money once through. Periodically monitor your winnings at 50 or 100 spin intervals. If you hit a cold streak or a tight machine your price for fun will shoot through the roof. When that happens you should take a break or play another machine.

Should you play winnings?

Let's assume you haven't exceeded your win-limit by winning a big jackpot. Our once-through money management strategies are designed to leave you with some winnings. Even Strategy number 1 will very likely produce a few coins. The original bankroll is gone. Should you put the winnings at risk? Remember, it's your money. Do you want to continue purchasing fun? Slot fanatics like Lois Maven (our hypothetical slot player from Chapter 1) will play it all in pursuit of one big jackpot. That's OK if you're prepared to end the session with zero dollars. Another approach is to walk away with your winnings. That makes cashing out a pleasure, but it stops the fun cold. A middle approach is to set aside half your winnings and use the other half to replenish your session bankroll. Repeat the process until the new bankroll produces no winnings or you hit a big jackpot and exceed your win-limit. Either way, you'll go home with money in your pocket.

Timesaver
Don't stay with a tight machine or one that has turned into a loser. Set a short limit for how many consecutive losses you will allow before moving on. If the machine teases you with a couple of coins during that time give it a couple more spins, but no more.

Coins instead of paper

Modern slots take coins or bills and give you play credits in return. Wins are registered in credits until you cash out. Some people use this convenient feature to keep track of their bankroll and winnings. They play coins exclusively and let the wins rack up as credits. It's simple and effective. The only drawback is repeatedly loading the machine with coins, but for some people that's an advantage. Credits can be abstract, but handling the coins means spending money.

Running total and the no-effort system

Another way to keep track of winnings is to write them down and keep a running total. When winnings equal credits you cash out or set aside that amount from your bankroll. If a running total is too much arithmetic, here's a no-effort system: Let's say you're playing maximum coins on a quarter machine ($1.25 per spin). Your bankroll is $100. Start with twenty five-dollar bills and load one. Play those four spins. No wins? Go to the next bill. Let's say you win on the second spin. Cash out and hand load the $2.50 for the next two spins. Leave the winnings in the coin tray. Are you feeling really lazy? Just cash out and go to the next five-dollar bill. You only miss two spins, and the less you gamble the less you lose.

A slot machine player's checklist

The best part of playing a slot is the dizzy anticipation of possibly winning it all. It's the lottery every ten seconds. The whole experience can be so intoxicating that some people forget practical considerations. For example, countless would-be slot players accidentally put quarters in dollar machines in their

Moneysaver
Don't pump money into a losing streak expecting the slot to eventually even the score. The RNG doesn't keep score (though a separate accounting mechanism does). Every spin decision is independent. The RNG doesn't remember previous spins, so it may never make up for the losing streak.

frenzy to begin playing. Mistakes like that are usually benign, but some are a nuisance, and some can be costly.

The following checklist is designed to help make the important things automatic so you can focus on the pleasures of playing.

1. Determine your bankroll, price for fun, and betting strategy before going into the casino.

2. Remember to take your slot club card and a picture I.D. with you when leaving home or the hotel room.

3. Choose a machine that fits your strategy. Know if you're playing a progressive.

4. Insert your slot club card into the machine and be sure the machine acknowledges the card.

5. Decide before playing how you will handle winnings paid by the machine. Stick to the system you choose.

6. Cash out when you're finished. You would be surprised how many people forget.

7. Remember to remove your slot club card when leaving the machine.

Handling jackpots

Jackpots above a certain level are paid by a slot host. If you hit a big jackpot, don't play the machine again and don't wander away. Stay right there until a host arrives and verifies your win. Have your I.D. ready because the host will ask to see it. If you look young be prepared for scrutiny. Underage and unidentified gamblers will not be paid. Period.

Even if the win doesn't require a host, be careful when you're ahead. Don't step away from the machine and leave money in the tray. Don't be distracted or turn your back. Slot areas can be loud and confusing. It takes just a moment for a thief to steal coins or a purse while you're helping someone, possibly a confederate, who is loudly in distress.

Slot myths

Slots seem to breed myths more than any other casino game. That's probably because players have so little control over what happens. The inscrutable inner workings of the machine only add to the mystery and the myths.

Myth: A slot that hasn't paid in a while is "due" to hit

A slot that hasn't paid in a while is probably tight and certainly not "due" to hit. The RNG picks numbers at random and the probability of hitting a jackpot is always the same for every spin. For the same reason, a slot that just hit a jackpot is now no less "due" or more "played out" than it was the spin before. A loose slot is a loose slot.

Myth: Someone played my machine and stole my jackpot

It happens all the time. A slot player steps away from a machine for a short break and returns to find another slot player grinning ear to ear having just won a major jackpot on that very machine. If the first player had stayed she would have won the jackpot. Right? Actually, no. The second player just happened to push the spin button at the exact moment when a jackpot was on the RNG. A millisecond more

Watch Out!
Nevada's Megabucks jackpot has repeatedly been hit by people who weren't playing maximum coins. The result? No jackpot. Always play maximum coins on a progressive slot. Always read the payout table to understand what kind of slot you are playing.

or less would have produced a different result. It is highly unlikely that the first player would have pushed the button at the exact same instant. In fact, two or three jackpots may have passed her by when she was scratching her head or sipping her drink.

Myth: I was one stop away from a big jackpot

Your heart skips a beat when the symbols almost line up, but not quite. Were you close? It may look that way, but there is no such thing as close for the RNG. The actual number that generated the sequence may have been hundreds, thousands, or even millions of numbers away from the nearly identical jackpot sequence. You were no closer or farther this time than the last time.

Myth: Playing faster increases my chance of winning

Playing faster and spending more increases the effect of the house edge and makes you lose more. The chance of winning on each spin is not affected by the speed of play.

Myth: Slots are looser at certain times of the day or week

Casinos can't change the way their slots pay out without changing the slot. The payback percentage is set at the factory. There is no switch or computer program that tightens or loosens a slot at a specific time or day of the week. See Chapter 13 for more information as to why such a switch doesn't exist.

Slot tournaments: a good way to even the odds

How would you like unlimited spins without having to pay the machine? And no worries about loose or tight! That's a slot tournament. Occasionally they are free promotions, but many casinos have paid tournaments. One fee gives you an opportunity to compete with other players to see who can win the most slot credits. The top prize can be thousands of dollars and (depending on the tournament size) the mid-range prizes are substantial, too. Some competitions even have a cash prize for last place. Larger tournaments usually include a hotel room, meals, and other goodies like show tickets and gifts. Add it up and the total value is often greater than the amount paid even when you don't win a top prize.

Of course, if you have really lousy luck and you finish tenth from last in a field of five hundred, you won't win anything, but you still get the room, meals, entertainment, and the pleasure of competing. The key, as always, is to do the arithmetic and figure a price-for-fun.

Just the facts

- Slot machines are negative expectation games. The house edge varies for each machine and (depending on local regulations) is typically set in a range from about one percent to an occasional 25 percent.

- Casinos in competitive markets have the lowest house edge, usually 10 percent or less on most machines.

- Slot spins are controlled by a random number generator. The way you push the button, pull the handle, or insert the coin has absolutely no effect on the outcome.

- A slot is never "due" to hit or "played out." Each spin is independent.

Moneysaver
Playing two side-by-side machines doesn't double your chances of winning, it actually lowers them. If one machine is loose then the other one is most certainly tight. You'd be better off playing the loose one exclusively. If both machines are paying off similarly then neither one is loose. Find another machine.

- Progressive, nickel, and quarter slots tend to be tighter than nonprogressive, dollar, and five-dollar slots. Don't play a progressive machine unless you're shooting for a big jackpot.

- Casinos put their loosest machines in high visibility slot areas. Machines near table games and in low visibility locations tend to be tight. Airports, gas stations, and other nongaming venues have the tightest slots.

- Slot tournaments are a good way to enjoy lots of slot play while strictly limiting your total cost. Look for free tournaments or competitions that pay back all or most of the entry fee in prizes and services.

GET THE SCOOP ON...

How a video poker machine works ▪ Video poker
machines that give players an edge ▪ Strategies
for playing video poker ▪ What it takes to get a
royal flush ▪ Video poker machines to avoid

Video Poker

Video poker exerts a near-mystical pull on America's gamblers. It's the nation's legendary frontier game plus the best elements of a slot machine. That is powerful stuff.

Video poker is also popular because it seems inherently fair. There's no hidden house edge or secretly tight machines. Each draw is from a freshly shuffled deck. Every player has a chance and a choice. Video poker is one of the few casino contests that can have a positive financial expectation. Play the right machine, long enough, in the right way and video poker is guaranteed to pay back more than it takes in.

On the whole video poker is one of the best values for your gambling dollar. We'll cover the positive expectation opportunities later in the chapter, but in the meantime please don't sell anything to go play video poker. The commitment required for positive returns is not for everyone; in fact, it's not for most people.

If you know poker then you know the basics of video poker. You want the highest hand. Card combinations that make the various hands are ranked in

Unofficially...
Wild Bill Hickok
was holding a
pair of eights
and a pair of
aces when he
was shot and
killed while play-
ing poker in a
Deadwood
saloon. The card
combination
became known as
a "dead man's
hand." If you're
playing Deuces
Wild and you
receive that
hand, drop one
of the pair or
your bankroll will
suffer the same
fate as Wild Bill.

Figure 4.1. Beyond that and the concept of the draw you should forget everything you know about the table game when playing the video version. You can't bluff the computer, raise, or call. There's no pot. The computer deals you five cards. You can keep all of them, some, or none. The computer deals replacements as necessary. The new combination is your hand. Winners are paid according to a pay table posted on the machine.

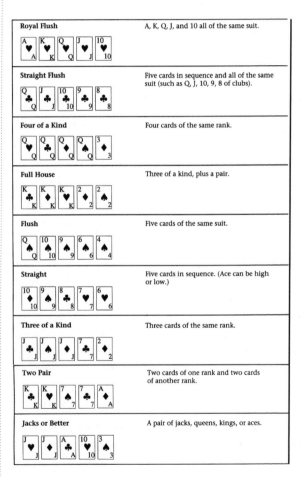

Video poker
hands for Jacks
or Better ranked
in winning order.

The most basic game is Jacks or Better; hands with two jacks or higher win. Other video poker versions include Deuces Wild where 2s count as any value the player requires. Joker Poker inserts a joker into the deck as a wild card. Double Joker Poker inserts two jokers. Poker Frenzy deals each card from a different deck making it possible for you to have five cards of the same rank and suit. There are many more game variations. In some cases a minimum win requires kings or better, three of kind, or two pairs. Whatever the game, the play remains the same for (nearly) every machine. Receive five cards, draw, the result is your hand.

Buttons on a video poker machine are similar to those on a slot machine (see Chapter 3) except that *Spin* is replaced by *Deal,* and each card has a button for holding. Newer video poker machines use touch screens and include computer-style help functions.

The single most important element of every video poker machine is the pay table. It shows the amount of coins or credits that will be paid for winning hands, and it completely determines the character of the game. To understand why let's take a look at the inside of a video poker machine.

Video poker's kinder and gentler RNG

The Random Number Generator (RNG) that we described in Chapter 3 is also at the heart of a video poker machine. Its basic operation is the same. The RNG randomly selects numbers in a range between zero to a few billion, one after another, at a rate of about one thousand numbers per second. In a video poker machine each number corresponds to a unique five-card hand and five replacement cards.

Watch Out!
Some players becomes excited and forget to hold cards when they're dealt a royal flush or another perfect hand. One more press of the deal button does not bring a big payout, but five more cards. Ouch! Be sure to press the hold button for every card you intend to keep. The screen should acknowledge your choice.

Timesaver
Do you wonder
how replacement
cards are dealt?
Is it sequentially
from a pile of
five or does each
card have a
unique replace-
ment from the
five? It's an
interesting ques-
tion, but the
answer has no
statistical effect
on the result.
Save your
brainpower
for strategy.

Video poker is so much more predictable than slots because the RNG is set only one way. It strictly simulates the probabilities of dealing from a shuffled deck of cards. No loose or tight machines. No mysterious house edge. No exceptions. Shuffle a deck at home and deal. The likelihood of any particular hand from a real deck is identical to a video poker deck.

Wild deuces or the addition of a joker or two change the probabilities, but only in a real-life way. The true odds are fixed. Casinos can only get an edge with house odds. That's why the pay table is so important.

The pay table IS the game

Table 4.1 is a pay table for the venerable original version of Jacks or Better. The far-right column shows (in rounded percentages) how often a player is likely to hit any particular hand when using an optimal playing strategy. Notice the payouts on a one-coin wager for a full house (9 coins) and a flush (6 coins). We'll refer to them again in Table 4.2.

TABLE 4.1: JACKS OR BETTER 9/6 PAY TABLE

Coins	1	2	3	4	5	
Royal Flush	250	500	750	1000	4000	0.0025%
Straight Flush	50	100	150	200	250	0.01%
Four of a Kind	25	50	75	100	125	0.2%
Full House	9	18	27	36	45	1.1%
Flush	6	12	18	24	30	1.1%
Straight	4	8	12	16	20	1.1%
Three of a Kind	3	6	9	12	15	7.1%
Two Pairs	2	4	6	8	10	12.5%
Pair of Jacks or Better	1	2	3	4	5	20.0%

Each coin increases payments proportionally except for a fifth coin which quadruples the payment for a royal flush. Win percentages in the far right column are rounded.

TABLE 4.2: COMPARING PAY TABLES

Machine Type	9/6	8/5	6/5
Royal Flush	250	250	250
Straight Flush	50	50	50
Four of a Kind	25	25	25
Full House	9	8	6
Flush	6	5	5
Straight	4	4	4
Three of a Kind	3	3	3
Two Pairs	2	2	2
Pair of Jacks or Better	1	1	1
Payback	99%	97%	95%

All three machines play Jacks or Better video poker. Win percentages are rounded and are based on maximum coin play (royal flush pays 4,000 coins).

Table 4.2 condenses the previous pay table into one column on the left (labeled 9/6). Two additional columns show condensed pay tables from other Jacks-or-Better machines. The game rules are the same, but the paybacks are different. Notice the lower amounts in the middle of the second and third columns. A full house receives only eight coins and a flush receives five in the second game. This

TABLE 4.3: DOUBLE DOUBLE BONUS POKER

Royal Flush	250/4000 for five coins
Straight Flush	50
Four Aces	160
Four Aces with 2, 3, or 4	400
Four 2s, 3s or 4s	80
Four 2s, 3s or 4s with an Ace, 2, 3, 4	160
Four 5s through Ks	50
Full House	9
Flush	6
Straight	4
Three of a Kind	3
Two Pairs	1
Pair of Jacks or Better	1
Payback	98.8%

This is the pay table for Double Double Bonus Poker. Look at all those ways to win, and it's a 9/6 machine too! But why has the overall payback dropped to 98.8 percent? Because two pairs are worth only one coin.

TABLE 4.4: SAMPLE PAY TABLES

Double Bonus Poker

Royal Flush	250/4,000 with maximum coins
Straight Flush	50
Four Aces	160
Four 2s, 3s or 4s	80
Four 5s through Ks	50
Full House	10
Flush	7
Straight	5
Three of a Kind	3
Two Pairs	1
Pair of Jacks or Better	1
Payback	100.2%

Joker Poker

Five of a Kind	250/4,000 with maximum coins
Royal Flush	100
Straight Flush	100
Four of a Kind	16
Full House	8
Flush	5
Straight	4
Three of a Kind	2
Two Pairs	1
Payback	97.2%

Notice the absence of a high pair in Deuces Wild and Joker Poker. Deuces Wild doesn't pay for two pairs either.

Deuces Wild

Royal Flush	250/4000 with maximum coins
Four Deuces	200
Royal Flush with Deuces	25
Five of a Kind	15
Straight Flush	9
Four of a Kind	5
Full House	3
Flush	2
Straight	2
Three of a Kind	1
Payback	100.7%

"8/5 version" pays about two percent less overall than the 9/6. In the third game, the overall payback drops to about 95 percent because a full house pays six coins and a flush pays five coins.

The 9/6 machine obviously pays more. In the early days of video poker when these three games were most common it was easy to look for a 9/6, settle for 8/5 and avoid 6/5. This clarity made some machines less popular so casinos countered with measures to muddy the water. The schedule in Table 4.3 is one example. It looks like a 9/6 with some exciting new ways to win, but the payout is actually lower because two pairs are worth only one coin.

These days more than four dozen versions of video poker can be found with paybacks ranging from 91 percent to 100 percent and occasionally higher. Some machines offer progressive jackpots, and that further complicates the equation. Professional gamblers and novices alike use computer programs to calculate the shifting odds, or they buy books like Lenny Frome's *Winning Strategies for Video Poker*. Frome covers fifty-five different games; each has a different strategy to maximize wins.

The result of so many choices is that the traditional wisdom of looking primarily for a 9/6 Jacks-or-Better machine doesn't work so well anymore. It's still a great game, but the market is swimming in machines. Some pay more, many pay less. The only way to know for sure how much a machine pays is to read the whole pay table. Math wizards then use a spread sheet. The rest of us simply compare it with a table that is proven to have a certain payback.

Table 4.4 contains pay tables for three common video poker games. You'll notice that it's easy to glance at a pay table, see the numbers, and miss the

Moneysaver
Some people rush through hands to increase the overall probability of hitting a royal flush. Bad idea. Going faster can make a royal come sooner, but it also tends to increase mistakes. That can cost money and may even cause someone to miss the royal they were chasing.

Bright Idea
Here's a good way to avoid being fooled by a near look-alike pay table. Write your preferred tables on a small piece of paper and then compare them line-by-line to the games in the casino. This works in reverse too. Carry a pen and paper with you while playing. Record the pay tables of unfamiliar games for later study.

required lowest hand. Joker Poker looks inviting until you realize a high pair won't bring you a win. Deuces Wild may look anemic in comparison, but it actually pays more. Beware of copycat Deuces Wild pay tables that are nearly identical but only pay 4 for four of a kind. That one coin difference drops the payback about six percent.

Stalking the elusive royal flush

One hundred percent plus games certainly look inviting. They really do pay what they promise, but you may not be willing to make the effort. Here's why.

A 52-card deck can produce 2,598,960 unique hands. Four of them are royal flushes. That's one royal flush that won't require a draw in every 649,740 hands. When we add the probability of drawing to a royal flush the chances increase to about 1 in 40,000. That number can go up or down depending on the type of strategy that is used. The critical point is that the payback on every video poker machine includes the value of the royal flush. The player must win the royal flush while playing maximum coins to reach those wonderful positive expectations. It's mathematically guaranteed, but only with no strategy mistakes (like accidentally throwing away a royal) and enough play time. And remember that 40,000 is an average. A royal is like the elusive head on a coin; it may not appear when expected.

What it takes to play a positive game

Let's say a player completes a game every ten seconds. That's six games a minute, 360 games an hour, and 111 hours to play 40,000 games. During this time smaller wins are accumulating and maximum coins are being wagered. The required bankroll is only three or four thousand dollars, but after 111 hours $50,000 worth of quarters has gone through the machine. If a royal comes during this time, and if the machine has a payback of 100.5 percent, the total return will be $250.00.

$$\$50,000 \times 100.5\% = \$50,250$$

A dollar machine will return $1,000. Not exactly a windfall. And here's the clincher. Most people don't use a strategy or they don't play maximum coins. That gives them a zero chance of seeing a 100 percent return in the long run.

Is 95.5 percent so expensive?

$250 profit for 111 hours of play may seem paltry, but compare it with a $2,250 loss. That's the cost of the same $1.25 per hand play on a 95.5 percent machine.

Do you play video poker more than one day per year? If you take two annual trips to Vegas, a once-a-week trip to Atlantic City, or an occasional afternoon on a riverboat, then your aggregate numbers will inevitably begin to resemble the average. Maximum quarters and 360 hands per hour produces a positive average return of $2.25 per hour on a 100.5 percent machine and a cost of $20.25 on a 95.5 percent machine. Four sessions of four hours each is $36 profit on a 100.5 percent machine compared with $324 cost when playing 95.5 percent.

Remember, this is an average over time and it includes winning the royal. The numbers are worse without the royal.

Once again the question is price for fun. How much are you willing to pay? Finding a higher pay machine is sometimes easy, sometimes it's a hassle. An unfavorable or unfamiliar pay table may be the only game available. If you'd rather just play and pay

Timesaver
High pay machines are nice, but don't waste time searching for them in markets without competition or in jurisdictions that restrict payouts. Some states like Louisiana simply don't allow non-casino locations to offer big video poker jackpots or a house edge that favors players.

Moneysaver
Casinos frequent-
ly adjust pay
tables to improve
a game's appeal
and profitability,
but sometimes it
backfires. New
games occasion-
ally pay more
than what was
expected. Savvy
players keep up
with the develop-
ments and hit
the machines for
tidy profits
before the casi-
nos realize the
mistake and
withdraw
the game.

for the pleasure then go right ahead. Just be sure you have a handle on the cost. We'll give you some suggestions for calculating that at the end of the chapter.

Finding high pay machines

Machines that pay much less than 100 percent don't usually advertise the fact. They only show the pay schedule and leave you wondering. High pay machines are often emblazoned with signs promoting their payback. One casino I visited had labels on the machines that said "100 percent certified." The very fine print added "with maximum coins wagered and optimum play."

The best machines are found in competitive markets, but video poker is like its cousin the slot machine. It tends to pay less in convenience stores and other offbeat locations. Bar and truck stop games often pay back only 94 percent. That's OK for a few quarters, but save the big bucks for a casino. If you're in a market with multiple casinos (like Las Vegas) it pays to shop around.

One more thing to consider. Any machine becomes high pay if it's progressive and the top jackpot is big enough. A quarter Jacks-or-Better 8/5 progressive is 100 percent when the meter reaches $2,200. Every dollar above that number pushes the machine higher into positive territory. But (as always) you've got to win the royal to see the positive return.

So many games, so many strategies

Imagine playing Jacks or Better with the goal of getting 10s or worse. Any video poker machine will oblige you and play this wacky game. Of course it won't pay on the "winning" hands, just the "losing" ones. And you will occasionally "lose." You might even "lose" with a royal flush. Our 10s-or-worse game is an extreme example of how a strategy affects the probability of seeing any particular hand. The royal flush becomes less likely but not impossible.

The best video poker strategies balance potential profits from every hand with the probability of winning any particular hand. In some cases pat hands are sacrificed for possibly better ones. In other situations it's the reverse. The resulting strategies are sometimes bizarre and run counter to everything a person learns playing traditional poker. Yet they work. Unfortunately every change in a pay table requires a change in strategy, so every game has a unique system of optimal play. A classic Jacks-or-Better approach used on a Deuces Wild machine, Joker Poker, or even another Jacks-or-Better game with a different pay table can result in poorly played hands and fewer wins. Some strategies are nearly identical. Some are radically different. That's something to keep in mind if you choose to play an unfamiliar game. Don't risk too much of your bankroll.

Basic strategies for popular games

Tables 4.5, 4.6, and 4.7 present abbreviated strategies for three popular video poker games. If they don't seem abbreviated consider this. Table 4.6 combines options such as a four-card flush that has three high cards, the same hand with two, one and zero high cards. Each hand has a slightly different probability of producing a win. On a more complete schedule they would be separated from each other by a three-card royal and hands that include a pair of jacks, queens, kings, but not aces. Did that cross your eyes?

TABLE 4.5: JACKS OR BETTER 9/6 STRATEGY

Keep	Discard	Hand
5	0	Royal Flush
5	0	Straight Flush
4	1	4 of a Kind
4	1	4 Card Royal
5	0	Full House
5	0	Flush
3	2	3 of a Kind
5	0	Straight
4	1	4-Card Straight Flush
4	1	Two Pairs
2	3	Pair of Jacks or Higher
3	2	3-Card Royal
4	1	4-Card Flush
2	3	Low Pair
4	1	4-Card Straight
3	2	3-Card Straight Flush
2	3	2-Card Royal
3	2	3 High Cards
2	3	2 High Cards
1	4	1 High Card
0	5	Everything Else

This strategy also works with most 8/5 and 6/5 machines.

> **"** Someone once gave me a hand-held video poker machine because they knew I loved regular poker. I played it every day for hours until I realized video poker strategy was ruining my regular game. I was unconsciously throwing away good hands at the table in pursuit of a royal flush.
> —Allen Brivic, poker player **"**

That's why we shortened the strategies. Strictly speaking they are not optimal, but they'll bring you closer to optimum play and they're easier to memorize or to copy and carry in your pocket. If you're serious about playing a complete strategy then check out one of the books in Appendix C. One more caveat; not everyone agrees (including the people who create these games) as to the optimal importance of the various incomplete hands and exactly how much on average a machine will pay back. Some strategists give greater weight to the opportunity of getting a royal.

TABLE 4.6: DOUBLE BONUS POKER (JACKS OR BETTER) STRATEGY

Keep	Discard	Hand
5	0	Royal Flush
4	1	4 Aces
4	1	4 2s, 3s or 4s
5	0	Straight Flush
4	1	4 5s through Kings
4	1	4-Card Royal
3	2	3 Aces
5	0	Full House
5	0	Flush
3	2	3 2s, 3s or 4s
3	2	3 5s through Kings
5	0	Straight
4	1	4-Card Straight Flush
4	1	Two Pairs
2	3	2 Aces
3	2	3-Card Royal
4	1	4-Card Flush
2	3	Pair of Jacks, Queens or Kings
4	1	4-Card Straight
3	2	3-Card Straight Flush
2	3	Low Pair
2	3	2-Card Royal
3	2	3-Card Flush
3	2	3 High Cards
3	2	3-Card Straight
2	3	2 High Cards
1	4	1 High Card
0	5	Everything Else

This is a strategy for the Double Bonus game in Table 4.4.

Bright Idea
One of the pleasures of playing video poker is the complete absence of pressure from dealers and other players to make a quick decision. Use this to your advantage and take all the time you need to consider each hand. Your resulting play will be more accurate.

TABLE 4.7: JOKER POKER STRATEGY

This is a strategy for the Joker Poker game in Table 4.4.

Keep	Discard	Hands Without Joker
5	0	Royal Flush
5	0	Straight Flush
4	1	4 of a Kind
5	0	Full House
4	1	4-Card Royal
4	1	4-Card Straight Flush
5	0	Flush
3	2	3 of a Kind
5	0	Straight
4	1	Two Pairs
3	2	3-Card Royal
3	2	3-Card Straight Flush
4	1	4-Card Flush
4	1	4-Card Straight
2	3	Pair
2	3	2-Card Straight Flush
2	3	2-Card Royal
3	2	3-Card Flush
3	2	3-Card Straight
0	5	Everything Else
Keep	**Discard**	**Hands With Joker**
5	0	Five of a Kind
5	0	Joker Royal Flush
4	1	4 of a Kind
4	1	4-Card Royal
5	0	Full House
4	1	4-Card Straight Flush
5	0	Flush
5	0	Straight
3	2	3 of a Kind
3	2	3-Card Straight Flush
4	1	4-Card Straight
4	1	4-Card Flush
1	4	Joker

Watch Out!
Traditional Jacks-or-Better winners, a high pair or two pairs, are worthless when playing Deuces Wild. The lowest paying Deuces Wild hands are three of a kind and a straight.

A closer look at the strategies

The way to use the tables is to match your hand to the highest one in the list and then play that strategy. Below are examples from Table 4.5.

$$2♥ \quad 7♥ \quad 9♥ \quad J♥ \quad J♣$$

The above hand should be played as a high pair instead of a four card flush because the pair is higher on the list.

$$3♥ \quad 4♥ \quad 5♣ \quad 6♥ \quad 6♦$$

This hand should be played as a low pair instead of a four card straight. Low pairs should also be held over a three card straight flush or any single high card.

$$A♥ \quad K♥ \quad Q♦ \quad J♥ \quad 10♥$$

People who play regular poker will quickly notice that video poker strategy is very different. This is a classic situation. A smart player will throw away a perfectly good hand for the chance of getting a royal flush.

$$3♣ \quad 3♦ \quad K♥ \quad 6♦ \quad 9♠$$

Don't hold a single high card, commonly called a "kicker," unless it's the only card you hold. Holding a kicker with anything else dramatically decreases the chance of improving a hand.

$$7♦ \quad 8♣ \quad 10♥ \quad J♥ \quad Q♠$$

Drawing to a an inside straight is always dicey business. Strategists recommend it under certain complex conditions. If your only other alternative is to hold high cards then keep those cards and draw to the straight. If the straight doesn't have high cards then dump it in Jacks or Better 9/6 and play it in Double Bonus and Joker Poker. This advice applies only to straights. Always draw to a four card inside straight flush and a three card inside straight flush unless your hand also includes something that's higher on the list.

2♣ 7♥ K♥ Q♥ J♥

This could be played as possible flush, but you should go for the gold and the royal.

8♦ 3♥6♥10♥ 2♠

This is a zero hand (draw five cards) when playing traditional Jacks or Better but when playing Double Bonus and Joker Poker you should go for the flush. The reasoning is simple. Double Bonus pays more for a flush; Joker Poker may fill in the flush with a joker.

Hunches and winning

Most video poker hands are losers. It is unfortunate, but strategy doesn't change this. The machine regularly wins nearly 60 percent of the time. Add in the hands that are a push and you're only ahead about 1 in 4 contests. High pay machines can be even stingier. You'll lose a lot before you win more.

Some players become frustrated with all the losing, so they abandon strategy and begin playing hunches. This is absolutely wrong from a mathematical point of view, but I disagree with people who say it should never be done. Playing a hunch is perfectly okay. Just realize that you are paying for the pleasure of making a guess. You might win, but on average you are more likely to lose. If you can live with that then by all means do what you "feel." Remember it's absolutely possible to throw away all five cards and still get a royal flush.

Video poker myths

Video poker machines breed their own brand of myths based mostly on the feeling that the machine is toying with the player. How else does one explain drawing to a four card royal and finishing with a regular flush, then on the next hand receiving another four card royal and drawing to trash. Is it the work of a sadistic programmer or just average luck? Most people forget they're ahead four coins.

Myth: Some machines are loose and hit royals more often

The more a machine is played, the more chances it receives to hit a royal. That's simple mathematics. The machine isn't hitting more because it's loose. There is no such thing as a loose video poker machine. The pay table alone determines how much a machine will pay back.

Myth: Maximum bets bring more trash hands

The RNG is not aware of how many credits have been wagered. It spits out thousands of numbers in the time you take to push in a $5 bill. Whatever is on the RNG at the moment you press deal is the only factor that decides the hand.

Myth: A machine that just paid a royal should be avoided

This falls into the slot machine myth category of "due" to hit or "played out." A video poker machine has an equal chance of hitting a royal on every hand. The last royal has no effect on the next one.

Myth: Playing quickly makes a machine pay more

Yes, and it will cost more too. One hand every six seconds or one every sixty seconds doesn't change the per hand chances of winning. Playing faster sim-

Watch Out!
Some games mimic high pay versions by offering a nearly identical pay table. The catch is one coin less on exactly one hand. It's easy to miss in the mass of numbers, but that translates into a nearly six percent house edge for one version of Deuces Wild.

ply increases the speed at which the house edge or player edge (on positive machines) takes effect. On a negative machine, the more you play, the more you pay. It's the same on a positive machine until you hit a royal.

Myth: A nearby machine paid a royal so this machine won't

A progressive pot is the only situation when one machine's win can affect another machine. If that happens you're out of luck, but regular five-coin jackpots aren't affected by other machines. When someone at the next machine hits a royal you may feel the luck has been sucked out of the area along with the money, but take comfort in the fact that your chances haven't changed one bit.

Myth: Someone stole my royal flush!

We covered this in Chapter 3, but it's good to repeat here. The issue comes up when one player leaves a machine and a second player wins on that machine. The first player didn't lose a royal or leave before a royal was due to hit. The second player just happened to press the deal button at the instant a royal was on the RNG. The first player probably missed ninety royals in the hour she was playing the machine. Think about it. The RNG produces 1000 numbers per second. That's a royal every 40 seconds!

The rest of the common slot myths are also invalid for video poker. Pushing the buttons or dropping the coins a certain way has no effect. Cold or hot coins out of the machine mean nothing. Casinos have no control over when or if a machine hits. And most important; the machine is not toying with you.

Money management, price for fun, and practical issues

As we said previously, about six out of ten video poker bets are losers. Another one or two hands are pushes depending on the game. High pay machines tend to produce more losing and winning streaks than their lower pay counterparts, and although this is a function of the pay table and not the RNG, it sometimes leads to the feeling that video poker is simply losing, losing, losing and never winning. The pleasure of a full house or a flush can be quickly consumed in a seemingly endless sea of trash hands and pairs.

The house edge is magnified without a royal. It's further magnified without an occasional straight flush or four of a kind. It's amazing, but video poker with a zero house edge can take a player's money faster than roulette. The following money management suggestions adjust for this dynamic.

Money management: short session

Our advice here mirrors the advice we gave for the slots. If you're playing a short session with one roll of coins or less be prepared to lose it all. That's highly unlikely, but it's better to think this way and be pleasantly surprised to have twelve coins left out of 40 than to expect that wonderful near-zero house edge to return most of your money. It usually doe not. Your price-for-fun should be the entire bet, one to five coins per hand.

Money management: medium session

A medium session is typically two or three hours, or about seven hundred to eight hundred hands. You probably won't see a royal or a straight flush. You may see four of a kind only once. If you play near optimum level on a Jacks or Better 9/6 and the best hand is an occasional full house then the house edge hovers around 10 percent. It increases to near 20 percent on a 6/5 or a positive machine that only pays one coin for two pairs. Playing $200 once through on a quarter machine, one coin per hand, should leave you with at least $160. Playing $100 once through and then playing your winnings once through will leave you with about $60. A bankroll of $50 will disappear completely with repeated play. Yes it's possible to win more (or lose less), but don't expect it.

Money management: the long haul

If you play multiple sessions over many days (more than 80,000 total hands) you will see royals and all the other combinations. With perfect play the house edge shrinks to less than one percent on a 9/6 machine and it goes positive on many others. Betting maximum coins on a 100.2 percent positive quarter machine with a minimum $3,000 bankroll should leave you ahead by about $100 after 40,000 hands, but only if you hit the royal once.

Should you bet the max?

Maximum bets are required if you want anything near a positive return. If $5 per hand is too much then go to a quarter machine. If $1.25 is still too much then find a nickel machine or accept the higher house edge and drop to lower bets. Remember that maximum coins only make a difference when winning a royal, and a $100 bankroll will disappear five times faster when betting the maximum. That's a once-through difference of 80 hands compared with 400. Betting either way is fine. Just be sure it matches your price for fun.

Advice for playing casino machines

Slots and video poker are identical when it comes to practical issues like coins or bills, tracking wins and losses, handling a big win, and avoiding confusion in the clamor of the casino. We covered those subjects extensively in Chapter 3, so we won't repeat them here, but the information is very helpful when playing video poker, particularly the slot player's checklist. All the items on the list apply to any casino machine game.

Just the facts

- Video poker true odds are identical to the odds when playing with a real shuffled deck.

- Some video poker games have a positive expectation for the player, but only when a player bets maximum coins and periodically wins a royal flush. The chance of hitting a royal flush is about 1 in 40,000.

- You should carefully check the entire pay table on a video poker machine before playing. Some machines pay slightly fewer coins on selected hands.

- 9/6 Jacks or Better is a good game but it may be hard to find. Beware of imitation machines that have lower paybacks.

- Optimal strategies change when a pay table changes. Be sure you're playing the right strategy for a particular video poker game.

- High pay machines tend to be more "streaky" with wins and losses. This is not a function of the RNG, but a function of the pay table.

- Video poker and slots are identical when it comes to practical issues like handling money and avoiding confusion.

Moneysaver
Many slot clubs award fewer points for video poker play than they do for regular slots. Some don't award anything when you play a positive expectation machine. Rules vary and they change like the wind, so don't assume a previous deal, sweet or sour, is still on. Check periodically, especially before playing a large bankroll.

Table Games

PART III

GET THE SCOOP ON...
Blackjack basic strategy ▪ Rules that
give players an edge ▪ Blackjack bets
you should never make ▪ Counting cards

Blackjack

Chapter 5

I f blackjack were invented today, casinos probably wouldn't offer the game; it gives too many
advantages to the player.

The first and most devastating advantage is that
blackjack, in some circumstances, is a positive expectation game. And you don't need to play 40,000 or
more hands (like video poker) to see that positive
return. Unlike table poker, players aren't strategiz-
ing against you while the casino sits above the fray.
Blackjack doesn't require other players. The dealer
follows strict rules. You play as you please.

Blackjack allows you to increase a bet as odds
improve, decrease it if odds are bad, and even insure
against loss. If you play well, you can turn the odds
against the casino to win more. There is not another casino game that allows you so many decisions
and options to positively affect your situation after
the initial bet. Compare that to Caribbean Stud
Poker and Let It Ride. Those are examples of what
casinos consider ideal table games; few player decisions and fat margins. Casinos would love good play-

ers to leave the blackjack table and move to one of those games or maybe the slots and video poker.

Notice that I said "good players." The bad players are why blackjack remains the most profitable of all the table games. It has evolved into a love-hate thing for casinos. They love the profits, but hate the fact that some players (mostly professional gamblers) can consistently win money. It's a powerful subtext to blackjack that occasionally overshadows having fun. That's a shame.

In this chapter we'll tell you how to maximize enjoyment and winning while minimizing your involvement in the casino's struggle with a few professionals. You'll learn how to beat the casino into a nearly even and occasionally positive contest. But before we continue, please heed a caveat similar to the one we gave you in Chapter 4: The commitment required for consistent positive returns playing blackjack is not for everyone; in fact, it's not for most people. Casual players should expect a good game, a good time, and a price for fun.

It's all about twenty-one

Blackjack is all about the number twenty-one. The suits of the cards mean nothing; their rank is of sole importance. Two through ten are counted at their number value. Jacks, queens, and kings are counted as ten. Aces can be one or eleven, as the player prefers.

Each player competes with the dealer to build a hand that has a point total closer to twenty-one but not over that amount. The initial hand is two cards. If it's a combination of a ten and an ace, twenty-one, it's called *blackjack* or a *natural;* the player automatically wins (assuming the dealer doesn't also have a natural). Blackjack is dealt about once in twenty hands. When the card combination totals less than twenty-one, the player can ask for additional cards in an attempt to get closer to twenty-one without going over. Receiving an additional card is called a *hit*. Refusing additional cards is a *stand*. Players who exceed twenty-one automatically lose. This is called a *bust* or a *break*. When all the players have finished hitting, standing, and sometimes busting, it's the dealer's turn to complete a hand. If the dealer busts and the player hasn't busted, the player wins. If the dealer has a lower total, the player wins. A tie (called a *push*) has no winner and no money changes hands. The only way a player can lose without busting is when the dealer is closer to twenty-one, so the house advantage rests primarily on the fact that players complete their hands first.

A natural win is paid 3:2. That means a ten dollar bet will win you fifteen additional dollars. All other bets are paid 1:1 (except insurance, which we'll cover in the next section).

How blackjack is played

Blackjack is played at a table like the one in Figure 5.1. You should always note the important rule information printed on the table cover and on the card next to the dealer. Some casinos offer single deck games where the dealer actually holds the deck as she distributes the cards, but most casinos have multiple deck games. Two to eight decks are stored in a box called a *shoe*. The dealer pulls cards from a slot at the front of the shoe.

A player's cards are usually dealt face down in a single deck game. Multiple deck games can be either face up or face down. Your chances of winning are the same either way, although face up gives

Moneysaver
Occasionally a casino will offer a promotion of 2:1 payouts for naturals. The additional edge (more than two percent) will push almost any blackjack game into positive expectation. If you see such a promotion, play it soon because it won't last long.

Watch Out!
Third-base play-
ers are some-
times harassed
by other players
for not correctly
playing blackjack
basic strategy.
Pulling a ten
that would oth-
erwise bust the
dealer is particu-
larly unpopular.
If you don't want
the attention,
don't play
third base.

you more information about cards that are in play and therefore unavailable.

The game begins when you sit down. Any seat is fine. You have an equal chance of winning at all of them. The seat to the dealer's far left is commonly called *first base*. The seat at the other end of the table, the dealer's far right, is *third base*. The terminology is of no consequence in the game, but it may help you in a conversation with an experienced blackjack player.

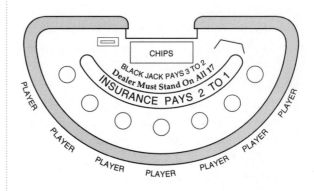

An example of a standard blackjack table layout. Note the house rules printed at the center of the table and on the upright card next to the dealer.

The cards will be shuffled and you or another player will be allowed to cut the deck(s). In a single-deck game, this is simply lifting a top portion of the deck and laying it next to the bottom portion. In multiple deck games you will use a plastic card-sized stop. Put it somewhere near the middle. The dealer completes the cut, and burns the new top card by discarding it in a tray or putting it face up toward the end of the deck. At this point it's time to bet. Put your wager in the circle in front of you and don't touch the chips again. You'll either lose them at the end of the hand or be given more chips by the dealer.

Starting on her left the dealer gives one card to each player and then one card face up to herself. A second card is dealt to each player and the dealer receives another card called the *hole card*. This time it's face down.

You can see only one of the dealer's card. Let's say it's a ten. Does the dealer have blackjack? Does the dealer have nineteen? Does the dealer have thirteen? If you have twenty-one or twenty it doesn't matter; you'll stand and probably win or tie. But what if you have thirteen? Should you hit? What's that other card?

Insurance

You have an option in most games to take *insurance* against a dealer blackjack if the dealer is showing an ace. It's an additional bet of up to one-half the value of your original bet and it pays 2:1. If you take insurance, in many casinos the dealer will check the hole card for a ten before continuing the hand. Let's say you have a $10 original bet and a $5 insurance bet; you don't have a natural but it turns out the dealer does. She will take $10 and pay $10. It's a push. If the dealer doesn't have blackjack, you lose the insurance bet.

If both of you have naturals it's a push without insurance, but with insurance you win the equivalent of even money on your original bet. If you take insurance and you have blackjack but the dealer doesn't, the two wagers still work out to even money. Insurance sounds like a wonderful thing, but it's actually a bad bet. We'll explain why later in the chapter.

Timesaver
An easy way to quickly calculate the value of aces in a hand is to always start with one and then add ten. Five and an ace would be six or sixteen; three and an ace would be four or fourteen.

Watch Out!
Most casinos that deal cards face up require that you don't touch the cards. This includes splitting. In this case simply put an additional wager next to the original bet (not on top of it) and indicate your intention to split. The dealer will separate the cards and hit as you request.

Hit, stand, double, and split

Most dealer hands aren't naturals, so players have an opportunity to either request additional cards or refuse them. The dealer works from her left to her right. Tapping or scratching the table with your index finger indicates your desire for an additional card. A small wave with one hand as if to say "stop" or "go away" indicates that you are standing. In games where the cards are played face down there is yet another way to indicate a stand. You simply push the edge of your cards a bit under the wager and move your hands away.

One variation of a hit is called a *double down* or *double*. It requires an additional bet, usually an amount equal to your original wager. You put the extra chips next to your original chips. The dealer gives you exactly one more card and that is your hand. No additional cards may be dealt. Most casinos restrict doubling to hands with two cards.

If your original hand has cards with an equal point value (two eights, two aces, two nines) you can split them for an additional wager equal to the first wager. You now have two hands. Each hand is played separately. You can hit or stand as necessary. Some casinos restrict doubling on splits. Most require that you take only one card on split aces.

The dealer's hand

If you don't bust it's up to the dealer to beat you. She turns over her cards and draws according to a strict rule. The dealer must stand on seventeen or over, and she must hit on sixteen or under. She has no decision in the matter. Some casinos require a dealer to hit a *soft* seventeen, which is any hand that totals seventeen but includes an ace counted as eleven. A *hard* seventeen would be a hand without an ace or one in which the ace is counted as one.

When your hand isn't a bust and the dealer goes over twenty-one, you win. Your point total doesn't matter. If the dealer doesn't bust, your point total suddenly matters a lot. You'll either win, push, or lose.

Losing bets are taken, winners are paid, the cards are collected, and the process begins again.

Rule variations

Some casinos offer *surrender*. If your initial hand seems hopeless you can take back half your bet and forfeit the rest. Surrender is usually restricted to situations when the dealer doesn't have a natural. This is known as *late* surrender. Occasionally, you may be allowed *early* surrender against an ace that turns out to be blackjack. Other rule variations include different payouts on naturals, not checking the hole card on insurance bets, restrictions on splitting and doubling, and a panoply of side bets that usually offer worse odds than the basic game. Every casino has its own unique combination of rules, so you should always check the specifics before playing. We'll talk more about the effects of rule variations later in the chapter.

A blackjack reality check

Okay, let's say you have a hard thirteen and the dealer's upcard is six. What should you do? Most people hit, and that's a mistake. What if you have a hard sixteen and the dealer's upcard is a seven? Most people stand. That's a mistake, too.

Multiply those mistakes by all the other card combinations and you'll find that most blackjack players unintentionally give casinos an enormous advantage. The built-in house edge hovers around zero to one percent. Average players give away about two percent more. Bad players stretch the combined number to four percent and higher.

Unofficially...
Blackjack is distantly related to baccarat, and like baccarat the early versions of twenty-one paid even money for naturals. This changed when gambling houses began offering a 10:1 bonus for an ace and a "black jack." The bonus was eventually reduced and applied to all naturals, but the name blackjack stuck.

Unofficially...
Divide 16/52 to
get the probabil-
ity of drawing a
ten (including
face cards) from
a freshly shuffled
deck, but remem-
ber the probabil-
ities change as
each card is
drawn. After a
ten is pulled, the
chance of get-
ting another ten
drops from 16/52
to 15/51, or
about two per-
cent. Multiple
decks reduce this
probability
change.

That's a house edge comparable to some slots, and slots require much less effort. In fact nearly every casino game requires less effort than blackjack. If you think the words effort and fun shouldn't be in the same sentence, blackjack is probably not your game. If you're the kind of person who prefers to see luck and the universe solely determine winning and losing, blackjack is most definitely not your game. On the other hand, if you're the type of person who loves squeezing money out of the house with strategy, then read on.

Basic strategy

The exciting thing about card games in general is that the results are somewhat more predictable than games involving dice and wheels.

Sixteen cards, a whopping 30 percent of the deck, are valued at ten when playing blackjack. That climbs to 38 percent when you include nines and 46 percent when you include eights. Consider the dealer's hole card. There's a really good chance it's an eight, nine, or ten. Does that change your impression of a six upcard? There is a nearly one in two chance the hand is a fourteen, fifteen, or sixteen. And consider what will come out of the shoe when the dealer hits.

Meanwhile you have a hard thirteen. What's coming out of the shoe for you? Hitting a hard thirteen against a dealer six doesn't seem so appealing anymore. With a six upcard the dealer will bust about 42 percent of the time. Why screw that up?

Mathematicians have worked out the various probabilities. The result is a basic strategy for playing blackjack that in most cases reduces the overall house edge to less than one percent. Favorable rules push the edge past zero and into positive territory. Table 5.1 contains a version of the strategy that is optimized for multiple deck games when the dealer stands on soft seventeen and when doubles are not allowed after splits. Variations of the strategy for hitting soft seventeen and doubling after splits are minor and we'll cover them in a later section.

Basic strategy is easy to use. Just find your card combination on the left and the dealer's upcard at the top. Follow the upcard column down and your card combination row across until the two intersect. That's how you should play the hand. If some of the strategy choices seem odd then you'll find Table 5.2 helpful. It shows the probable outcome of a dealer's hand based on the upcard.

At first glance, basic strategy may seem complicated, but it's simple. About one-third of the hands should always be played the same way, regardless of what the dealer is showing. The rest of the hands, with a few exceptions, should be played one of two ways. This is determined by the dealer's upcard.

Surrender

You will rarely use it, but surrender options should be considered (and hopefully found unnecessary) first. If late surrender is offered, you should take it on a hard sixteen against a dealer nine, ten, or ace. You should also surrender on a hard fifteen against a dealer ten. If you can't surrender, then hit. Early surrender is much less common and the strategy for it is a bit more complicated. It is not reflected in Table 5.1, but if you're fortunate enough to find a game that offers early surrender, use it when the dealer has an ace and your hand totals five, six, seven, or hard twelve through hard seventeen. You should also early surrender hard fourteen against a ten.

Be sure not to confuse early surrender with late surrender. Early surrender allows you to take back half your bet even if the dealer's ace turns out to be a blackjack; late surrender means you lose the entire bet when the dealer has blackjack. Our strategy table is optimized for late surrender, which is much more common.

Timesaver
You'll find basic strategy easier to remember if you break it into consecutive sections. First look for a surrender, then a split, stand, double or hit in that order. Follow this pattern, and the decisions will eventually become automatic.

Watch Out!
You may be tempted to play an early surrender strategy in a late surrender game, but don't do it. Early surrender strategy saves you money when the dealer has a natural. Late surrender rules won't give you that money. Stick to basic strategy when late surrender is offered.

TABLE 5.1: BLACKJACK BASIC STRATEGY

Dealer's Upcard

Player's Hand	2	3	4	5	6	7	8	9	10	A
A-A	sp	sp	sp	sp	sp	sp	sp	sp	sp	sp
10-10	NC	NC	NC	NC	NC	NC	NC	NC	NC	NC
9-9	sp	sp	sp	sp	sp	NC	sp	sp	NC	NC
8-8	sp	sp	sp	sp	sp	sp	sp	sp	sp	sp
7-7	sp	sp	sp	sp	sp	sp	h	h	h	h
6-6	h	sp	sp	sp	sp	h	h	h	h	h
5-5	db	db	db	db	db	db	db	db	h	h
4-4	h	h	h	h	h	h	h	h	h	h
3-3	h	h	sp	sp	sp	sp	h	h	h	h
2-2	h	h	sp	sp	sp	sp	h	h	h	h
Soft 19-21	NC	NC	NC	NC	NC	NC	NC	NC	NC	NC
Soft 18	NC	dbN	dbN	dbN	dbN	NC	NC	h	h	h
Soft 17	h	db	db	db	db	h	h	h	h	h
Soft 16	h	h	db	db	db	h	h	h	h	h
Soft 15	h	h	db	db	db	h	h	h	h	h
Soft 14	h	h	h	db	db	h	h	h	h	h
Soft 13	h	h	h	h	db	h	h	h	h	h
Hard 17-21	NC	NC	NC	NC	NC	NC	NC	NC	NC	NC
Hard 16	NC	NC	NC	NC	NC	h	h	sr	sr	sr
Hard 15	NC	NC	NC	NC	NC	h	h	h	sr	h
Hard 14	NC	NC	NC	NC	NC	h	h	h	h	h
Hard 13	NC	NC	NC	NC	NC	h	h	h	h	h
Hard 12	h	h	NC	NC	NC	h	h	h	h	h
11	db	db	db	db	db	db	db	db	db	h
10	db	db	db	db	db	db	db	db	h	h
9	h	db	db	db	db	h	h	h	h	h
8	h	h	h	h	h	h	h	h	h	h
7	h	h	h	h	h	h	h	h	h	h
6	h	h	h	h	h	h	h	h	h	h
5	h	h	h	h	h	h	h	h	h	h

This version of blackjack strategy works well for single- and multiple-deck games when the dealer stands on soft seventeen and doubling is not allowed after splitting.

sr=surrender
sp=split
NC=stand
db=double
dbN=double, stand if double not possible
h=hit

TABLE 5.2:   DEALER BUST PROBABILITIES

Dealer's Upcard	17+	18+	19+	20+	21	BJ	Bust
2	65%	51%	37%	24%	12%	0%	35%
3	63	49	36	24	12	0	37
4	60	47	35	23	11	0	40
5	58	46	34	22	11	0	42
6	58	41	31	20	10	0	42
7	74	37	23	15	7	0	26
8	76	63	27	14	7	0	24
9	77	65	53	18	6	0	23
10	71	60	49	38	4	8	21
A	58	45	32	19	5	31	11

This table shows how the upcard affects the probability of a dealer bust. Numbers are rounded and reflect multiple decks when the dealer stands on a soft seventeen. Hitting soft seventeen will produce slightly different numbers.

Split

Always split aces and eights. The reason is obvious. Two aces together are a problem, but apart they have a good chance of becoming naturals. Remember that tens appear more than any other value. Similarly, two eights together are also a problem. Sixteen has a high probability of busting and an even higher probability of losing if you don't hit. Single eights can make eighteen or nineteen with one card, or you might pull a three and a ten or some other combination for twenty-one.

Always split nines except against a dealer seven, ten, or ace. Hitting a single nine might produce a nineteen and that's great unless the dealer has a twenty, so splitting against a ten or ace isn't smart. You should split nines against a nine or eight because the dealer may have nineteen (an ace or a ten in the hole). If the dealer shows seven and that becomes seventeen, splitting the nines isn't necessary, but if the dealer shows less than seven you should split because he will definitely hit. If the dealer doesn't bust, he will probably beat your unsplit eighteen.

Watch Out!
A casino table is
not the best
place to learn
basic strategy.
You're better off
practicing on a
computer version
of the game, or
just buy a pack
of cards and play
by yourself. It's
easy because
the dealer's
moves are
predetermined.

Never split fives or tens. Their combined values are more desirable. Never split fours unless doubling is allowed on splits; in that case you should split fours against a dealer five or six, but not against any other card.

Twos, threes, sixes, and sevens should not be split against a dealer upcard of eight or more. They should be split against a dealer four, five, or six. The reasoning behind these decisions may not be as obvious as the other splitting situations, but it's a good example of how basic strategy improves your play. All these choices are statistically more likely to produce favorable results.

Stand

Always stand on nineteen, twenty, or twenty-one. Always stand on a hard seventeen or eighteen. Always stand on a hard thirteen through sixteen against a dealer's two through six. In each of these situations your probability of losing is greater if you hit and possibly bust than if you stand and let the dealer bust or possibly lose on points.

Double down

Doubling down is an ingenious way to increase a bet when the odds are in your favor, but some people resist doubling because it limits their ability to hit again. They forget that doubling situations will rarely require an additional card. Let's say the dealer shows a four. You double down on a ten and pull a five. Bad news, but you wouldn't draw an extra card anyway because now you have a hard fifteen. Strategy says to stand because the dealer has a high probability of busting. Most doubling situations will produce hands that you shouldn't hit even if you could.

Some casinos allow players to double for less than the full wager. This defeats the mathematical purpose of doubling. If the additional bet is too much for your bankroll then just hit.

Hit

Anything that doesn't call for a surrender, split, stand or double is a hand for hitting. Except in doubling situations, you should hit any point total less than eleven and any soft thirteen through soft seventeen. Hard twelve through hard fourteen should be hit against a dealer seven or higher. Table 5.3 has basic strategy converted to a list that some people find easier to memorize than the chart.

TABLE 5.3:   BLACKJACK BASIC STRATEGY

SURRENDER the following:

Hard 16 against dealer 9, 10, and ace

Hard 15 against dealer 10

SPLIT the following:

Aces or 8s against every dealer card

9s against every dealer card EXCEPT 7, 10, and ace

7s against dealer 7 or lower.

6s against dealer 3-6

3s or 2s against dealer 4-7

STAND on the following:

Hard 17 or higher against every dealer card

Hard 13-16 against dealer 6 and lower

Hard 12 against dealer 4-6

Soft 19 or higher against every dealer card

Soft 18 against dealer 2, 7, and 8

DOUBLE DOWN on the following:

Hard 11 against dealer 10 or lower

Hard 10 against dealer 9 or lower

Hard 9 against dealer 3-6

Soft 17-18 against dealer 3, 4, 5, and 6

Soft 15-16 against dealer 4, 5, and 6

Soft 14 against dealer 5 and 6

Soft 13 against dealer 6

Table continues

Timesaver
It pays to learn
the exact strate-
gy variations for
hitting soft sev-
enteen if you
play exclusively
in casinos that
offer that game.
If only some of
the casinos
where you play
hit soft seven-
teen, then don't
bother learning
the nuances until
you've mastered
basic strategy.
The differences
are minor.

TABLE 5.3:   BLACKJACK BASIC STRATEGY

Continued

HIT on the following:

Hard 16 or lower against dealer 7 or higher (except when surrendering)
Hard 12 against dealer 2 and 3
11 or lower against every dealer card (except when doubling)
Soft 18 against dealer 9 or higher
Soft 13-17 against every dealer card (except when doubling)

Hitting soft seventeen and doubling on splits

Basic strategy is slightly modified when the dealer hits soft seventeen. Double eights should be surrendered against an ace if possible; if not, they should be split as they would be normally. Soft nineteen should be doubled against a six, and if that's not possible then stand. Soft eighteen should be doubled against a two. If that's not possible then stand. Hard seventeen should be surrendered against an ace if possible; if not, you should stand. Hard fifteen should also be surrendered and if no surrender is available, then hit. Eleven should be doubled against an ace.

Basic strategy also changes a bit if doubling is allowed after splits. If it is, then you should split twos and threes against the dealer's two or three. You should also split sixes against a dealer's two and fours against a dealer's five or six.

Should you insure?

The probability of finding a ten under the dealer's ace is about 30 percent and insurance pays 2 to 1. That works out to a house edge of about eight percent, so insurance costs money in the long run. When you have a natural, the cost may seem lower because naturals pay more and insuring them guarantees even money, but the actual cost of the insurance bet doesn't change. Over time, when the wins and pushes are combined, you'll earn four percent more on naturals when you don't insure. Insurance is a bad bet. Don't make it.

Favorable and unfavorable games

I recently played in a casino that offered three different blackjack games. The first game was played with one deck of cards; you could double only on nine, ten, or eleven and not after splits; the dealer hit soft seventeen. The second game was played with two decks and no restrictions on doubling even after splits; you could resplit aces and the dealer stood on soft seventeen. The third game used six decks, offered late surrender, double after splits, resplit aces, and the dealer stood on soft seventeen. Which was most favorable?

Let's figure it out. Assuming you play perfect basic strategy, the house edge is zero in a single-deck game where the dealer stands on soft seventeen and doubling is allowed but not after splitting. That's our baseline. Table 5.4 shows the relative advantages and disadvantages of the most common rule variations.

Do the arithmetic and you'll find the single-deck game has a house edge of 0.3 percent. The six-deck game is a nearly identical 0.29 percent, but the two-deck game is a slender 0.11 percent. Of course all three games are still negative expectation, but remember, these numbers are all significantly less than one percent. You're better off playing any one of these games than almost any other game in the casino, and that includes most video poker.

Bright Idea
Everyone likes a smooth-flowing game, so it's a good idea to be prepared for a split or a double down. You might want to set aside chips equal to your original wager at the beginning of a hand. That way you won't be simultaneously trying to count chips and card numbers.

TABLE 5.4

Unfavorable Rules

Two decks	-0.35%
Four decks	-0.52%
Six decks	-0.58%
Eight decks	-0.61%
Dealer hits soft 17	-0.20%
Double only on 9, 10, or 11	-0.10%
Double only on 10 or 11	-0.20%
No splitting of aces	-0.17%
Naturals pay 1:1	-2.29%

Favorable Rules

Resplit aces	+0.10%
Double after split	+0.14%
Late surrender	+0.05%
Early surrender	+0.62%
Double on more than two cards	+0.21%
Five-card automatic winner	+1.40%
Six-card automatic winner	+0.15%
Naturals pay 2:1	+2.29%

This table shows the effects of various rules on the house edge. The baseline is a zero percent house edge in a single deck game where the dealer stands on soft seventeen and doubling is allowed but not after splitting.

Side bets, bonuses, and Double Exposure

Blackjack's skinny margins frequently inspire casinos to offer side bets. You might be offered an opportunity to bet that the next card will be over or under seven, or that your two-card total will be over or under thirteen. Another such bet is predicting the color of the dealer's next card. These are usually sucker bets. You'll get better odds playing craps or roulette.

Bonuses are another matter. They're basically off-beat favorable rules designed as a promotion. One example is giving an automatic win to players with five cards in their hand, or paying more for hands with triple numbers. Bonuses cost you nothing unless you deviate from basic strategy to pursue them. Chasing bonuses can be complicated and expensive. You're better off sticking with basic strategy unless you play a particular bonus game exclusively. Then you should learn a strategy that optimizes for the bonus.

A special strategy is also required for Double Exposure, a popular variation of blackjack in which both dealer cards are face up. The game is also known as Show & Tell, Peek-a-Boo, Face-Up and other similarly descriptive names. Seeing both dealer cards sounds great, but Double Exposure naturals usually pay even money, doubling is restricted, dealer wins a push, and surrender is never allowed. Combine the advantages and disadvantages, and Double Exposure usually has a larger house edge than regular blackjack. Also, the required changes to basic strategy can be confusing and cause some people to play poorly. Double Exposure isn't a bad game, but regular blackjack is usually better. If you choose to play Double Exposure, just remember that the probability of any particular card coming out of the shoe is the same as in regular blackjack. For example, you should stand on a hard thirteen if the dealer has sixteen. Appendix C has information about books with strategies for Double Exposure.

Hunches and luck

Great pleasure comes from confidently standing on a hard twelve against a dealer five and watching the dealer bust. It's so much fun you might forget that your hand had a 58 percent chance of losing. Luck is luck. Basic strategy doesn't fix a bad hand; it simply tells you the best way to play it. Nothing guarantees a win because blackjack is gambling. It is subject to streaks like any game. You can play perfectly and the dealer can win ten hands in a row. Basic strategy won't beat a blackjack or a dealer twenty when you double on eleven and pull an eight.

Watch Out!
Playing video blackjack is a good way to polish your basic strategy skills, but beware of the payoff on naturals. Many video games only give you even money on blackjack. The pay table may show 2:1 or just 2, but the machine is including your bet in this amount. Even money on naturals costs you more than two percent.

Some people get frustrated and start playing hunches when cards repeatedly fall the wrong way. Even when cards are falling the right way, some people want to follow a "feeling." As we said in Chapter 4, hunches aren't mathematically correct, but it's your money. Just realize that you are paying for the pleasure of making a guess. You might win, but on average you are more likely to lose. If you can live with that, then do what you "feel."

Counting cards

You've probably heard about counting cards, but you may not know the degree to which it is a source of ongoing conflict between casinos and professional gamblers. Card counting is perfectly legal, but it's very unpopular in the gaming business. Players who exhibit counting behavior for any reason will invariably find casino hospitality cut short. Many of these behaviors would seem quite innocent to the average player.

That's why you should understand how counting works even if you don't count cards. We're not encouraging you to do it, nor discouraging you, but you're likely to find this information helpful either way.

The origin of card counting

Blackjack was once like roulette, craps, and all the other casino games. It looked easy to beat, but it actually gave the house a nice edge. Then someone did the unthinkable. In 1962 Edward O. Thorp published *Beat the Dealer*, a best-selling book that described a system for beating blackjack. For once it was true; the gambling system worked.

At first it was only a handful of professionals who earned a tidy living playing blackjack, but the numbers grew and the casinos realized they were losing

Moneysaver
The odds bet in craps is often called "the best bet in the house" because it has no house edge. Unfortunately, you must also bet the pass line to make an odds wager. The two craps bets combined usually have a higher house edge than a blackjack bet when playing basic strategy. Blackjack is truly "the best bet in the house."

money. Multiple decks, frequent shuffling, and other measures were put in place to discourage card counting. That helped, but the basic mathematics of blackjack couldn't be changed. Every measure brought a countermeasure. Every casino response was studied and new counting systems were invented.

How counting works

There are many methods of counting cards. Contrary to popular belief, none of them involves memorizing all the cards in the deck. We're going to explain one of the simplest counting systems. It's called Hi-Lo, and it operates on the principle we demonstrated in Chapter 2. When a card leaves the deck it changes the probability of receiving any one of the remaining cards. You've probably noticed that tens favor players because they make nice pat hands and usually cause the dealer to bust when he hits. Small cards have the opposite effect.

A player using Hi-Lo simply scans the cards as they are revealed during play and assigns a number to each one. Cards with a value of two, three, four, five, and six become +1. Seven, eight, and nine are zero. Tens, face cards ,and aces are -1. The numbers are added and the result is a measure of how many tens and aces are left in the deck compared to smaller cards.

Let's say it's only you and the dealer playing with a freshly shuffled deck. At the end of the first hand you have two tens and the dealer busted with a ten, a three, and another ten. Great for you, but on a single deck the count is now -3. The cards remaining in the deck favor the dealer. You might win the next hand and the next one after that but those little cards will come back to haunt you. Conversely, if the count is positive you can expect big fat tens to come out of the deck at some point, even if you're losing.

Card counting is definitely not for everyone, and is more trouble than it's worth for the vast majority of casual players. But for a "math freak" like me, card counting actually adds to the fun instead of detracting from it, and it sure makes the game a lot more interesting.
—F. S.,
card counter

Watch Out!
Card counting isn't easy. Take a shuffled deck and deal the cards face up, two at a time, into a pile. Do it in forty-five seconds. An average card counter can consistently follow the count from zero to zero and never make a mistake. A good counter can do the entire deck in thirty seconds.

Card counters divide the running count by the number of decks remaining in the shoe to get the "true count," so -4 is only -1 when playing a six-deck game with four decks left in the shoe. All this information is used to make decisions including when to deviate from basic strategy, when to take insurance, and how much to bet. Bets are raised when the count is up and lowered when the count is down.

That's how counting works. Casinos really hate it. A good card counter can turn a slim house edge into a plump 1.5 percent player advantage and (with luck) win thousands in a matter of minutes.

How casinos fight counters

Card counting is legal, so casinos can't have a counter arrested. How can you prosecute someone for using a mental process? Without a clear legal recourse, casinos have resorted to a combination of techniques to discourage counters. Multiple decks and frequent shuffling are the first line of defense. One sophisticated procedure uses surveillance systems and a computer to follow the count and find correlations with a player's bet size.

The most common and particularly crude technique involves a dealer and pit boss evaluating a player's behavior. This is unfortunate because truly good counters rarely exhibit overt counting behavior, but normal people who aren't counting sometimes do.

Card counting requires mental effort; counters (mostly mediocre ones) must concentrate and this causes them to look preoccupied. They lower bets when decks are shuffled. They raise and lower bets frequently, by wide margins, and in a seemingly random fashion because they're following the count. Counters prefer seats at first base or third base because this allows them an easy view of the table.

They carefully watch the cards in play and constantly glance at the discard pile. Sometimes they observe
a game and enter "mid-shoe" when the count is positive.

Dealers and pit bosses are trained to spot such
behavior. People suspected of counting are "backed
off" the game with frequent shuffling and unfriend-
ly service. If that doesn't work they are asked to cash
out, and they may be ejected from the casino. Ejection is not allowed in Atlantic City, but it happens
regularly in Las Vegas and other locations. If a suspected counter happens to be staying at the hotel,
his comp privileges are permanently over and he
may find his possessions on the sidewalk.

Griffin Investigations, Inc., a Las Vegas company,
provides a subscription service to most of the casinos in the United States. It's a book with pictures
and information about gamblers who cheat. Suspected card counters comprise a large portion of
the Griffin book in spite of their legal standing. A
person who is listed in the book can never gamble
in a normal way again. That person can never again
check into a casino hotel, join a slot club, or receive
a comp using a real name.

How to stay out of the card counting conflict

If the last few paragraphs have caused you to consider avoiding blackjack, please don't. It's a wonderful
game. Issues about card counting won't arise unless
you are indeed counting or you exhibit certain
behaviors associated with counting. Remember that
counting is legal, but not welcome. Here is a list of
actions you should avoid when playing blackjack.

■ Don't vary your bet by more than four base betting units unless you're using a positive progression. For example, don't jump from ten dol-

lars to one hundred dollars and then back to
ten dollars on three consecutive hands.

▪ Don't lower your bet when the deck is shuffled
unless the previous hand was a loss.

▪ Don't change your bet after a push.

▪ Don't increase your bet after a loss.

▪ Don't sporadically take insurance.

▪ Don't split tens.

▪ Don't watch a table and then enter mid-shoe
with a big bet.

▪ Don't look nervous or act as if you're thinking
too hard.

A couple of these behaviors are inconsistent with
basic strategy. That's another reason why they
arouse suspicion. You'll find some dealers and pit
bosses more vigilant than others; some are zealous
and some don't care. Chapter 13 has more information about dealing with casino employees. Chapter
15 has tips for handling problem situations and suggestions for keeping the overall mood upbeat.

One thing you should do is occasionally *toke* (tip)
the dealer. Card counters are notoriously tight with
tokes because they're in business and they operate
on a slim margin. If you're losing, don't bother giving more away, but if lady luck is smiling on you, it's
not a bad idea to "bet one for dealer." See Chapter
15 for an extended discussion about toking.

Final words about card counting

Counting cards is not a spigot to a money machine.
Profitable counting is hard work and it takes a big
bankroll. $10,000 is the minimum necessary before
the law of averages consistently returns $60 per

hour. Bad luck can still put a card counter out of business. Sloppy counting, missing a few hands, and guessing are worse than forgetting the count and playing basic strategy. And, of course, dealers and pit bosses are always looking for counters.

So if you decide to count cards, don't do it for the money. Do it for the pleasure of counting, and bet responsibly. What you do inside your brain is your business, and the casinos will never know and never care unless you try to make a killing.

Blackjack's price for fun and money management

Blackjack pays even money on most wagers and that makes it easy to calculate a price for fun. It's the house edge on every bet, usually less than one percent, plus whatever you're willing to spend for bad luck. You'll win a few and lose a few. Do the arithmetic every ten to twenty hands and be sure you're not falling behind too quickly. Take a break or lower the bets if your session bankroll is disappearing.

Blackjack is typically played at a rate of about sixty hands per hour. It is not uncommon to see streaks of wins and losses. An hour session might produce twenty-two wins and thirty-eight losses with twenty losses coming in the first twenty-five minutes. The next hour could be reversed. The key to riding out the slumps is keeping your bets small in relation to your bankroll. Don't play at a table with a high limit just because seats are available.

Positive betting progressions for blackjack

Blackjack players often bet using positive progressions (see Chapter 2). A positive progression is OK. Just remember that it will cost you if the table goes choppy. Don't blow your bankroll on a series of alternating wins and losses. Below is one very conservative progression that requires two wins before you increase the bet. Drop back to the beginning of the progression after a loss.

1, 1, 2, 3, 4, 4, 4 (4 continues until a loss)

This progression wins *less* than straight betting if a loss occurs in the third level (two units) or fourth level (three units). A loss in the first, second, and fifth level is equal to straight betting. A loss in any level after five will leave the progressive bettor ahead. It's a good idea to see how this progression works on a computer or when playing with a deck at home before you try it in a casino. Remember, this is a *positive* progression. Don't use a negative progression. Don't increase your bet after a loss. Learn basic strategy first before using a positive progression.

Handling cash and chips at the table

Chapter 14 has a detailed explanation of the casino procedures for changing money into chips, but here's a brief summary that you'll find helpful when playing blackjack and most other table games. Put money on the table; never hand it directly to the dealer. The dealer will take the money and give you chips in whatever denomination you request. When it's time to cash out you must take the remaining chips (and hopefully many more) to the *cage* where a cashier will exchange the chips for money.

Just the facts

- Blackjack's house edge is usually in the range of zero to one percent, but you must play perfect basic strategy to reach that number. Players who don't use basic strategy give the house a three percent edge and sometimes more.

- Every rule change affects the house edge. Some rule combinations can turn blackjack into a positive expectation game. You should always check the rules before playing.

- Card counting adds to a player's edge and can turn blackjack into a positive expectation game, but counting can be difficult and can sour your relationship with a casino. Don't do it unless you're willing to take that risk.

- Dealers and pit bosses are constantly looking for card counters. Even if you don't count cards, you should avoid card counting behaviors. Remember, card counting is legal, but it is not welcome.

- Don't take insurance or make side bets. The house edge is much larger on these wagers.

- Blackjack can be "streaky." Be prepared for multiple losses even if you play perfect basic strategy.

GET THE SCOOP ON...
The best and the worst roulette bets ▪ Tips
for protecting your roulette bankroll ▪ Betting
systems that don't work ▪ Bias and other
methods for beating roulette

Roulette

R oulette inspires a unique fascination in some
people. The game is ordered and precisely
mathematical in its arrangement, yet the outcome is thoroughly random. Enthusiastic players are
often unwilling to accept this contradiction, and that
leads them to endlessly look for patterns in the winning and losing. It is not a coincidence that many
betting systems focus on roulette. The facade of pre-
dictability and symmetry is beguiling, but roulette
(on an unbiased wheel) is simply unbeatable. It is the
archetype of a negative expectation game.

So should you play roulette? Yes, if you will accept
a rock-solid 5.26 percent house edge (when playing
on an American wheel). Yes, if you will believe that
roulette produces an uncontrollable and unpredictable pattern of wins and losses. Do you see? Even
those two truths seem to be a contradiction.

Roulette's layout: order in disorder

Roulette has its origins in an ancient Chinese contest, but the game that we see today is a reflection of

Unofficially...
Modern roulette is a French invention, but it was originally played in Germany during the mid nineteenth century because gambling was illegal in France. The game was such a hit in Hamburg that Charles III, Prince of Monaco, invited roulette developer François Blanc to bring the game to Monte Carlo.

the European Age of Reason. It was a time in history when scientists and mathematicians believed the universe and everything in it was ordered and predictable. There is evidence that famed mathematician Blaise Pascal contributed to the design of roulette, but the modern layout was finalized by Francois and Louis Blanc in 1842. Their wheel had thirty-seven slots and a single zero. When the game came to America it was given an additional slot, double zero. This difference continues between European and American roulette wheels to this day. We'll focus on the American wheel in the next few sections and discuss the European version later in the chapter.

A double-zero identifies this as an American roulette wheel. The European version has only one zero. All other wheel characteristics are identical in both versions.   Image courtesy of the *Unofficial Guide to Las Vegas* by Bob Sehlinger.

An American roulette wheel's thirty-eight slots are numbered one through thirty-six, zero and double-zero. The wheel rotates counterclockwise. A dealer spins a marble-like ball clockwise around the wheel's perimeter; centrifugal force keeps the ball on a grooved track as it moves. When the ball loses speed it falls into one of the numbered slots, and the various attributes of the number determine winners and losers.

The wheel's numbers are arranged in what seems to be a haphazard fashion, but it's actually a complex system designed for maximum variability. Red and black alternate; pairs of odd and even alternate; pairs of high and low alternate. Every odd number has its even successor directly across the wheel.

The roulette table is equally marvelous. The numbers are arranged sequentially, but the patterns of red, black, high, low, odd, and even create betting options that correspond to the wheel's variability layout and ensure that no bet has an advantage over any other bet. The table can accommodate dozens of unique wagers; all of them have various probabilities of success and yet all of them (with one American exception) have an exactly identical house edge.

Roulette is simply a product of genius, relentlessly systematic yet utterly unpredictable. It is no wonder that wise and scholarly people have lost fortunes betting on the wheel. In the next few sections we will explain their mistakes and help you to minimize the cost of enjoying this fascinating game.

Watch Out!
Some roulette computer simulations inexplicably alter the perfectly balanced wheel design and move the numbers around. This can cause confusion when the player switches from the simulation to a real casino.

How roulette is played

Roulette uses a unique system of colored chips that distinguish one bettor from another. This allows two or more people to make identical bets without confusion, and it creates some interesting contrasts. Your chips may be worth five dollars each. The player next to you may be betting one hundred dollars per chip. There is no way to know unless you watch a person buy in.

Most roulette tables can accommodate six to eight players. Just walk up and lay down your money (never hand it directly to a dealer). Players may buy in with casino chips or cash. As with every table game, it's a good idea to read the upright card that has information about the game and table limits. Roulette often has different restrictions on minimum amounts that can be bet *inside* and *outside* the layout. Figure 6.2 is a typical roulette layout with examples of the various wagers.

Moneysaver
Don't leave the table with your roulette chips. The dealer should not allow it, but if there's a slip-up and you do walk away with chips, they will be worthless everywhere else (including at other roulette tables).

Inside Bets

[Figure 6.2: A standard roulette table layout showing numbers 0, 00, 1–36 arranged in the grid, with columns marked 2 TO 1, and outside bet areas for 1ST 12, 2ND 12, 3RD 12, 1 TO 18, EVEN, RED, BLACK, ODD, 19 TO 36]

Outside Bets

This is a standard roulette table layout. Wagers placed directly on numbers or combinations are "inside" bets. 1:1 and 2:1 wagers are "outside" bets.

A roulette dealer in Europe is called a *croupier* (pronounced KROO-pee-ay) but in America they are simply called dealers. The dealer will give you a stack of chips and you'll have an opportunity to make a bet before the ball is spun on the wheel.

Inside bets

Inside bets have the highest payoff and highest risk. A straight or straight up bet on one number has a 1/38 chance of winning. A payoff equal to the true odds (zero house edge) would be 37:1, or thirty-seven times the wager, but the casino only pays 35:1. That loss of two units works out to a 5.26 percent house edge. Players make a straight bet by simply putting one or more chips directly on a number.

Split bets are made by putting a wager on the line between two numbers. Either number can be a winner. The casino pays 17:1 on split bets. A true odds payoff would be 18:1. That works out to a familiar 5.26 percent house edge. We won't bore you with the true odds for the remaining wagers but be assured that every roulette bet (except for one) has a 5.26 percent house edge.

Street bets are made by putting a wager at the end of a row of three numbers or at the intersection of three numbers at the top of the layout. The bet pays 11:1.

Square or *corner* bets are made by putting a wager at the intersection of four numbers. The bet pays 8:1.

Six-number bets are placed on the intersecting lines at the end of two rows. They pay 5:1.

American roulette has a five-number bet. It's made at the end of the row where the one and the zero intersect and it covers zero, double-zero, one,

Unofficially...
The rump of a horse is called a *croup*. A person who rode there in centuries past was an assistant or servant of the master riding in the saddle. The French called the servant a *croupier*. Eventually the word was used exclusively for servants of casino patrons. American casinos prefer the much more egalitarian term *dealer*.

Bright Idea
If a number or combination you want is already covered with wagers, simply stack your bet on top of another player's bet. Roulette is the only game that allows this because each player has different-colored chips.

two, and three. It pays 6:1 and it is the only exception to the 5.26 percent rule. A five-number bet has a house edge of 7.89 percent. Pascal would not have approved. This bet is not available on a European wheel.

Outside bets

Bets on the outside of the layout are less risky, but they pay less. Betting a group of twelve, 1-12, 13-24, or 25-36 pays 2:1. You can also bet a column of twelve numbers for the same payoff.

The rest of the outside bets pay even money, 1:1. They are red, black, 1-18, 19-36, even and odd.

Winning and losing

One dealer can run a roulette table, but very busy tables usually have two dealers. On a crowded night people will be leaning across the layout to place multiple bets. Dealers will assist players if they can't reach numbers. There will be a frenzy of activity that will heighten as one of the dealers spins the ball on the perimeter of the wheel. A few additional seconds of betting is usually allowed and then the dealer will wave her hand over the layout to indicate that bets are no longer accepted.

All eyes will turn to the wheel and the table will go silent. A few seconds later the ball will slow down and fall into one of the wheel slots. Players will either gasp or sigh. The dealer will put a plastic token (usually a small upright cylinder) on the layout over the winning number. Losing bets are raked in like autumn leaves. Winning bets are paid off starting from the outside of the layout and proceeding in. When the last straight bet has been paid, the process begins again.

Roulette reality: finding ways to lose less

Roulette is a relentlessly negative expectation game. It is mathematically impossible to come out ahead in the long run unless the game is biased. We'll cover bias in later sections, but right now let's just say it's not common. Besides bias, there is no other way to win. There is no system, no strategy, no method, no pattern for playing roulette that produces positive expectation. It's as certain as subtracting five from four. The result is consistently negative.

People who play roulette should accept this and enjoy the inevitable streaks of winning and losing because roulette can be exciting. Two or three well-placed bets can put a player ahead by thousands of dollars. It happens all the time. The key to making it happen is stretching your bankroll, giving yourself the maximum chance to win, and then quitting when you're ahead.

European wheel

An excellent way of stretching your bankroll is to play a European wheel. This is roulette without a double-zero. One less slot cuts the house edge in half. That's 2.63 percent. Happily you don't have to visit Monte Carlo to play a European wheel. Many American casinos have them, but it's often with a catch. The European wheel will have a higher table minimum than a double-zero version sitting just a few feet away. No problem if you were planning to risk the extra money, but don't play for higher stakes just to get a lower house edge.

Avoiding five-number bets

A five-number bet (zero, double-zero, one, two, and three) is only available on American wheels. The house edge is a hefty 7.89 percent. It's a bad bet; don't make it. If you truly have a vision that one of those numbers will win, then bet it straight up or make a street or split bet. That will cut the house edge by more than two percent and will return between two to six times more than a five-number bet.

Surrender

Some American casinos offer surrender, a modified version of the European custom *en prison*. Under this rule even money wagers that lose to zero or double-zero are only half-lost. You can leave the bet on the layout and hope for a push or take half back. Casinos in Atlantic City have this option and it cuts the house edge on even money bets in half to 2.63 percent. Surrender on a European wheel drops the house edge on even money bets to 1.32 percent. The extra spin is mandatory in Europe, which is why they say "en prison."

TABLE 6.1: MULTIPLE BETS COMPARED TO COMBINATION BETS

NUMBERS	17 & 20	7,8,9	1,2,4,5	4-9	1-18
Straight bets	2	3	4	6	18
Win	35	35	35	35	35
Losing bets	-1	-2	-3	-5	-17
Total after win	36	36	36	36	36
Combo bet	2	3	4	6	18
	(split)	(street)	(box)	(2 rows)	(any)
Win	34	33	32	30	18
Losing bets	0	0	0	0	0
Total after win	36	36	36	36	36

Combining chips into one bet for multiple numbers returns the same amount as splitting the wager and betting each number individually.

Outside bets versus inside bets

A straight bet obviously has more risk and offers more reward per spin than an even money bet, but in the long run both bets actually cost exactly the same. That's the heart of the roulette paradox.

People who spread chips around the table lose at the same rate as those who bet single numbers or groups. Table 6.1 shows why. Betting multiple chips on one combination is identical to dividing the bet on individual numbers. For example, $10 on the line between seventeen and twenty will return the same amount as $5 straight up on seventeen and $5 straight up on twenty. This is also true for multiple combinations. A six-number bet for $10 returns the same as two $5 street bets. Betting $10 on a dozen returns the same as two sixes for $5 each.

There's nothing wrong with spreading bets around, but there's nothing right about it. In the long run it doesn't make any difference. This is true for combinations, multiple straight bets, and for every other roulette wager. For example, $10 on a single number may seem riskier and more expensive than $10 on even money, but in the long run they have the same cost (assuming surrender is not offered). Table 6.2 shows the results from a typical day of roulette play with an exactly average outcome.

Of course, results are hardly ever exactly average. That's the lure and the heartbreak of roulette. Normal streaks of winning and losing make some people think that particular bets or combinations of bets win more than others. Some bets do win more frequently, but none of the bets win more money on average. They all lose by exactly the same percentage over time.

> "
> There are ways of altering probability in your favor. We reveal documented probability analysis from an English professor of mathematics and statistics detailing how to sway the random chances of nature in your direction.
> —Advertisement for a roulette gambling system
> "

TABLE 6.2: STRAIGHT BETS
COMPARED TO EVEN MONEY BETS

Straight Bets 35:1		$10 wagers
Total decisions	380	
Wins	10	$3,500
Losses	370	$3,700
Net Loss		-$200
Even Money Bets 1:1		**$10 wagers**
Total decisions	380	
Wins	180	$1,800
Losses	200	$2,000
Net loss		-$200

This chart shows an exactly average outcome after 380 decisions (approximately seven hours of roulette play). Surrender is not offered.

Squeezing and stretching risk

Take another look at Table 6.2. Both bets cost the same over time, but the total amount won and lost is much higher when betting single numbers. Roulette's house edge is unyielding, but squeezing and stretching risk is quite easy. This is where many people get confused and get into trouble. They imagine that it's possible to bet a certain way and squeeze the risk right out of roulette, or stretch it so thin that it has no effect. That can't be done. Fortunes have been lost by people who tried. The following betting systems are examples of squeezing and stretching risk. It's OK to use them, but keep in mind that they won't put you ahead in the long run unless you're lucky, and they'll cost more money than regular betting if your luck is anything less than exactly average. Remember, there is no system that can beat the wheel.

Betting two groups of twelve

This is a well-known system that is popular among people who like to see the dealer frequently pushing them money. The bettor simply puts an identical amount on two groups of twelve. For example, $5 on 1-12 and $5 on 13-24. If the ball lands on one through twenty-four, the bettor wins an aggregate $5 ($10 on the winning dozen less $5 on the losing dozen). Betting two dozen wins 63 percent of the time. The wins and losses together add up to a predictable 5.26 percent average loss, but it's certainly fun to "win" more than six out of ten times.

Betting one group of twelve and even money

A system that "wins" even more frequently is betting two units on a group of twelve and three units on a totally opposite even money contest. An example would be $10 on 1-12 and $15 on high numbers. This combined wager pushes the risk into only eight numbers, 13-18, 0 and 00. A win either way pays an aggregate of $5. A loss costs the bettor $25. Losses occur 21 percent of the time, on average about one in five spins. Wins occur the other four times, so five spins will usually cost the bettor $5. Of course you could easily win ten consecutive times and be ahead $50. Or you could get a run of 20, 24, and zero. That would cost you $75. The wins and losses will add up to a 5.26 percent loss in the long run, but if the wrong numbers come up in the short run this system can cost big bucks.

Betting one number with a closed-end progression

We said previously that negative progressions are dangerous and should be avoided (Chapter 2), but there is one limited exception to this rule. Table 6.3 shows a closed-end progression that increases the bet after a loss (so we must call it negative), but it has a predetermined limit. The entire amount of the progression is equal to the price for fun, and it doesn't foolishly chase small returns with big stakes. We are betting on one number to pay 35:1. There is

Bright Idea
One very exciting bet is a *parlay* (leaving the original bet and winning chips on the layout for another spin). Money can quickly multiply, or it might disappear. A $5 straight-up win with one parlay will bring $6,125. The odds of this happening are 1 in 1,444.

TABLE 6.3

CLOSED-END PROGRESSION				FLAT $20 BETS			
38 Spins Costs $751				38 Spins Costs $760			
Wager	Prior Losses	Single Win	Gain	Wager	Prior Losses	Single Win	Gain
5	0	175	175	20	0	700	700
5	5	175	170	20	20	700	680
5	10	175	165	20	40	700	660
5	15	175	160	20	60	700	640
5	20	175	155	20	80	700	620
6	25	210	185	20	100	700	600
7	31	245	214	20	120	700	580
8	38	280	242	20	140	700	560
9	46	315	269	20	160	700	540
10	55	350	295	20	180	700	520
11	65	385	320	20	200	700	500
12	76	420	344	20	220	700	480
13	88	455	367	20	240	700	460
14	101	490	389	20	260	700	440
15	115	525	410	20	280	700	420
16	130	560	430	20	300	700	400
17	146	595	449	20	320	700	380
18	163	630	467	20	340	700	360
19	181	665	484	20	360	700	340
20	200	700	500	20	380	700	320
21	220	735	515	20	400	700	300
22	241	770	529	20	420	700	280
23	263	805	542	20	440	700	260
24	286	840	554	20	460	700	240
25	310	875	565	20	480	700	220
26	335	910	575	20	500	700	200
27	361	945	584	20	520	700	180
28	388	980	592	20	540	700	160
29	416	1015	599	20	560	700	140
30	445	1050	605	20	580	700	120
31	475	1085	610	20	600	700	100

Both the progressive bettor and the flat bettor are wagering on a single number. Wins pay 35:1. This progression should only be used when the bettor is willing to spend the total $751 (the figure at the bottom of the second column) as a price for fun.

CLOSED-END PROGRESSION				FLAT $20 BETS			
38 Spins Costs $751				38 Spins Costs $760			
Wager	Prior Losses	Single Win	Gain	Wager	Prior Losses	Single Win	Gain
32	506	1120	614	20	620	700	80
33	538	1155	617	20	640	700	60
34	571	1190	619	20	660	700	40
35	605	1225	620	20	680	700	20
36	640	1260	620	20	700	700	0
37	676	1295	619	20	720	700	−20
38	713	1330	617	20	740	700	−40
0	751	0	−751	0	760	0	−760

a 1/38 chance of winning on each spin, and we're giving it thirty-eight chances. The columns on the left side of the table show the progression. The right side shows a person betting a flat $20 per spin on the same number.

Notice that the flat bettor's potential gain is constantly dropping, while the progressive bettor's gain is going up. At no time does the progressive bettor risk more of the total session bankroll than the flat bettor.

But remember, the house edge hasn't changed. We're just pushing the risk and reward around a bit. Flat betting costs more, but it also returns more if the bettor is lucky and wins in the first fifteen spins.

This closed-end negative progression is designed for a roulette table with a five-dollar inside minimum and a bettor who would typically risk $20 per spin. The bettor should be willing to spend $751 for about forty-five minutes worth of excitement. If that price is too rich for your blood, then don't use this progression.

- ▪ Don't continue the progression beyond thirty-eight steps.

- Don't continue after a win; go back to level one or quit for the session.

- Don't use the progression on a table that has a maximum payout limit below $1,330.

- Don't modify this progression while playing in a casino; do it first on a spreadsheet to see the result.

- Above all, don't *expect* your number to come up.

You have a better chance of winning using this progression than if you put the entire amount on one even money spin, but it's still a only a chance. If you have any hesitation about possibly spending $751 in less than an hour, this is *not* a progression for you.

Table 6.4 has a modified version of the progression for a $10 per spin bettor and a $5 inside minimum. The same caveats apply. Be prepared to spend $388 for about forty-five minutes of fun. If that's too much money, then don't use the progression.

TABLE 6.4

The total cost for this progression is $388 (the figure at the bottom of the second column). The progressive bettor spends less than the flat bettor in the first thirty-six levels and only $8 more than the flat bettor at the end of the progression.

CLOSED-END PROGRESSION				FLAT $10 BETS			
38 Spins Costs $388				38 Spins Costs $380			
Wager	Prior Losses	Single Win	Gain	Wager	Prior Losses	Single Win	Gain
5	0	175	175	10	0	350	350
5	5	175	170	10	10	350	340
5	10	175	165	10	20	350	330
5	15	175	160	10	30	350	320
5	20	175	155	10	40	350	310
6	25	210	185	10	50	350	300
6	31	210	179	10	60	350	290
6	37	210	173	10	70	350	280
7	43	245	202	10	80	350	270
7	50	245	195	10	90	350	260

| CLOSED-END PROGRESSION | | | | FLAT $10 BETS | | | |
| 38 Spins Costs $388 | | | | 38 Spins Costs $380 | | | |
Wager	Prior Losses	Single Win	Gain	Wager	Prior Losses	Single Win	Gain
7	57	245	188	10	100	350	250
8	64	280	216	10	110	350	240
8	72	280	208	10	120	350	230
8	80	280	200	10	130	350	220
9	88	315	227	10	140	350	210
9	97	315	218	10	150	350	200
9	106	315	209	10	160	350	190
10	115	350	235	10	170	350	180
10	125	350	225	10	180	350	170
10	135	350	215	10	190	350	160
11	145	385	240	10	200	350	150
11	156	385	229	10	210	350	140
11	167	385	218	10	220	350	130
12	178	420	242	10	230	350	120
12	190	420	230	10	240	350	110
12	202	420	218	10	250	350	100
13	214	455	241	10	260	350	90
13	227	455	228	10	270	350	80
13	240	455	215	10	280	350	70
14	253	490	237	10	290	350	60
14	267	490	223	10	300	350	50
14	281	490	209	10	310	350	40
15	295	525	230	10	320	350	30
15	310	525	215	10	330	350	20
15	325	525	200	10	340	350	10
16	340	560	220	10	350	350	0
16	356	560	204	10	360	350	-10
16	372	560	188	10	370	350	-20
0	388	0	-388	0	380	0	-380

Timesaver
If you're playing a game with a minimum $10 bet on the inside, and you want to use the progression in Table 6.3, here is an easy way to do it. Just start the progression at $10 for the first ten spins and move to $11 on the eleventh spin. This will increase the total cost for thirty-eight levels to $786.

Betting zones

Another very popular betting strategy is to cover contiguous sections of the wheel. If the ball falls anywhere in the covered sections then you're assured a win. One example would be betting 1-6, 13-24, and 31-36. The statistical result is identical to betting two groups of twelve, but it can be psychologically pleasing to know that a one slot difference will rarely make you a loser (or a winner).

Betting 1-6, 13-24, and 31-36 covers contiguous numbers on both sides of the wheel.

The opposite of this strategy is betting numbers that are spread around the wheel. Wherever the ball lands you have a chance of winning. The ultimate example of this is simply betting one of the even money propositions, but there are many more complicated systems, including one known as Shotwell. It's a progression that uses a combination bet on 1-6 and straight up bets on 8, 10, 20 and 26. The ball will always land on those numbers or near them. You'll always win or have the comfort of knowing that you were close, even as the dealer is taking your chips.

The power of zero and double-zero

It's difficult to comprehend, but roulette's entire house edge rests on two green slots floating in a sea of red and black. Without zero and double-zero the game is an even contest. With the extra slots it gains a punishing house edge. Don't ever forget that. There is a great temptation to focus on the winning potential of a particular system and ignore the possibility that the ball will fall into the green. It's a nice fantasy, but casinos were built on money earned from zero and double-zero. Covering the numbers won't help. The mathematics of the payouts and probabilities remain inflexible. If you play roulette, then you simply must be prepared to lose. The only alternative is playing a biased wheel. Bias is not common, but in the next section we'll explain how it works.

Bias and other methods of beating the wheel

Roulette's randomness requires a perfectly balanced wheel. Anything less creates a bias toward certain numbers. Roulette wheels are built with extreme precision and are frequently checked for balance and wear, but biased wheels occasionally remain undetected. Unfortunately they don't have a big sign announcing a player edge, so you must hunt them down or (more likely) stumble across them.

Hitting a particular number two or three times in a row is not in itself an indication of bias. A number must consistently hit more than once in thirty-six trials (thirty-eight minus the house edge) over an extended period, usually at least 1,000 spins. The process of recording spin results is called clocking a wheel, and it's usually done in shifts by a team of professional gamblers. It's a twenty-four-hour operation because any breaks during or after clocking allow the casino time to move the wheel to another table. If the team finds a biased wheel, another group moves in and bets millions to earn millions.

Nice for them, but how can you benefit from a biased wheel? In most cases you can't, but here's a system that will at least give you a chance.

How to find a biased wheel

Clock a wheel for fifty spins while betting normally. After fifty spins, bet on any numbers that have won four or more times. Straight-up bets or combinations are fine. Meanwhile, expand your sample to 100 spins, and bet on any numbers that win at least eight times. Exclude numbers that turn cold and include numbers that heat up. Expand the sample by increments of fifty spins and four occurrences. Any numbers that consistently reach these criteria will be appearing *much* more frequently than normal.

Just remember, most wheels aren't biased. You might clock 100 wheels before you find one that is out of balance, and the next day it might be gone. It's a lot of work, and usually not worth the effort unless you really love roulette or you're a professional gambler.

Dealer signature

Dealing is often a monotonous job. Certain actions become automatic, including the ball spin. When an experienced dealer is on mental autopilot the ball's speed and trajectory are amazingly consistent from spin to spin. The big variable becomes the metal stops on the wheel that are designed to deflect the ball as it comes off the track. If no deflection occurs then it's possible to accurately predict where the ball will drop. Even with deflection it's possible to predict the winning zone.

The key is finding a consistent dealer and carefully watching where the ball is released and where it lands. If you see a pattern, you'll have just a few seconds after the spin to calculate where the ball will stop and to make a wager. Becoming familiar with the wheel layout will help you quickly bet zones. Most dealers don't have predictable signatures, but it doesn't hurt to check. The nice part about roulette is that even when a system doesn't work, the result is never worse in the long run than the alternative, a wild guess.

Roulette's price for fun and money management

Roulette's price for fun on an American wheel is 5.26 percent (2.63 percent on a European wheel) for every dollar wagered, plus whatever you're willing to spend for bad luck. If your luck is exactly average, a $100 session bankroll will be reduced to about $95 after twenty $5 even money wagers. If your luck is not average, you'll see streaks. Four or five identical decisions on even money wagers are not uncommon, but it's unlikely you'll see anything beyond six or seven consecutive wins or losses. Straight up bets and other inside bets will quickly gobble your bankroll. Don't make them unless you have staying power for at least thirty-five to fifty spins.

Roulette is not a good game for a small bankroll, but it's the kind of game where lightning strikes. You put a $5 split wager on eight and eleven. The ball falls into the eight slot and pays you $85. You leave $40 on the same split and eleven comes in right after that. You've just won a total of $765. The person next to you lost $200 in the same two spins. It seems he was covering every number on the table except for yours.

66

My own personal superstition is that I won't leave a casino until I have played at least $50 on roulette. I bet the minimum on only the number 23. That's my birthday.
—Julie Marie Irvin, roulette player

99

Timesaver
Most roulette tables have an electronic display that shows the results of the last twenty contests. It's an excellent tool to use when clocking a wheel, but consider this: If the information is so valuable, why would the casino help you get it?

Just the facts

- Roulette is a relentlessly negative expectation game with an inflexible 5.26 percent house edge on an American wheel.

- European roulette wheels don't have a double-zero slot. That lowers the house edge to 2.63 percent. You can find European wheels in some American casinos, but they may have higher table limits than double-zero games.

- A five number bet of zero, double-zero, one, two and three is the worst roulette wager. The house edge is 7.89 percent. Don't make this bet. You'll get better odds and a better payoff by choosing those numbers another way.

- Look for *surrender*. It's a rule variation offered by some casinos; even money bets that lose to zero or double-zero are only half lost.

- Roulette uses a unique system of colored chips to distinguish one player from another. You must buy in before playing roulette and exchange the colored chips for regular casino chips when leaving the game.

- There is no betting strategy or method that will change roulette's house edge on an unbiased wheel. Most strategies simply push the risk into fewer numbers or stretch it in an attempt to make the risk disappear. It never does.

- Biased wheels and dealer signatures are the only factors that can predictably influence roulette's outcome. Both can be difficult to detect. If you find bias or a dealer signature, use it, but don't expect roulette to ever be a consistently positive expectation game.

GET THE SCOOP ON...
The best bet in the casino ▪ Lowering the
craps house edge ▪ Sucker
bets ▪ Tips for handling the dice

Craps

C raps is the game your grandfather played on a battleship in the Pacific during World War II, or it's the game your uncle learned as a young man in Brooklyn. It was extremely popular in the middle of the twentieth century, but craps' reputation as a "man's game" eventually contributed to its decline. The men became old guys smoking cigars, and younger people of both sexes began to see craps as an anachronism, not very refined and difficult to understand.

That's a shame because craps isn't difficult and it isn't exclusively a tough guy's game. Yes, Frank Sinatra and Marlon Brando played craps in *Guys and Dolls*, but the dice originally came from a pharaoh's court in Egypt and the rules of the basic contest were developed in England and France. Wealthy aristocrats played an early form of craps, but they called it *hazard* or they used a nickname, *crabs*, which were the double-ones that could make you lose. The French pronounced *crabs* as "creps" when they brought it to the New World, so Americans simply called it *craps*.

Craps is about dice

Many people take one look at a craps table and immediately go somewhere else in the casino. The layout seems so complex. It's ironic because craps doesn't require a table; the game is really about the dice. That's how craps got its tough guy image. Dice are really small, even smaller than cards, and they're less cumbersome. You can carry them anywhere, even on a boat, even into battle. Soldiers and sailors played craps during World War II and in Korea. The game could last ten minutes or all night. Any number of people could play, and the dice (and money) would disappear in a moment if a mortar shell came arcing over or the captain suddenly walked past.

That's why so many old men love craps. Baby boomers never shared the enthusiasm and by the 1990's craps had nearly disappeared in a sea of slots and video poker; less than four percent of gamblers played the dice.

But an interesting trend has developed in the last few years. Men and women are rediscovering the camaraderie and visceral pleasure of a game once played by heroes in foxholes and in the shadows of tanks. Craps is making a comeback. Players are learning what their fathers and grandfather knew before them. The game is about the dice.

So forget the layout for now. We'll use it later to help organize the bets. In the next few sections, let's talk about "rolling the bones."

How will the dice roll?

A standard pair of dice can make thirty-six combinations that total eleven numbers (2 to 12). Table 7.1 shows the various possible sequences.

TABLE 7.1: POSSIBLE DICE COMBINATIONS

Number	Ways to Roll	Combinations	True Odds	Percent Probability
2	1	1-1	35:1	2.8%
3	2	1-2 2-1	17:1	5.6%
4	3	2-2 1-3 3-1	11:1	8.3%
5	4	1-4 4-1 2-3 3-2	8:1	11.1%
6	5	3-3 2-4 4-2 1-5 5-1	6.2:1	13.9%
7	6	1-6 6-1 2-5 5-2 3-4 4-3	5:1	16.7%
8	5	4-4 2-6 6-2 5-3 3-5	6.2:1	13.9%
9	4	3-6 6-3 4-5 5-4	8:1	11.1%
10	3	5-5 4-6 6-4	11:1	8.3%
11	2	5-6 6-5	17:1	5.6%
12	1	6-6	35:1	2.8%

A pair of dice can create thirty-six possible combinations. Each cube has six sides and $6 \times 6 = 36$. Percent probabilities in the far right column are rounded.

Let's say you're the *craps shooter* (the person throwing the dice). On your first roll, called the *come-out roll*, there are two numbers that can win and three that can lose. The winners are seven and eleven. If you roll seven or eleven the contest is over. You rolled a *natural* and *passed*.

If you roll two, three, or twelve, it's "craps"; you *don't pass*. The contest is over and you lose.

Most of the time you won't roll a natural or craps; the come-out roll will be four, five, six, eight, nine, or ten. When that happens the number becomes your *point*. You must roll the same number again to pass. There is no limit to the attempts allowed for a pass. You can pass in one roll or 100. After a point is established the only way to lose is to roll a seven. Yes, it was good for the come-out, but now it's bad. All the other numbers (including eleven and craps) have no importance at this stage. Roll the point and you win; roll seven and you lose. End of contest; the next roll is a come-out.

Unofficially...
Dice have been found in Egyptian tombs that were built before 2,000 BC. The ancient cubes have the same design as modern dice, six sides with one to six spots. The sum of opposite sides is always seven. Look at a pair of dice and see for yourself.

That's it. That's basic craps. It's stunningly simple. Table 7.2 shows the various rolls required for a pass along with probabilities for each outcome.

TABLE 7.2: WINNING AND LOSING ROLLS FOR THE SHOOTER

Come-Out Roll	Numbers	Probability of Rolling
Pass (Win) with natural	7,11	22.2%
Don't pass (lose) with craps	2,3,12	11.1%
Point	4,5,6,8,9,10	66.7%
Rolling to repeat the point		
Pass (win) with point	point	variable
Don't pass (lose) with seven	7	16.7%
No effect	all other numbers	variable

A come-out roll is twice as likely to pass with a natural than be craps. The most likely outcome is establishing a point. If a point is established, the shooter must roll the point number again to pass. Seven becomes a loser. Rolling seven after the come-out is called a *seven-out*.

Of course, there is much more to craps than pass and don't pass, but it's mostly centered around the shooter and this contest. If you understand how to pass, you understand craps.

The table and the crew

Craps is played on a table like the one in Figure 7.1. It's big, typically five by ten feet. The sides are high to prevent dice from coming off the layout. The top edge has a rail with grooves to hold your chips, and below that is a ledge for drinks. It's everything necessary to shoot craps like a member of the Rat Pack.

The dealer at the center of the table is the *stickman* (some people say "stickperson" but the old-style terminology is still prevalent). The stickman retrieves dice after a throw, returns them to the shooter, and is responsible for all other issues concerning the cubes.

Bright Idea
Many casinos provide craps classes. They're free and usually take an hour or two. A knowledgeable dealer will teach you the game at a real craps table.

The Craps Table

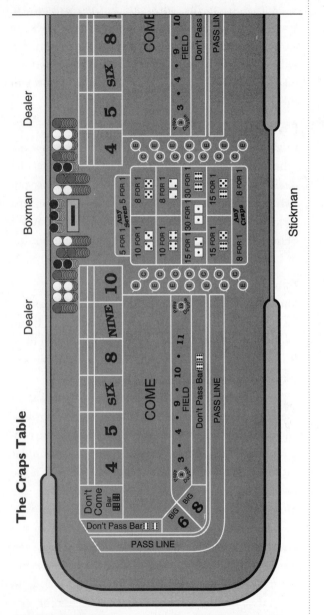

Standard craps layout. The section on the left is the same as the section on the right. Image courtesy of the *Unofficial Guide to Las Vegas* by Bob Sehlinger.

Timesaver
Throw dice hard
enough to hit
the end of the
table, but don't
throw them so
wildly that they
come off the
table. The game
will be delayed
until the dice are
found and
checked for tam-
pering. Supersti-
tious shooters
request "same
dice" if the
cubes escape
because chang-
ing dice will sup-
posedly cause a
seven-out.

Across from the stickman is the *boxman*. He keeps an eye on the bank of chips and supervises the game. Most disputes are settled by his decision. On either side of the boxman are dealers who pay bets, take chips, place bets for players, and generally run the game.

Buying in

Buying into craps is a little different from some other table games because you may have to get the dealer's attention. Put your money on the layout (when the dice aren't rolling) and say "change" in a clear voice. A dealer will give you chips in whatever denomination you request. We'll talk about betting in later sections, but first let's talk about shooting.

Throwing the dice

Shooting is optional. When the stickman offers you dice, simply choose two and throw, or decline. If you decline, the person next to you will be offered dice. If you decide to throw, you'll hear the stickman say, "Shooter coming out!"

Throw the dice hard enough to hit the wall at the other end of the table. This is very important. Dice that don't take a bounce at the end may be considered a *no roll*. This will make you very unpopular with the crew and the other players, especially if the invalid numbers would have paid someone big money.

Time-consuming rituals before throwing are equally unloved. It's OK to rattle the dice for a few moments or whisper a mantra, but elaborate performances are not appreciated. Keep your hands in sight at all times when holding the dice, and be sure your hands are off the layout when someone else is shooting.

You may throw the dice indefinitely, as long as you continue to pass on the come-out, roll craps, pass with a point, or roll numbers other than seven after a come-out. If you roll seven instead of your point this is called a *seven-out*. You lose and the dice are offered to the person standing next to you.

This entire performance will be watched and wagered upon by a dozen or so people. Craps is a communal experience, thoroughly unlike any other casino game. Video poker is solitary; blackjack is you against the dealer; roulette is dignified and ordered; craps is shooting the rapids with a bunch of strangers.

Mostly good bets

Craps offers a multitude of betting options. Some are closely tied to the shooter's attempt to pass. Others are simply wagers on the next number to be rolled. It's not like roulette, where each spin necessarily ends all contests. A craps bettor can have wagers *working*. One roll of the dice might win three, lose two and leave three more unaffected. Multiply that by each player and the action becomes fast and furious.

Of course, multiple bets are not a requirement. You can always wager just one contest, but much of the fun comes from two or three bets working and collecting money on sequential rolls. And, of course, much of the sadness comes when the shooter throws the wrong numbers and the bets lose sequentially, or sometimes all at once.

Moneysaver
A casino is not the place to test a new craps betting system. Use a computer simulation first. The best simulations do more than just play the game. They log the sequence of rolls, bets, and decisions, and compare your results with the expected average.

Pass-line bets and taking odds

The most basic craps wager is a bet that the shooter will pass. It's called a *pass-line* wager and to make it you simply put chips on the *pass line;* the marked space closest to the edge of the table. The wager is normally made before a come-out roll. It pays even money. Remember, the shooter may win or lose on the come-out or may roll many times before passing with a point or losing with a seven-out. Your *line* bet must remain on the layout until the contest is over.

A pass-line bet has an overall house edge of 1.4 percent, but that's a combined number. You actually have a greater chance of winning on the come out roll, and less of a chance after the point has been made. The possibility of winning also depends on which point is rolled; passing with an eight is more likely than passing with a four. So rolling a point is better than rolling craps, but it's certainly not ideal. One way to take the sting out of the situation is to *take odds* on your pass-line wager after the point is established. Odds is an additional bet that the shoot-er will make the point. It's paid at true odds, so it has zero percent house edge. Table 7.3 shows the vari-ous odds payoffs.

TABLE 7.3: ODDS THAT A NUMBER WILL ROLL BEFORE SEVEN

Point	True Odds	$20 Odds Bet Returns
4	2:1	40
5	3:2	30
6	6:5	24
8	6:5	24
9	3:2	30
10	2:1	40

You take odds on a line bet by putting an additional amount just off the pass line behind your original chips. Odds are allowed in multiples of the original *flat* bet and there is usually a limit, so if the flat bet is $10 and the odds allowed are 2×, you can take odds in any amount up to $20. If odds allowed are 10×, you can take odds in any amount up to $100. Odds limits will be posted along with the other table limits and important information on a card attached to the side of the table.

The important thing to remember about taking odds is to do it in multiples that the casino can pay. If the point is six and you take $8 odds, the payoff would be $9.60. The casino will only give you $9. To get the full payout you must take odds in multiples of $5 for points six and eight, and $2 for points five and nine. Any whole-dollar amount is fine for points four and ten.

Odds are often called "the best bet in the house" and if you don't include some blackjack rule combinations then this is certainly true. But remember that odds can only be taken in conjunction with another bet, and the other bet invariably has a house edge. We'll examine the pros and cons of taking odds in a later section, but it's basically the best bet you can make on a craps table.

One other great thing about odds is that you can make the wager any time after the point is established, and you can take odds off the table as you please. The casino doesn't care because it has no edge in the contest. Just pick up your chips when the shooter isn't rolling and the bet is off.

Don't pass and giving odds
The opposite of a pass-line bet is a wager on the *don't-pass bar*. It's often called *don't* while the pass

Watch Out!
The pass line (do) and the don't pass bar (don't) are also often called *right* and *wrong*. This is a clue to the mentality of some sensitive craps shooters. If you're betting wrong it's often a good idea to be discreet; leave the shouting and cheering to the right players.

Bright Idea
A player can take a don't bet down at any time after the point has been established, but it's foolish to do so because a don't wager has a solid edge after the come-out. If you see someone retrieving a don't bet, offer to buy it. Your purchase will be better than laying odds.

line is called *do.* Nearly everything operates in reverse when betting the don't. Seven and eleven lose on the come-out. Two and three win. Making the point loses. Seven-out wins. The only variance is that twelve on the come out is a push rather than a win. This small change gives the house its edge. It's an average 1.4 percent which is identical (after rounding) to the house edge on a pass-line bet. Some casinos push two instead of twelve. This has no effect on the probability of winning. The chances for a don't win are lowest on the come-out and grow if a point is established. In fact, the house advantage resides entirely in the first roll. After the first roll the probability of winning solidly favors the don't bettor.

A bet on the don't-pass bar can only be made before a come-out roll. It pays even money.

Don't bettors can take advantage of a zero percent house edge on odds just like pass-line bettors, but they must give (or *lay*) odds rather than take them. Don't players bet more to get less because the odds are in their favor, so the payouts in Table 7.3 are reversed. If the point is four, then the bettor must give odds of $40 to win $20.

Giving odds has limits identical to taking odds, but the limits are figured on the payoff, not the bet. Let's say that odds allowed are 2×. If the original wager is $5 and the point is four, you can wager a maximum of $20 for a $10 win. And, of course, bets should be made in multiples that the casino can pay. If the point is eight and you make a $10 odds bet, the payoff would be $8.33. The casino will only give you $8. To get the full payout, you must give odds in multiples of $6 for points six and eight, $3 for points five and nine, and $2 for points four and ten.

You make an odds bet on the don't-pass bar by putting the additional chips next to the original wager. The bottom chip of the odds stack should be off-center so the stack will be crooked. This will show it as an odds bet. Some casinos have different requirements for indicating odds. The dealer will show you how to do it.

Odds bets on the don't can be made or withdrawn at any time like odds on the pass line. The original don't bet can also be withdrawn at any time (unlike the do). In fact the casino wants you to withdraw a don't bet after the come-out because their best chance of winning is gone; the player has the edge. So the rule is that the flat portion of a don't bet can be withdrawn at any time, but it cannot be replaced. Pass-line bets can be made or increased at any time, but they can't be withdrawn. Making or increasing a pass line wager after a come-out is called a *put* bet. It's an uncommon wager (some dealers don't even know that it exists) and it's ill-advised except when used in conjunction with odds. We'll cover put bets later in the chapter.

Come and don't come

Betting *come* is where most people become confused about craps. Part of the problem is the word itself. It has no obvious meaning. *Pass* and *don't pass* are clear enough. But why *come*?

The original purpose of the word has been somewhat obscured over the years as craps developed and moved from Europe to America, but you'll find it helpful to consider come as a hearty welcome to gamblers who have arrived at the game during the shooter's attempt to pass.

Timesaver
Shooters are usually required to make a line bet (a bet on the pass line or don't-pass bar). This ensures that they have a stake in the way the dice are rolled, but there's no rule that says a shooter must continue shooting. If you want to stop then just decline the dice.

It's simple. A come bet works like a pass-line bet except that a come bet is made *after* the shooter establishes a point. A come bet is not a put bet; it has a full opportunity for a natural on the first roll.

The key to understanding come (and its opposite, *don't come*) is to forget about the shooter's contest and simply focus on the numbers as the shooter rolls them. Remember, the rules for winning, losing, payouts, and odds are exactly the same for pass and for come. The only difference is when the bets can be made.

TABLE 7.4: DO AND DON'T BETTING EXAMPLES

Dice Roll	Pass	Don't Pass	Come	Don't Come
7	win come-out	lose come-out	no action	no action
4	point est.	point est.	no action	no action
3			lose craps	win craps
10			point est.	point est.
12				
5				
6				
10			win point	lose point
2			lose craps	win craps
3			lose craps	win craps
2			lose craps	win craps
4	win point	lose point	point est.	point est.
8	point est.	point est.		
4			win point	lose point
7	lose (7 out)	win (7 out)	win come-out	lose come-out
11	win come-out	lose come-out	no action	no action
4	point est.	point est.	no action	no action
9			point est.	point est.
7	lose (7 out)	win (7 out)	lose (7 out)	win (7 out)
Total	3 wins 2 losses	2 wins 3 losses	3 wins 5 losses	5 wins 3 losses

For example, a come wager will win on the first roll (its come-out) when the shooter rolls seven or eleven, and it will lose with craps. A winning seven on a come bet might be a seven-out for the shooter, but the shooter's contest doesn't matter to the come bettor. Craps for the shooter mean nothing for the come. A come bet has its own point, and odds are figured on that point. Come is entirely independent of the shooter's attempt to pass except that both use the same dice number sequence.

Table 7.4 shows how this works. Imagine that four players have simultaneously arrived at the table. Each player bets only one way and waits for a win or loss before placing another bet. The various wagers are shown side by side. They all occur during the same random rolls of the dice. Empty spaces indicate no effect from the roll.

Notice that the first seven is a come-out roll and has no effect on the come and don't-come bettors because action is not allowed for them. The second seven is a win for the come but a loss for the shooter. The third seven changes this; the come bettor loses with the shooter.

There is no limit to the number of come and don't-come wagers a player can make alone or in tandem with other bets. Betting on multiple successive rolls is common, though it can get expensive. If a shooter throws seven, the current come bet will win, but the others that are waiting for a point will be lost. On the other hand, if the shooter is hot and seven is nowhere to be seen, multiple come bets will earn a lot of money. And, of course, the opposite is true for multiple don't-come bets; one seven brings rich reward, but a hot shooter will knock off multiple don't-come bets like Annie Oakley in a shooting gallery.

Watch Out!
When a come or don't-come bet wins, it is promptly paid and returned to the appropriate space on the layout. Don't delay in retrieving the chips or the entire amount will be in play for the next roll. The rule is "if it lays it plays."

Working with the dealer

Come and don't come belong to a category of craps bets that are handled in whole or in part by the deal-er. The mechanics of placing and removing such bets are different from pass and don't pass because they involve moving chips into the numbered squares or the center section of the table. This is done only by a dealer. Here's how it works for come.

You begin by noting whether the shooter is com-ing out. Do this by looking for the *puck*. It's a large disk that's black on one side and white on the other. "on" is printed on the white side; "off" is printed on the black side.

The puck will be near or in the don't-come box with the off side up when the shooter is coming out. It will be moved to the corresponding number box and turned to the on side after a point has been established. If the puck is on, you can make a come bet.

Simply reach across the layout and put your chips on the come. Come bets that win or lose on the first roll are handled like any bet; they're either paid or taken. If a point is rolled, a dealer moves the come bet to the corresponding number box on the layout. The exact placement of the chips in the box will reflect where you're standing at the table. The chips will stay there until a seven or the point is rolled. A seven makes them disappear, but a point will bring them back to the come box with a match-ing pile of chips.

If you're making multiple come bets of equal value and a previous one happens to win while the current one has just established a point then the dealer won't bother switching equal stacks of chips. She'll just pay the bet. This is called *off and on* and it's one of the many informal customs that makes craps so charming.

Another one involves taking odds on come. The mathematics are the same as pass-line odds, but making the wager requires dealer assistance. You do this by putting chips on the layout (preferably over one of the lines that separates betting spaces). Tell the dealer what you want, "odds on the come," and the dealer will pick up the chips and place the wager accordingly. The charming part involves a subsequent come-out roll. A seven is good for the shooter but bad for your come bet. Most players betting come and the pass line want come odds "off" (not working) during a come-out. Retrieving the wagers and replacing them on the next roll would be time consuming, so the casino shortens the process by considering come odds automatically off during a come-out unless you request otherwise. If you don't care about what's happening on the pass line, tell the dealer you want odds to stay on.

Of course, the flat bet (the original bet) is always on, but you can turn odds on or off at any time for any roll. Just tell the dealer. If the shooter is giving you a cold feeling, you can remove odds entirely by telling the dealer to take your "odds down." The chips will be returned to you.

Don't-come odds are handled in a similar fashion. They can be on or off as you prefer, but they're not automatically off when the shooter is coming out because don't-come bettors are rooting with the pass line (only on that roll) and hoping for a seven.

Unofficially...
Craps is a very balanced game, with the do and the don't evident everywhere. Are you wondering why a place bet seems to be all alone? Well, it's not. Place is technically place to win, and there is a bet called place to lose, but most casinos don't offer it.

Place, buy, and lay bets

Betting the line can be frustrating if the shooter keeps rolling craps or if he rolls every number repeatedly except the point and then (after twenty rolls) finishes with a seven. Some bettors avoid this by wagering on or against individual numbers to be rolled before a seven. The wagers work essentially like taking or giving odds except that they don't require a line bet, and, of course, the house has an edge. Table 7.5 shows the various bets and how they pay.

TABLE 7.5: PLACE, BUY, AND LAY BETS

Place

	True Odds	House Odds	$60 Bet Pays	No Vig	Place House Edge
4	2:1	9:5	108	108	6.7%
5	3:2	7:5	84	84	4.0%
6	6:5	7:6	70	70	1.5%
8	6:5	7:6	70	70	1.5%
9	3:2	7:5	84	84	4.0%
10	2:1	9:5	108	108	6.7%

Buy

	True Odds	Vig	$60 Bet Pays	Payoff After Vig	Buy House Edge
4	2:1	5%	120	117	4.8%
5	3:2	5%	90	87	4.8%
6	6:5	5%	72	69	4.8%
8	6:5	5%	72	69	4.8%
9	3:2	5%	90	87	4.8%
10	2:1	5%	120	117	4.8%

Lay

	True Odds	Vig	$120 Bet Pays	Payoff After Vig	Lay House Edge
4	1:2	5%	60	57	2.4%
5	2:3	5%	80	76	3.2%
6	5:6	5%	100	95	4.0%
8	5:6	5%	100	95	4.0%
9	2:3	5%	80	76	3.2%
10	1:2	5%	60	57	2.4%

Place and buy bets are similar to taking odds on the pass line. Lay bets are similar to giving odds on the don't. Place, buy and lay bets are different from odds because they don't require a previous wager, and they do have a house edge. They can be taken down at any time.

The term *vig* used in the payoff column is short for *vigorish*. It's basically a fee or percent charge for making a bet. The word is not unique to craps. Strictly speaking, vigorish is synonymous with any casino house edge. Slots, video poker, and all the other games have vigorish, but the word is mostly used in situations that involve a betting fee.

Let's start with a $60 place bet and no vig to see how it works. A *place* bet is similar to a pass-line odds bet. It's a bet that the number will be rolled before a seven. Place bets don't require a line bet, but they also don't pay at true odds. For example, betting correctly that four will appear before seven returns $108. True odds would return $120. That $12 difference is the house edge and it works out to 6.7 percent of every 4/10 wager (about $4) when all the wins and losses average out.

A *buy* bet on the four to roll before seven pays the entire $120, but the casino charges five percent vig on the wager; that's $3, for a total of $63. The actual house edge is a bit lower than five percent; it's 4.8 percent when the wins and losses are combined.

A *lay* bet (sometimes called a *no* bet) is the opposite of a buy, and it's similar to giving odds on the don't. The bettor is wagering that a seven will be rolled before the number. If the number is four and the bet is $120, then the casino pays $60 if a seven appears. This is a true odds payoff, but once again the casino charges a vig; it's five percent of the payoff or $3, for $60. The total bet would be $123. That's a 2.4 percent house edge.

The mechanics of making place, buy, and lay bets are similar to taking odds on come and don't come. Put your chips on the layout and tell the dealer what you want. The dealer will move the chips to

Moneysaver
Some casinos only charge vig on winning bets. This drops the house edge considerably. The revised edge is identical for buy and lay wagers. Points four and ten are 1.6 percent, five and nine are 2.0 percent, and six and eight are 2.2 percent.

Watch Out!
5 for 1 is not the
same as 5 to 1
on propositions.
Many craps
tables play this
cute little trick
in the center.
They pretend
that they're pay-
ing one more
because they
take your origi-
nal wager. The
actual payout on
5 for 1 is 4 to 1;
10 for 1 is
actually 9 to 1.

the appropriate box and take the vig when necessary. The bets can be turned on and off as you
require and can be taken down at any time. Vig will
be returned. And, of course, place and buy bets are
handled like come odds during a come-out roll;
they're considered off unless you request otherwise.

Not-so-good bets

All of the remaining craps wagers fall into a spectrum that starts with not-so-good and progresses to
embarrassingly-bad-and-strictly-for-suckers.

Playing the field

Just below the area for come and above the don't-
pass bar is a section on the layout known as the *field*.
A bet here can be made without dealer assistance.
It's an even money wager that the next roll of the
dice will be three, four, nine, ten, or eleven; if the
dice roll two or twelve, the casino pays double the
wager (some casinos pay triple). Five, six, seven, and
eight are losers. Eight winning numbers and only
four losers may seem like a good bet but the true
odds are 20:16 against the field. The house edge on
a field bet is 5.6 percent when two and twelve pay
double. It drops to 2.8 percent if two and twelve pay
triple. That's comparable to roulette, and certainly
not one of the better wagers available in craps.

Big six and big eight

Big six and big eight are found in the corner of
some layouts and they are perfect examples of sucker bets. Each is a wager on one number, either the
six or the eight, to roll before the seven. It works
exactly like a place bet except that it only pays even
money. That's right. $60 on the big six wins $60. The
same money "place the six" will bring $70. Big six
and big eight are clearly intended for suckers. The
bet is so bad that it's not allowed in Atlantic City.

Hardway or all-day bets

A four, six, eight, or ten thrown as a double is called a hard number. Betting the *hardway* is a wager that a particular number will be thrown hard before a seven and before it is thrown the easy way. Hard four and hard ten pay 7:1. Hard six and hard eight pay 9:1. These bets are sometimes called all-day bets because they can stay on the layout for quite a while if the shooter doesn't throw the number or seven. The bet can be made at any time and withdrawn at any time; it requires dealer (stickman) assistance. The house edge for six and eight is a painful 9.1 percent. It's an excruciating 11.1 percent for four and ten.

Propositions

The rest of the center bets aren't better and are frequently worse. Except for the hardways they're all one-roll propositions. Table 7.6 shows the various bets, true odds, house odds, and the house edge.

TABLE 7.6: PROPOSITION BETS

Bet	True Odds	House Odds	House Edge
Any craps	8:1	7:1	11.1%
Two	35:1	30:1	13.9%
Three	17:1	15:1	11.1%
Eleven	17:1	15:1	11.1%
Twelve	35:1	30:1	13.9%
Hard 4	8:1	7:1	11.1%
Hard 6	10:1	9:1	9.1%
Hard 8	10:1	9:1	9.1%
Hard 10	8:1	7:1	11.1%
Hop (2 ways)	17:1	15:1	11.1%
Hop (1 way)	35:1	30:1	13.9%
Horn	20:4	17:4	12.5%
Whirl	10:5	8:5	13.3%
Any seven	5:1	4:1	16.7%

Odds and payoffs for horn and whirl are an average. Individual wins will pay differently. Proposition bets are placed and taken down by the stickman.

Betting the center is where the craps jargon really explodes. For example, horn is a combined bet on two, three, eleven, and twelve. The payoff is calculated as if you had bet each number separately. Your wager is divided into quarters, so if you make this long-shot bet it's a good idea to put money down in multiples of four or request a horn high and indicate on which of the four you want the extra money: "Horn high twelve!"

Whirl is a horn bet with the seven added. The bet is divided into five parts. A *hop* bet is a wager that a single number will be thrown a particular way on the very next roll. Some casinos will allow you to bet on any combination even if it's not on the layout. *C&E* is any craps plus eleven. *Buffalo* is a combination of the four hardways plus a seven or sometimes a "yo" eleven.

It's a cornucopia of colorful names and slang for basically rotten bets. There isn't a single proposition that has a house edge of less than nine percent. Betting the seven is a whopping 16.7 percent, not as high as keno, but that isn't saying much. The whole bunch of them should be avoided except maybe when you're red-hot. On those rare occasions when everything you bet comes back three or four times, throw a few chips into the center. That will be the true test of your luck.

Craps strategies

Craps' cornucopia of betting options tends to obscure the fact that it's a negative expectation game. There is no combination of wagers or any system for playing that will win money in the long run. In fact the game is often used as a cover for blackjack card counters to "prove" to the casino that they're playing contests that are guaranteed to lose.

But consider why card counters choose craps and not roulette or another game. It's because they can make a combination of bets that reduce the house edge to less than one percent. Luck is still luck, but at least the contest can be pushed to nearly even.

Reducing the house edge

The first step to reducing the craps house edge is to avoid anything that increases it. That includes any bet in the center of the table. It's OK to throw a few chips in there once a year, but you'll pay for the fun. No craps strategy should include propositions. There is no system or wagering combination that can improve these bets even when they are used as "insurance."

For example, some "clever" bettors insure the pass line by also betting any craps. That supposedly turns the first roll into a can't-lose bet. Right? Wrong! They didn't do the arithmetic. Table 7.7 shows why insuring the pass line is a mistake.

TABLE 7.7: CRAPS INSURANCE

	Craps Ways To Roll	Pass Ways To Roll	Point Ways To Roll	Craps Results	Pass Results	Point Results	Total
No craps insurance $20 line bet	4	8	24	-80	160	0	80
With craps insurance $20 line bet $3 any craps	4	8	24	4	136	-72	68

In this example $20 is wagered on the pass line and $3 is wagered on any craps. This combination guarantees that the first roll will always win $17 or $1, or establish a point and lose at most $3; but look at the total winnings over time: The line bet alone will always eventually win more.

Moneysaver
Most casinos charge a minimum $1 vig for buy and lay bets, so a bet for any amount less than $20 effectively increase the five percent vig. It's also customary to round down fractional vig amounts, so a $39 bet would also be charged only $1.

This is an example of "craps insurance." It's a very bad bet. Pass-line bets without insurance will always return more over time.

TABLE 7.8: FLAT BETS COMBINED WITH ODDS

Pass Line/Come	1.41%
With 1× Odds	0.85%
With 2× Odds	0.61%
With 3× Odds	0.47%
With 5× Odds	0.33%
With 10× Odds	0.19%
With 20× Odds	0.10%
With 100× Odds	0.02%
Don't Pass/Don't Come	1.40%
With 1× Odds	0.69%
With 2× Odds	0.46%
With 3× Odds	0.34%
With 5× Odds	0.23%
With 10× Odds	0.12%
With 20× Odds	0.07%
With 100× Odds	0.01%

The house edge on odds is always zero percent. The figures in the right column show the overall house edge when odds are combined with a line bet.

Of course it's tough when a shooter rolls craps two or three times in a row. That's what drives people to insurance bets; the cost seems so low. And who cares if you win less as long as you win? Right? Wrong again. They forget that craps is the least likely way a pass-line bet will lose. What usually happens is either a win on the come out or a loss with a seven-out.

That realization causes people to search for new ways to protect their wager against loss. Betting the field? Betting any seven? Betting an equal amount on the come? Don't waste your time. It can't be done. The smart way to bet craps is to pick a wager with a low house edge and make it even lower. Let us show you how.

TABLE 7.9: FLAT BETTING
COMPARED WITH TAKING ODDS

Dice Roll ->	Natural	Craps	Pass 4/10	Seven-Out
Probability ->	22.2%	11.1%	8.3%	16.6%
Pass $30 Wager				
Odds $0	+30	-30	+30	-30
Pass $10 Wager				
Odds $20	+10	-10	+50	-30
Pass $6 Wager				
Odds $24	+6	-6	+54	-30
Pass $30 Wager				
Odds $20	+30	-30	+70	-50
Don't Pass $30 Wager				
Odds $0	-30	+30	-30	+30
Don't Pass $10 Wager				
Odds $20	-10	+10	-30	+20
Don't Pass $6 Wager				
Odds $24	-6	+6	-30	+18
Don't Pass $30 Wager				
Odds $80	-30	+30	-110	+70

Natural and craps percentages reflect the come-out roll. Pass and seven-out percentages are for points four and ten after the point has been established. Other points would produce different amounts. Remember that don't bets win most frequently after the come-out.

Betting the line with odds

A line bet has a house edge of 1.4 percent. That's pretty low, but look what happens when odds are added to the equation. Table 7.8 shows the overall house edge when a flat wager is combined with various multiples of odds wagers.

Remember, the actual house edge on the flat bet doesn't change. $120 on the pass line will always be subject to a 1.4 percent house edge regardless of the odds allowed. But what if you didn't put $120 on the pass line? If you wager $60 on the line and take $60 in odds (1×) then the overall house edge on the total amount will be 0.85 percent. $20 on the line and $100 in odds (5×) will bring the house edge down to 0.33 percent.

Unofficially...
Pressing a bet means to increase the wager, usually by the amount of winnings from the last decision. This bit of craps jargon was the genesis for the common phrase "pressing your luck."

Putting less on the line and more in odds always lowers the combined house edge. This works for all wagers that allow odds including pass, don't pass, come and don't come. Of course, luck is luck. Don't confuse a lower house edge with an altered probability of any number appearing on the dice. Strategy to affect the contest is only possible in blackjack and poker. Craps strategy affects how much the casino pays and takes.

This leads to interesting objections from some players because odds is a separate wager. Reducing the amount on the line causes them to win less money if the dice tumble their way on the come-out. Table 7.9 shows this effect.

They're absolutely correct. The pass line's biggest opportunity is on the come-out. With less money on the line they win less for that particular wager if a natural appears. The temptation then is to take odds but leave the line bet unchanged. But that means more is on the table and more can be lost if the dice fall the wrong way. Not good. Odds should never be used as an excuse to increase the amount of the total wager.

A superior strategy is to bet less on the line and use the additional funds to take odds. The extra bet has a zero percent house edge, so in the long run you will always lose less money by shifting the largest portion of your wager to the odds. In the short run you may be frustrated by alternating naturals and seven-outs. Dice can be cruel, but this doesn't change the fact that over time odds is the best bet in craps.

Giving odds on the don't presents it's own challenge and temptations. Players must risk more to win less because the odds are in their favor. Small

Bright Idea
A *put* bet is a come or pass-line wager that is made or increased after the point has been established. Why would anyone do that? It's a rotten bet unless the player takes odds. A put bet with 10× odds has a lower house edge than a buy or place bet.

and frequent wins are not exciting enough for some players. They want big bucks, so they lay bigger odds to make the don't payouts comparable with the do. That's really dangerous, especially if the point is four or ten. One unlucky roll can sink an overextended player.

Some don't players avoid these sticky issues altogether by avoiding odds. They simply load the bar and pray that a natural won't appear. It's a great strategy for 77.8 percent of come out rolls, but it's not so hot for the other 22.2 percent. Giving odds in the proper amount is always a safer (if less exciting) bet.

This leads to the only logical argument that can be made against taking and giving odds. It's an even contest, and that can be boring for some players. They prefer to beat a game that is clearly against them; winning is sweeter and losing is more acceptable this way. It may not make sense mathematically, but fun is fun. If this describes you, then don't sweat it. Not taking odds and betting on something else is perfectly OK; just realize that you're paying for the pleasure of more risk.

Place six and place eight

Place six and place eight have a house edge of 1.5 percent, just a smidgen more than a line wager and still a pretty good bet. Players who bet the don't sometimes place the six and eight as a hedge when the shooter is hot and rolling numbers. This is not insurance as you'll see, but it is a gut call. You're predicting the shooter won't throw seven in the next two or three rolls

The best way to do this is to be sure the combined total of the six and eight is not greater than the don't wager. Let's say $15 is on the bar and the point is five. $6 would go on six and $6 would go on

Moneysaver
Buying the six or eight is a waste of money. You can place the same numbers for less and win more. On the flip side, buying the four and the ten is cheaper than placing them, but the question always comes back to odds. Why not just take odds?

eight. If the shooter suddenly rolls seven, then the total win (after losses) will be $3. It's not ideal, but, hey, that's gambling and you're ahead. If the shooter rolls the point it won't affect the place bets and you would have lost the don't wager anyway. If the shooter rolls six or eight a few times, the dealer will be giving you money. Just remember that the seven is more likely than the point. Don't be greedy. Take the place bets down after two or three rolls. The wager on the don't will usually win and then you can savor multiple victories.

A craps strategy list

Take another look at Table 7.5. Besides place six and place eight, the remaining wagers all have a house edge of 2.4 percent to 6.7 percent. That's comparable to roulette and better than keno and some slots, but for craps it's really mediocre. Don't waste your money. Below is a short list that summarizes craps optimum betting strategy.

- Bet the pass line, don't pass bar, come or don't come.

- Take or give maximum odds but avoid overbetting.

- Bet place six or place eight if your gut tells you the shooter is hot, but take the wagers down after a few rolls.

- Don't waste time or money on place, buy, or lay bets for the remaining numbers because odds wagers are better.

- Avoid proposition bets.

Follow this strategy and the overall house edge will always be less than 1.5 percent and usually less than one percent. That's nearly an even contest. Combine strategy with the discipline to walk away at the right time, and you'll often leave the table with chips stuffing your pockets.

Craps' price for fun and money management

Every craps bet is different, but if you follow our strategy then the overall price for fun should be less that 1.5 percent of your bankroll when wagered once through, plus whatever you're willing to spend for bad luck. The game is typically played at a rate of about thirty line decisions per hour (an average of four rolls per decision).

Craps is notorious for hot and cold streaks. If the dice are rolling against you, don't fight them. Reduce your bets and if that doesn't work, then take a break. Don't leave too many wagers on the table. A typical heartbreak scenario is being ahead but having five or six bets working, four of which can be taken down. The table suddenly goes cold. Nothing is happening. You don't move swiftly and suddenly the shooter throws a seven; they all disappear.

Rhythm and superstitions

Craps is a game with many superstitions, but unlike slots and video poker, the beliefs surrounding craps don't need to be debunked. Everyone knows they're not logical. Yet everyone (including the casino crew) heeds them. That's because there is a rhythm to the game and a feeling at a hot table that simply defies logic. Below are some of the more common superstitions.

- A don't bettor increases the chance of a seven-out.

- Cashing out will cause a shooter to seven-out.

- Breaking the shooter's rhythm will cause a seven-out.

- Mentioning seven or touching the shooter will cause a seven-out.

- Dice hitting a person's hand will cause a seven-out.

- Dice leaving the table will cause a seven-out, unless the shooter continues with the same dice.

- An empty or recently opened table will be cold, and not good for a streak.

- A female who is shooting craps for the first time will always pass, and will likely pass a number of times after that.

Yes, they're silly, and smart craps players don't believe any of this malarkey. But it's still not a good idea to touch the shooter while she's on a roll, OK?

Just the facts

- The shooter's attempt to pass is the basic contest in craps. Players can wager with the shooter on the pass line or against the shooter on the don't-pass bar. These do and don't bets have a house edge of 1.4 percent.

- Come and don't-come bets are made after a point has been established. They are independent of the shooter's contest, but otherwise they operate by the same rules as pass and don't-pass. Come and don't-come have a 1.4 percent house edge.

- Odds is an additional bet made in conjunction with a pass, don't pass, come or don't come wager. Odds wagers have a zero percent house edge; this makes them the best bet in craps.

- Taking or laying odds in combination with a flat bet reduces the house edge on the overall wager. It's always a good idea to bet maximum odds and lower the flat bet accordingly.

- Place bets and buy bets are similar to taking odds on the pass line, but they don't require a previous wager. Unfortunately the house pays less than true odds for winning place bets and charges a vig (fee) for buy bets.

- Lay bets are similar to giving odds on the don't. A previous wager is not required, but the house charges a vig for the bet.

- Bets in the center of the table are called proposition bets. They have a high house edge. You should avoid them.

- Big six and big eight are sucker bets.

- Avoid *insurance* bets. They're a waste of money.

GET THE SCOOP ON...
Baccarat versus mini-baccarat ▪ Rules
for banker and player ▪ A baccarat
bet you should avoid ▪ Casino
"shills" ▪ Baccarat betting strategies

Baccarat

Chapter 8

B accarat is the spiritual opposite of games like craps, roulette, and blackjack. It has no pretense of player control, no psychological room for being crafty, smart, or skillful. Bettors have three options; none involve how the contest is played. The result is purely karmic. Baccarat is a symbolic measure of a person's luck. Consider the following pop culture examples:

James Bond, agent 007 (Sean Connery), was winning handily at European-style baccarat, chemin de fer, when the world first saw him in *Dr. No.* Bond predictably trounced a beautiful and aristocratic female opponent, Sylvia Trench (Eunice Gayson). When she upped the stakes, he said, "I admire your courage, Miss..." She responded, "Trench. Sylvia Trench. I admire your luck, Mr..." And he delivered the immortal line, "Bond. James Bond."

John Gage (Robert Redford) was losing at baccarat in the movie *Indecent Proposal* when he asked Diane Murphy (Demi Moore) to play with him "for luck." Baccarat pronounced its verdict on both characters. She promptly lost an additional $100,000 of

"

What we want,
what we need is
a nine.
—John Gage
(Robert Redford)
to Diane Murphy
(Demi Moore) in
the movie *Inde-
cent Proposal*

"

his money. It was the more amiable and ostensibly plebeian craps that broke the rules of the universe and gave them $1 million.

Baccarat in real life plays like a tarot reading. Perhaps that's because the game was originally played with tarot cards. It came from Italy during the Middle Ages and was a big hit with sixteenth-century French nobility.

These days casinos promote baccarat's mysterious and portentous image with velvet ropes, crystal chandeliers, and high table limits. A minimum $25 to $100 per hand is common. That's too bad because baccarat is a lot of fun, and the house edge is slim. Mini-baccarat is a low-stakes version with identical rules for winning and losing. It can be fun too, but as you'll see the game is less about the rules and more about presentation.

Roots and rules

American baccarat (the game described in this chapter) is actually a modified version of the French game *chemin de fer*, which itself is a modification of the original European baccarat. We're telling you this in case you wander into a casino in Bucharest and sit down to play a game that looks like American baccarat. The European rules are different.

There is evidence that baccarat was also the genesis for blackjack. The two games are similar in their basic structure. The critical difference is that baccarat allows no decisions in the play. The cards are drawn for both hands by a strict rule. Think of it as a casino-imposed basic strategy. Baccarat makes up for this disadvantage by allowing players to wager on either hand.

The game is about nine

Two hands are dealt in baccarat regardless of how many people are sitting at the table. One hand is called *banker* and the other is called *player*. Each hand initially receives two cards. The suits of the cards mean nothing; their rank is of sole importance. Two through nine are counted at their number value. Tens, jacks, queens, and kings are counted as zero. Aces are counted as one. Hands that total more than nine are reduced by ten. This is easily done by dropping the first digit; fifteen becomes five, twelve becomes two, eighteen becomes eight. The highest possible hand is a nine. It's called a *natural,* or more formally *le grande natural.* An eight is *le petit natural.* A natural automatically wins unless it is tied (nine beats an eight).

Unofficially...
Baccarat is pronounced bah-kah-rah; the t at the end is silent. It's a French spelling of an old Italian expression that meant "zero." Modern Italians no longer use the word (except to describe a card game). They say "zero" when they mean "zero."

TABLE 8.1: BACCARAT RULES FOR DRAWING

1. Naturals automatically win or are tied (nine beats an eight). No cards are drawn.

2. If neither side has a natural, then the following applies:

If Player's Hand Is		*Player Must*
0-5		Draw
6-7		Stand
If Player Does Not Draw *And Banker's Hand Is*		***Banker Must***
0-5		draw
6-7		stand
If Player Draws *And Banker's Hand Is*	*Banker Will Draw If Player's Third Card is*	*Banker Will Stand If Player's Third Card is*
0-2	banker always draws	banker always draws
3	1-7, 9 or 0	8
4	2-7	1, 8, 9, or 0
5	4-7	1-3, 8, 9, or 0
6	6 or 7	1-5, 8, 9, or 0
7	banker always stands	banker always stands

Two hands are dealt in baccarat, one for player and one for banker. Each hand initially has two cards. Player and banker will receive one additional card according to these rules. Player always draws first. The highest point total wins.

Drawing and betting

If neither hand is a natural, then each hand will receive exactly one additional card as specified by the rules. Player draws first. After the draw, the hand with the highest point total is the winner. Table 8.1 on page 163 shows the rules for how cards are drawn in baccarat. They're interesting, but don't give yourself a headache trying to learn them. It's the dealer's job to know when a card should be drawn.

Bettors can wager on either player, banker, or a tie. A win on player or banker pays even money; a tie is a push for these bets and no money changes hands. A winning wager on tie pays 8:1 (some casinos pay 9:1). The true odds for a tie are about 9.5:1. The mathematics for winning somewhat resemble blackjack, so banker has a positive expectation. This is reversed with a *vig* (commission) on bank wins. It's usually five percent but some casinos charge four percent. No vig is charged for losses. Table 8.2 shows the house edge for each bet.

Wagers on player and banker pay even money. A tie is a push for player and banker and a win for a tie bet. Vig is charged only on banker wins.

TABLE 8.2: BACCARAT'S HOUSE EDGE

Player	1.24%
Banker 5% vig	1.06%
Banker 4% vig	0.60%
Tie Pays 8:1	14.36%
Tie Pays 9:1	4.84%

We'll talk about betting and playing strategy in a later section, but the basics are self-evident. Never bet a tie; always bet banker or player.

Baccarat on a grand scale

Baccarat is played at a table like the one in Figure 8.1. Two or more baccarat tables together are called a *baccarat pit*. The pit is usually separated from the regular casino area and easy to spot. Look for velvet ropes, dealers in tuxedos, and high rollers. If you have the money to wager, don't be put off by the continental airs. Walk into the pit and choose a seat as you would at any casino table.

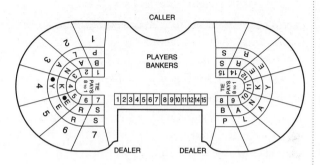

CALLER

PLAYERS
BANKERS

TIE PAYS 8 to 1

TIE PAYS 8 to 1

DEALER   DEALER

This is a baccarat table. Each number around the edge indicates a player seat.

Unofficially...
Baccarat players are by definition high rollers. This gives them certain privileges. One perk is being allowed to bend or mutilate cards. It's not uncommon to see the banker making an origami duck out of a jack. The casino will gladly sacrifice decks (and ducks) to keep a person wagering.

Many casinos use special baccarat chips (more correctly referred to as *cheques*) that are larger than normal. This is yet another touch intended to enhance the continental feeling. You obviously don't have to shout "change" here as you would playing craps. Put your money down and ask for cheques. A crew of three dealers and a concierge or two will attend to your every need.

The grand shuffle

The shuffle for baccarat is like everything else, an elaborate affair. Eight decks are mixed in an elegant performance. One player is offered the cut. The decks are then placed into a shoe similar to one used in blackjack. In baccarat the shoe is called the *bank*. The first card is turned over and its number indicates how many additional cards will be *burned* (discarded).

Moneysaver
Don't bank European baccarat unless you have a lot of cash and you understand the rules. Players are required to finance the game when they bank the continental version. It's similar to being the casino. That's why the banker is allowed an advantage.

Dealing and playing

One dealer, known as the *caller,* runs the game. Two additional dealers across the table handle the financial matters. At the beginning of the game (assuming all the players have just arrived) the first player to the caller's right is offered the bank and an opportunity to deal the cards as banker. It sounds important, but the procedure is simple and is done completely at the direction of the caller.

Players (including the banker) bet player, banker, or tie by placing chips in the appropriate space on the layout in front of them. When the wagering is finished, the caller instructs the banker to deal four cards face down into two hands: "Card for the player. Card for the banker." It's easy to follow. The banker pushes the first and third card (player's hand) to the center of the table and tucks the second and fourth card (banker's hand) slightly under the edge of the shoe. The caller uses a long paddle to pick up the player's hand and deliver it to the person who made the highest wager on player. That person looks at the cards and then turns them over with an appropriate expression of either smugness or disgust. The caller retrieves the hand (or the player pushes/tosses it to the caller) and the two cards are placed at the center of the table.

The banker then reveals his hand. An additional card or two may be drawn at the caller's direction, and the contest is finished. If banker wins, the shoe stays with the person who is dealing. A win for player moves the shoe counterclockwise to the next person. Banking is not mandatory and you (like James Bond) may offer your regrets and pass the shoe to André.

Of course, none of this elaborate ritual has any effect on the game. The moves are predetermined. One dealer could do everything. And that is exactly how the low-stakes version of baccarat works.

Mini-baccarat

Mini-baccarat is played at a standard casino card table like the one in Figure 8.2. Players buy in as they would for blackjack or most other table games. The dealer shuffles six decks in a normal fashion, and one player cuts them with a plastic stop. The dealer puts the deck in a shoe, reveals the value of the first card and then burns that number of additional cards. Bettors wager on player, banker, or tie by placing chips on the various marked areas of the table. The dealer then draws cards according to baccarat rules and pays or collects bets. Players never touch the cards. Mini-baccarat is not as fancy as the big version, but the minimum bet limits are much lower, typically $5 to $10 per hand.

Watch Out!
A baccarat pit can be intoxicating, and you may be tempted to wager more so you can play there. Don't do it unless you can comfortably bankroll at least $500 for $25 per hand play, and $2,000 for $100 per hand play. If that's too much, play mini-baccarat instead.

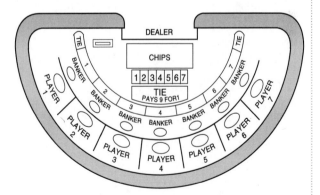

Mini-baccarat is played at a regular casino card table with only one dealer. Players don't touch the cards in this version.

Bright Idea
Baccarat pits often have a dress code that is different from the main casino. Time of day may also be a factor, so it's a good idea to ask. On the other hand, if you're an ultra-high roller (casinos call them *whales*), the staff won't care if you play in a bathing suit.

The game moves quickly, about one hand every thirty seconds. This can create an interesting cost similarity with the big version. A $10-per-hand player at a quickly moving mini table may wager as much or more in an hour as a $25 per hand player at a slower big table.

Big or mini?

Your bankroll will probably be the biggest factor in determining which version of baccarat you should play. If money isn't a factor then you may want to consider some other practical issues, most having to do with your mood.

Wealthy people play baccarat. If you like rubbing elbows with monarchs and magnates then head for the pit. The atmosphere there is quieter and the drink and food service is better than in the main casino.

On the other hand, that whole scene may seem stuffy to you. Too many perfectly coiffed women and too many men wearing dinner jackets or sweaters tied around their necks may be an irritation. Also, you may not enjoy watching other people carelessly drop $1,000 per hand.

Another thing to consider is that many casinos employ *shills*. These are people who are paid to play baccarat so that the pit won't look empty. Shills are usually women, attractive, and expensively dressed. If you choose a table with only a couple of players, it's possible that one or both will be shills. Their presence won't affect the outcome of the game, but if it bothers you, discreetly ask a concierge or dealer to tell you who is who. You're not required to play with shills, but the woman who looks like one may actually be a countess.

Mini-baccarat doesn't present such strange questions. It's less ostentatious and it plays faster. That can be an advantage or a disadvantage depending on your point of view. If you're the kind of person who likes casino hubbub and prefers to hop from game to game, the big version will bore you. You can quickly play five or ten hands of mini-baccarat and then move to another game with little fanfare.

Baccarat strategy

Part of baccarat's allure is the way it resists strategy. Players have no say in how the cards are dealt. Betting is the only variable, and there are only three options. The preferable bet is obviously banker because it wins most frequently and has the lowest house edge. This is especially true if the vig is only four percent.

Bets on player don't win as often, but the no-vig payoff brings the house edge for player nearly even to banker. The difference between player and banker in all cases is less than one percent.

Tie is the only wager that offers a clear choice, and that choice should be no. This is particularly true if the payoff is only 8:1. The 14.4 percent house edge qualifies it as a sucker bet. Combining a tie bet with a simultaneous bet on player or banker drops the overall house edge to about 12 percent. That's still an edge for suckers. There is simply no way to improve tie. You'll get better odds betting craps propositions.

Following trends and counting cards

Some people think it's possible to predict future baccarat results by analyzing previous wins and losses. That's why you'll often see players studiously scribbling notes. Casinos offer paper and writing instruments to assist them. This is an obvious indication that such systems don't work.

> 66
>
> Tell me Miss Trench, do you play any other games besides *chemin de fer*?
> —James Bond (Sean Connery) in the first 007 movie, *Dr. No*
>
> 99

Bright Idea
If you're not paying the vig until the end of the shoe, one way to track the total (and check the dealer's figures) is to buy additional chips in a small denomination. Set aside five percent of every win. Accounting will be easy when the time comes to settle.

Counting cards is also not effective. Repeated analysis has shown that baccarat's rules make the game impossible to accurately predict until the very end of the shoe. A millionaire could earn about $10 an hour with perfect counting.

So baccarat remains an unbeatable game and an elegant mystery.

Paying the vig

The only thing more painful than losing at baccarat is losing and then having to pay a large accumulated vig. Winning bank wagers are recorded by the dealer and the vig is usually collected at the end of the shoe, but there's no rule that says you can't settle up sooner. Some players pay after every winning wager. Whatever you choose to do, just remember that properly accounting for the vig as you play will help you avoid an unpleasant surprise.

Baccarat's price for fun and money management

Baccarat is a negative expectation game. There is no strategy to get around this. Happily, the maximum price for fun is a slim 1.24 percent if you avoid betting tie and you have average luck. A $500 bankroll will turn into about $490 after fifty $10 wagers. That's approximately thirty minutes of mini-baccarat action. Regular baccarat moves at half that speed. Of course, your luck will probably be better or worse than average, so be prepared to win or lose more. If you hit a losing streak, don't stick it out. Stop after four or five bad hands. Yes it's tough to walk away, especially if you just started, but the alternative is possibly blowing your session bankroll in about twenty minutes. If that's an acceptable price for fun then go ahead, but otherwise go for coffee.

Remember, the chances for winning don't change if you play now or later. You won't miss an inevitable hot streak and you're not avoiding a cold stretch. Stopping is just a way to keep money in your pocket. The goal is to have fun, not to run cash through the casino system.

Just the facts

- Baccarat is a high-stakes game played in an elegant setting. The American version is similar but not identical to European baccarat, or *chemin de fer*.

- Players make no decisions in baccarat except for the wager. They can choose banker, player, or tie. Cards are drawn according to a strict rule.

- Mini-baccarat is a low-stakes version of regular baccarat. The rules for betting, winning, and losing are the same, but mini-baccarat is less ostentatious and players never touch the cards.

- Baccarat is a negative expectation game, but it has a slim house edge, 1.24 percent or less if you don't bet tie.

- The best bets in baccarat are on banker or player. Tie is a sucker bet and should be avoided.

- There is no effective strategy for reducing baccarat's house edge or predicting wins. This includes counting cards. There is no effective strategy for reducing baccarat's house edge or predicting wins. This includes counting cards.

Poker

Poker isn't really a casino game. Yes, it's played in casinos (among other places), but the poker mindset has more in common with golf than it does with blackjack or craps. Blasphemy? Before picking up the rocks, please hear me out.

Regular casino games put players on one side and the house on the other. Professionals can squeeze out a positive edge in some situations, but in most contests the casino has an absolute advantage; it's typically between one and 30 percent. That's why there are no professional roulette players, slot players, keno players and craps players. It's not mathematically possible to win at those games in the long run.

There are a few professionals who earn a living playing blackjack, and even fewer who sustain themselves playing video poker, but it's tough. Perfect play will produce a one to two percent player edge. Skill has a part in those contests, but luck and the percentages still hold the greatest sway.

173

Chapter 9

Unofficially...
The World Series of Poker is held every spring in Las Vegas at Binion's Horseshoe. The biggest event is "no-limit Texas hold 'em." Top prize is $1 million. The entry fee for the "big dance" is $10,000 per player.

It's the other way around in poker. Bad luck can hurt, but skill always beats luck over time. Consider the people who play poker. Many are professionals, either big money winners or small players who grind out a reasonable living. Some are semi-professionals; they supplement their regular income with poker winnings. And then there is a throng of casual players who love the game and play once or twice a week. It all sounds a lot like golf.

Why is this distinction important? Because your money is potentially at greater risk when playing poker. The house edge slowly bleeds you dry in most casino games, but it protects you as well. The mathematics are set. Sometimes you win and more times they win. You have a predictable chance even if you're a beginner. Not so in poker. If you're a beginner or mediocre, it's like playing golf against Tiger Woods. You'll never win. Ever. At least not in a casino.

Casino poker

Poker, not baseball, is the national pastime. Think about it. How many people actually play baseball? Every week millions of people across America gather in kitchens and dining rooms to play the game that enthralled Wyatt Earp, Buffalo Bill, and countless other historic personalities. Most people's poker knowledge begins with this communal experience. It's further influenced by a ubiquitous scene from films and television. Four or five people are sitting at a round table. A single bright light shines from above. The year is 1880 or maybe 1920. Each person is holding five cards. The bad guy throws some cash into the pot and says, "I'll see your $800 (dramatic pause) and raise you $3,000." Then he tosses another stack of bills onto the pile.

Casino poker is nothing like that. Even the basic game is different. You'll be hard-pressed to find five-card draw or any contest with wild cards. The two most popular poker versions for professionals and semi-professionals (whom you will surely encounter in a casino) are seven-card stud and Texas hold 'em. Other common poker versions include Omaha and lowball. The list goes on, but we're going to concentrate on the two leaders.

Ranking the hands

Figure 9.1 shows the ranking of poker hands. Most versions of the game use it, but there are a few exceptions. The most notable is lowball, where the lowest hand wins. Seven-card stud and Texas hold 'em (or just "hold 'em") use the standard ranking.

Poker's unpredictable process of determining a winner is what separates genuine poker versions from the downpour of quasi-poker games that have flooded the market in the past few decades. Video poker, Caribbean Stud Poker, Let It Ride, and all the other recent inventions have an absolute standard for winning and losing. You can read it on a pay table. Real poker has no such thing. No hand is an automatic winner (besides a royal flush), and no hand is an automatic loser.

In fact, the object of poker is not necessarily to have the best hand. The object is to win the biggest *pot* (the combined bets of all the players). Having the best hand may allow you to do that, but it may not. Keep this in mind as we explain how the game works.

Obviously, the best hand wins in a *showdown*. That's when two or more people reveal their hands to see who will win the pot. If two players have iden-

Unofficially...
In 1909 a bill to regulate and license poker players was proposed in the Missouri state legislature. Its purpose was to save "millions of dollars lost annually by incompetent and foolish persons who do not know the value of a poker hand."

Bright Idea
People some-
times confuse
poker hands,
especially when
the pressure is
on. They'll forget
that a full house
beats a flush,
and a straight
beats *trips* (three
of a kind). Don't
allow yourself to
be unnecessarily
flushed. Refresh
your memory and
study a list of
poker hands
before sitting
down to play.

tical hands (two flushes, two straights, two full houses), the rank of the cards in each hand will determine the winner. For example, a queen high straight
flush would beat a seven high straight flush. Three
kings beat three jacks. Two aces beat two queens. A
jack high flush would beat a flush that has a high
card of nine. If both players have identical combinations (both have four jacks, both have two aces),
then the highest singleton (single unsuited card)
determines the winner.

Royal Flush	A, K, Q, J, and 10 all of the same suit.
Straight Flush	Five cards in any *sequence*, all of the same suit (such as Q, J, 10, 9, 8 of clubs).
Four of a Kind	Four cards of the same rank, one in each suit, plus an additional card that doesn't matter.
Full House	Three cards of one rank plus another two cards of another rank.
Flush	Any five cards of the same suit, in any order.
Straight	Any five cards in sequence.
Three of a Kind	Three cards of the same rank, plus two additional cards.
Two Pair	Two cards of one rank and two cards of another rank, plus an additional card
One Pair	Two cards of the same rank and three additional cards.
No Pair	All five cards of different ranks and not all of one suit.

Poker hands ranked in winning order.

If neither hand has a combination, the hand with the highest singleton wins. The pot is split when all five cards match in rank. Suit is never used to determine a winner. In games (like seven-card stud) where the player creates a five-card hand from a greater number of cards, the sixth and seventh card are not considered.

TABLE 9.1: FREQUENCY OF POKER HANDS

Royal Flush	4
Straight Flush	36
Four of a Kind	624
Full House	3,744
Flush	5,108
Straight	10,200
Three of a Kind	54,912
Two Pair	123,552
One Pair	1,098,240
Everything else	1,302,540
Total possible combinations	2,598,960

The probability of drawing any particular card is 1 in 52 or 51 to 1 against. The odds of a royal flush are 1 in 649,740. If you play 100 hands every day you'll see one royal flush about every 17 years.

What are the chances that a straight flush will materialize to beat four aces? Table 9.1 shows the total number of possible card combinations that can be dealt from a fifty-two-card deck. Remember, the actual probability of getting any hand changes as the cards are dealt. For example, if you have four cards to a regular flush and you have received only four cards, it's likely (but not certain) you will get the fifth card after three more cards are dealt.

Playing the games

Not every casino has poker, but if they do it's usually in a space set apart from the hubbub of the main casino areas. There will be a reception desk at the

Watch Out!
Don't touch the
pot. The proper
way to bet is to
take chips off
your stack and
put them in front
of you. The dealer
will count the
chips and then
move them to the
center of the
table. If you win
a pot, wait for
the dealer to push
you the chips.

entrance. A host there will be organizing games. If a seat is not immediately available the host will put your name on a list and call you when something opens up. Games are identified by the type of poker (seven-card stud, hold 'em, Omaha) and betting limits, 1-5, 4-8, 10-20, or some other number combination. In a *fixed-limit* game the first number is the amount that can be bet or raised in the early rounds (usually round one and two); the second number is the amount that can be bet or raised in later rounds. A *spread-limit* game allows any bet between the two amounts at any time.

The game will also have a minimum *buy-in* amount that is usually about five times the higher limit. Ten or twenty times the limit is a better buy-in if you're serious about staying in the game. We'll explain why in a later section.

Tables usually accommodate eight people including the dealer. That's you and six strangers who want your money. Get ready to swim with the sharks.

Seven-card stud

Seven-card stud requires an *ante* (a bet before receiving cards). The amount can vary, but it's usually something less than the minimum bet. The dealer will collect the ante, then shuffle the cards and begin the hand.

Cards are dealt clockwise starting on the dealer's left. Each player receives three cards for the first round known as *third street*. Two cards are face down and one is face up. Players carefully lift the cards that are face down and look at them, then put them back on the table. The person with the lowest upcard is now required to make an opening bet. If two people have matching low cards, the suits of the cards determine who bets first. They're ranked alphabetically: clubs is highest, then diamonds, hearts, and spades. So a five of spades would bet before a five of diamonds.

The opening bet is called the *bring-in*. The required size of the bet can be the table minimum or something less, depending on the game. The player to the left of the bring-in now has the following options:

Fold: This is an unconditional surrender. The cards are taken and the player is out of the hand.

Call: Match the previous bet. This allows the player to stay in the game and continue playing for the pot.

Raise: Match the previous bet and then bet at least that much more. This allows the player to remain in the game and requires everyone else to call the increased amount, raise, or fold.

Check: Neither bet nor fold. This option is only available in rounds where a bet has not yet been made. For example, everyone could check in round two. Players who check can't subsequently raise in the same round unless check/raise is allowed.

Here's how it works: John is the bring-in bet of $1. Tom sits to John's left, so Tom must fold, call $1, or raise at least $1. If Tom raises $1 then Margaret must fold, call the entire $2, or raise $2 or more. The betting continues clockwise around the table and returns to John. If one or more players have raised, then John must call the most recent amount (minus his original bet), fold, or raise. If John raises, the betting continues around for a second time. Most games permit at least three raises per round, so it's possible to raise, call, and later fold in the same round.

Timesaver
There is no need to exchange chips if the ones you have don't exactly match the size of a bet you want to make. Let's say the last bet was $2. Tell the dealer you want to call and put a $5 chip out. The dealer will take the chip and return the appropriate amount before dealing the next round.

Bright Idea
A winner is not required to reveal his hand if everyone folds, but in most casinos every player at the table has the right to see winning and losing hands involved in a showdown. The rule is intended to discourage cheating, but you can occasionally use it to aid in strategy. Ask to see the cards.

When all bets have been called the game proceeds to *fourth street*. One card is dealt face-up to each player who is still in the hand. The person showing the highest hand (of the two cards that are exposed) bets or checks first. If it's a check, the next player may either check or bet. The next player could also fold, but this would be foolish because a check will cost nothing. If someone bets, the rest of the players must either fold, call, or raise. Fifth, sixth, and seventh street follow with betting at each round. The fifth and sixth card are dealt face up and the seventh is face down. The person showing the highest hand always opens in the later rounds.

The hand ends in one of two ways: Either all the players fold somewhere on the way to seventh street leaving one player with the pot, or two or more players make it to seventh street. When all the bets have been called, the players reveal their cards and the highest hand wins.

Hold 'em

The most obvious difference between hold 'em and seven-card stud is that each player receives only two cards in hold 'em. They are face down. Five additional cards are dealt face up on *the board* (the table) as community cards. The players use the community cards and their two *pocket cards* or *hole cards* to build a poker hand. The hand can include one, both, or in rare circumstances none of the pocket cards.

Hold 'em doesn't have an ante. Instead it uses a rotating system of blind betting to start the pot. Each player is designated in turn as dealer for one hand. This doesn't mean the person handles the cards, but it does mean a disk called a *button, puck,* or *buck* is put in front of the player. The two players to the left of the designated dealer must make blind bets to start the pot. The first player to the left makes a *small blind* bet which is usually half the table minimum. The second player make a *big blind* bet, which is usually the minimum. The first two cards are dealt, and the rest of the players must either call the big blind, raise, or fold. If everyone calls, the small blind bettor must either fold or put in an additional amount to match the other bets. Both blind bettors can also raise when the betting returns to them.

After everyone has either called or folded, the dealer burns a card. Then he deals three cards face up. This is known as the *flop.* The first remaining player to the left of the designated dealer starts the betting in this round and in every subsequent round. Another card is burned after the betting, and a fourth card is revealed. This round is called the *turn.* More betting, another burned card, and the last card is revealed. Players have reached the *river.* Anyone left either folds to the winner or there is a showdown. The hand ends, the button moves clockwise to the next player (the former little blind bettor), and the new hand begins.

Poker strategies

Poker doesn't have a basic strategy like blackjack or video poker. The best way to play a particular hand will change with every game and every player. For example, a showdown is not necessarily the preferred outcome. *Tight* (conservative) players with *rags* (poor hands) will quickly fold rather than put money in a pot that someone else will ultimately win. A good poker player with a bad hand will some-

Unofficially...
Poker's buck was originally a buckhorn knife. In later years a silver dollar was used. That's why dollars are called bucks. The poker term was the genesis for the phrase "passing the buck" and the sign on U.S. President Harry S. Truman's desk: "The buck stops here."

Moneysaver
It is a tradition to *toke* (tip) the dealer when you win a pot. The amount is usually determined by the size of the pot and local custom. A dollar or so is common in low to medium stakes games. If the pot is very small or split, you should toke less or not at all.

times turn this to an advantage and *steal the pot* with aggressive betting. The same player with a good hand will lure unsuspecting bettors into the pot with tentative betting. Of course, other good poker players will recognize this obvious ruse and wager accordingly. It turns into an intricate game of, "He thinks that I think that he thinks that I think that he thinks that I have four kings. But I know that he knows that I know that he knows...." And the game goes on.

As a result, strategy for poker inevitably becomes a series of instructive stories and examples. Here are a few to consider when playing seven-card stud:

Seven-card stud: bluffing and tells

Let's say your first three cards include a pair of aces and a four. One of the aces is face up. It's a nice start, but if the hand doesn't improve there are a lot ways you can lose. One strategy would be to bet in a manner that suggests you indeed have two aces, or maybe three. This would drive other players out of the game and lessen the chance that you would lose in a showdown. Of course, if the other aces are face up somewhere on the table this semi-bluff won't work.

Now consider that your first three cards are all hearts, five, six, and nine. The nine is exposed. Very exciting, but your chances of making the straight flush are not good. Your chances for a flush are better, but still not overwhelming. Nevertheless, in this situation you would want everyone in the pot because you may develop a killer hand. The strategy here would be to draw other players in. How? That depends on how they're playing, loose or tight. Also, you should be ready to bail if you're holding rags on sixth street.

Now let's put the examples together. It's fifth street. The situation appears reversed and the other person has three hearts exposed on the table. You're holding the aces from the first example, and you've been lucky to catch a third ace. You're trying to push him out, and he seems to be trying to keep you in. The two of you may be locked in a little betting war if you don't fold. Of course he may not have the flush. Look around the table. If you see nine cards with hearts then he will never have a flush. If you don't see any hearts, his chances are good, maybe better than your chances of catching the fourth ace or a pair to make a full house. He's looking tentative. This might be a ruse. The smart move may be to fold. Or maybe not. Is your opponent the kind of person who frequently bluffs? Maybe those two down cards are spades. Now multiply this scenario by every person at the table.

Players gather information about their opponents' hands by analyzing betting patterns, noting exposed cards, and by reading player *tells*. These are unconscious movements or body positions that indicate what a person is thinking and therefore playing. A tell can be an ear scratch, a lean forward, or a heavy sigh. It can be the way someone fiddles with the chips or sips a drink. Some people nonverbally scream, "I'm holding aces!" Others telegraph the message "I've got trash!" Poker pros see this and use it.

Hold 'em: holding the nuts

Hold 'em is somewhat more volatile than seven-card stud. There is no ante and no reason to stay in if the first two cards are not good (unless you're the big blind). On the other hand, this makes pot stealing rather easy. Betting aggressively tells everyone you

Watch Out!
Don't ignore a dealer or player mistake if it puts you at a disadvantage. Speak up and be sure the error is corrected. The game shouldn't continue until you're satisfied. On the other hand, if you're the beneficiary of a dealer or player error, bow to the greater judgment and wisdom of the table. Keep your mouth shut.

have two aces or two kings. Sometimes the other players will bow out, or they might think you're bluffing and call you.

The most promising and occasionally the most dangerous situation is believing you hold the required cards, the *nuts*, to the best hand. Let's say you have two aces in the pocket. You bet aggressively. Some people drop out, but a few stay with you. The flop reveals another ace, a ten, and a four, all unsuited. You have the nuts, so you change strategy and decide to draw people in. You bet modestly. It works. Nobody folds. The turn brings a two. Everyone checks to you. Again you bet modestly. Everyone calls. You still have the nuts, and you prepare for the kill. The river reveals another ten. Now there is a problem. One of the remaining players could have four tens. Happily, there is no indication of this because everyone checks to you. You push out a big pile of chips. The first live player to the dealer's left raises. Everyone folds to you. Now you must fold with a lot of money in the pot, or you pay even more to possibly lose.

At times like this, an ability to read other players is crucial. Let's take a closer look at the hand. We'll call the person holding the aces "Hotshot." The person holding tens is "Killer."

Anatomy of a poker hand

The Pocket: Hotshot has two aces and decides to bet aggressively in a bid to push out the other players before they have a chance to improve their hands. Few take the bait. Everyone thinks Hotshot is on tilt (flustered and betting wildly) because he has been losing for the last two hours.

Most of the players call and Killer raises. She is holding two tens. She is also the big blind. In other circumstances Killer would have folded, but this time her money is already in the pot. She (incorrectly) believes that Hotshot is trying to steal it. Hotshot re-raises and Killer calls. Now she begins to suspect Hotshot has two aces or two kings.

The Flop: An ace, ten, and four appear. They are unsuited. Hotshot knows he has the best hand. It's the first one that night. Finally! He decides to string the other players along and pretend the flop didn't improve his situation. The trick works, but it will be Hotshot's undoing.

Meanwhile, Killer's hand also improved on the flop to three tens. She bets modestly. Hotshot puts on a show of thinking about it and then he calls. If Hotshot had raised big, Killer would have folded in the sure knowledge that Hotshot had three aces, but his ruse draws her in. Everyone else is fooled, too. Nobody folds.

The Turn: The dealer reveals a two. Killer and everyone else check to Hotshot. More theatrical thinking. He modestly bets and everyone calls. Hotshot begins mentally counting his money.

The River: Lightning strikes; the fourth ten appears and Killer is now firmly holding the nuts. She sees a momentary flash of panic cross Hotshot's face as he scans the table looking for a reaction. Killer shows nothing, but now she's sure that Hotshot has two aces in the pocket. She opens the betting with a check to draw Hotshot into the trap. Hotshot interprets this as weakness. He relaxes and decides that he still has the nuts. Hotshot makes a big bet. Killer raises. The rest of the players take a long look at the cards on the board and toss their hands. Hotshot is stunned, but he thinks Killer is bluffing. He raises. She raises again. Does she have four tens? Hotshot has no way out.

Timesaver
A pair that's ten or higher is good to keep as an opener in hold 'em. A lower pair is passable, but toss it at the first sign of trouble. Ace-King is strong. Any other high card combination is less than ideal unless the cards are suited. Lower suited connectors (6-7 of diamonds, 4-5 of clubs) can be played, but be ready to fold.

Watch Out!
Calling a bet and then suddenly raising is known as a *string bet*. It's a ruse to get a reaction, and it's not allowed. String bets only happen in the movies: "I'll call your $100...and raise you $500." In casino poker such a bet would be restricted to a call.

The moral is, if you've got the nuts, then don't back down, but be absolutely sure that you've got the nuts.

The reverse moral is, if you're definitely holding the nuts, don't wither in the face of an aggressive player who thinks you're bluffing. Don't just call him; raise him. Make him fold or make him feed the pot to see your cards. Remember, the goal is not necessarily to have the best hand, it's to win the biggest pot.

Hotshot was indeed on tilt. He wasn't thinking clearly, and he became greedy. The biggest mistake was playing it cool after the flop. Hotshot needed to establish credibility and prevent the others from improving their hands. He did neither. That's why Killer and the other players took his money all night long.

Poker economics and practical matters

Where is the casino during all this heated action? They're sitting above the fray collecting a portion of every pot. This is called the rake. Five to 10 percent is common. Or they may charge an hourly fee per player. Other casinos simply collect a flat amount for every hand. Whatever the method, you'll pay about $10 per hour to sit in a low stakes game. That amount will more than double in a higher stakes game.

Let's say seven people bring $300 each to the table. That's a total of $2,100. The house will steadily extract money as the game continues, so the total amount that can be won will decrease. The good players will take the money that is left and the not-so-good players will see their chips disappear.

Remember, poker is not like other casino games. It's not a series of decisions with a predictable edge for the house. There is no comforting once-through percentage to calculate. Weaker poker players lose. That's it. Playing conservatively just slows the flow of chips. What happens if you get a dream hand? Superior players read you like a clock and fold. Congratulations; you won the antes. Or they pull you in and skewer you with an even better hand.

Following the rules

Poker has a multitude of rules about how to bet and how the cards should be handled. Following the rules is important, especially in situations that involve the integrity of your hand. Remember, it's easy to lose a pot on a technicality. The other players won't be rooting for you to receive a lenient judgment as they would in blackjack or craps. With that in mind, here are some of the more important rules you'll want to remember.

- Your cards must be in sight at all times. Leave them on the table. Don't show them to other players or anyone else. Revealing your face down cards to others before a showdown can be grounds for having your hand declared dead.

- Your hand is dead if you or someone else throws all or part of it into the *muck* (discard pile). This can happen if the dealer incorrectly thinks you're folding. Or it may happen this way: You have a pair of kings in a showdown. The other person tells you he has aces, so you muck the cards in disgust. Then he reveals his hand and you realize he said "eights," not "aces." It's too late. Your hand is dead.

> 66
> If you can't spot the sucker in your first half-hour at the table, then you're the sucker.
> —Mike McDermott (Matt Damon) in *Rounders*
> 99

Moneysaver
Don't automatically *muck* (throw away) your cards in a showdown when you think the other person has a better hand. People often overlook a winning combination. The rule is that "the cards speak." Just turn the cards over and let the dealer declare the winner.

- Your hand is dead if you lose control of the cards while revealing them and one or more fall off the table.

- If another player's cards touch your cards, then both hands are dead.

- Buying chips during a hand is not allowed. You can only play with *table stakes*, the chips you have available. Running out of chips while competing for a pot is called being *all-in*. You can still win everything that has been collected to that point, and all the bets calling your last wager, but you will miss any bets raised beyond your limit. That new money will go into a side pot. Remaining players can win both pots, or just the second one if you win the first.

- If you win a pot, hold on to the winning cards and leave them face up until the chips are pushed to you. There is no proof that the pot is yours if the hand is mucked before that.

Tips for playing and poker etiquette

Following the rules is mandatory, but winning at poker requires something more. The best players develop a unique style that seems unguarded to opponents yet is ultimately inscrutable. The key is being comfortable within yourself. Here are a few tips that will help you develop a relaxed demeanor and put others off guard.

- **Wait your turn**. Folding, calling, or taking any action out of turn is rude. It creates an unfair advantage or disadvantage for other players, and it focuses attention on you in a negative way. Don't do it.

- **Don't be bullied** into making a quick decision. If you need time to think, then ask for it by saying "time." This is especially important in loose games when players are eager to interpret your silence as a check. And don't tap or rap the table while you're thinking. This action is interpreted as a nonverbal check.

- **Don't hesitate when it's time for a showdown.** Show your cards. If all players check in the last round, they should reveal their cards together. Some people are rude and want you to go first. It doesn't matter; show your cards.

- **Don't appear too smart at the table.** The less people think of your ability, the more they will underestimate you. Let them believe you're half-witted or on tilt. Just be sure you're not.

- **Take a break when you're tired or hungry.** It's no big deal. Just ask the dealer how long you can be away from the table. Twenty or thirty minutes is usually allowed. Count your chips and leave them there. It's the dealer's job to be sure they are untouched until you return.

Watch Out!
There is nothing more frustrating and wasteful than having the nuts but too few chips to properly compete. Poker's table-stakes rule prevents you from buying more chips during a hand, so be sure you're properly loaded before the cards are dealt.

Poker's price for fun and money management

The house rake is obviously only a part of poker's price for fun. The rest depends on who is playing. Are you better than everyone else at the table? If the answer is yes, then the price for fun will usually be zero or less. Poker will pay you money. On the other hand, if you're the worst player at the table, it is realistic to expect that nearly every dollar you put into the pot will disappear. It's like a Sunday golfer play-

Watch Out!
The kindly old gentleman with the sparkle in his eye and the caramels in his pocket is a poker pro. He earns $50,000 "fun money" every year by winning pots from tourists like you. The cute blonde with the goofy dress and ponytail is a semi-pro. She's putting herself through college with poker winnings.

ing in a pro tournament. He might be good with his weekend buddies, but he'll be creamed by the people who play for a living.

You may not think professionals play in low-stakes casino games, but they do. It's usually young people on their way up or tired champions on their way down. You'll find semi-professionals who like to fleece tourists, and eager beginners building a bankroll. Pro or amateur, the whole mindset is different here than anywhere else in the casino. These people are serious. It may be fun, but it's a different kind of fun from spinning the reels on a slot or throwing dice.

You can have fun, too: just remember that these people want to take your money. The only way to stop them is to play better or walk away. If you can't play better, and you're not in the mood to pay for an education in poker at that moment, then you should walk. That's always an option. You can fold anytime for any reason. They can't stop you. Just take your chips and go.

But keep practicing and learning. Eventually it will be you who is taking the money, stealing pots, and otherwise tweaking noses with style and aplomb. You'll be the one who can say with confidence that poker is the ultimate positive expectation game.

Just the facts

- Poker attracts a lot of professional and semi-professional players because it is a positive expectation game. This means your money is at greater risk (depending on your level of skill) than it would be when playing other casino games.

- Poker strategy is based in part on the ranking of the various hands and how often they appear. You should be thoroughly familiar with this ranking when playing the game.

- The goal when playing poker is NOT necessarily to have the best hand; the goal is to win the biggest pot. You'll need skill more than luck to do that.

- Never put money directly into the pot or touch the pot. Only the dealer should handle money that is in the middle of the table.

- Poker doesn't have a basic strategy like blackjack or video poker. Every situation is different. Good players use a combination of methods to consistently win. This includes understanding the odds, reading the other players, and properly pressing each advantage.

- It's important to follow the rules. Your hand may be declared *dead* if you don't, and this could cost you a pot.

- Beginners generally lose to more experienced poker players. If you're a beginner and you don't want to lose, you should avoid playing in a casino.

Other Table Games

I n a casino, as in life, context is everything. For example, a $5 bet is considered by most players to be a low wager at a table. Yet $5 is a sizable bet on video poker. Same money, same player, different opinion about the value of the contest.

Casino executives discovered this when players abandoned tables for machines. Red and green chips were mostly exchanged for quarters and dollar tokens. The newest table games are intended to reverse this trend and lure people back to higher wagering. They are also designed to "fix" the shortcomings (from the casino's standpoint) of traditional games like craps, blackjack, and baccarat.

Most of the newer table games share these common elements:

1. They're based on poker or other classic card games.

2. They don't require as much mental effort or calculation as blackjack, craps, or regular poker. They're easy to learn.

3. The house edge on the basic bet is larger than in blackjack, craps, and baccarat.

4. There is no winning strategy.

5. The rules give the impression that players have multiple choices and options for winning.

None of the newer games (with the exception of pai gow poker) have the character of the older, more venerable contests, but they also don't have puzzling terms and inexplicable outdated customs. It's a trade-off. Traditional table games and video poker still draw more patrons, but most casinos now have space set aside for the newer contests. Playing them can be fun. Just don't expect to win in the long run.

Caribbean Stud Poker™

If you like poker, but you're not in the mood for the mental effort required to win against a table full of wily opponents, then Caribbean Stud Poker is definitely the game for you.

It's easy to play. The contest somewhat approximates traditional poker, but the dealer is your only opponent. She has strict rules to follow, so it's really just you against the odds. Unfortunately, they're stacked against you, but hey... you're paying for convenience and the chance for a big win. The curse of regular poker is getting a dream hand when the pot tops out at $20. Caribbean Stud Poker guarantees a fat payout when the perfect once-in-a-lifetime combination of cards comes your way. Of course, it may take a lifetime before you see that combination, but before we get to that bad news let's see how the game is played.

Rules for holding and folding

Caribbean Stud Poker is played at a standard black-jack-sized card table. The hand begins with a player ante (a bet equal to at least the table minimum) and an optional side bet on a progressive contest. We'll discuss the side bet in a later section. The dealer gives each player five cards face down and deals herself four cards face down and one face up.

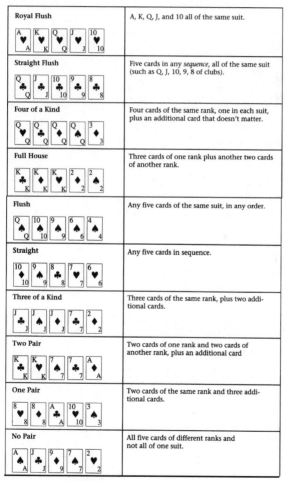

Royal Flush	A, K, Q, J, and 10 all of the same suit.
Straight Flush	Five cards in any *sequence*, all of the same suit (such as Q, J, 10, 9, 8 of clubs).
Four of a Kind	Four cards of the same rank, one in each suit, plus an additional card that doesn't matter.
Full House	Three cards of one rank plus another two cards of another rank.
Flush	Any five cards of the same suit, in any order.
Straight	Any five cards in sequence.
Three of a Kind	Three cards of the same rank, plus two additional cards.
Two Pair	Two cards of one rank and two cards of another rank, plus an additional card
One Pair	Two cards of the same rank and three additional cards.
No Pair	All five cards of different ranks and not all of one suit.

Poker hands ranked in winning order.

Unofficially... Caribbean Stud Poker was played on cruise ships and in Caribbean resorts for many years before it came to the U.S. One of the reasons for its popularity is that marginal hands often win. An unsuited ace and king or a pair of fours can earn even money. Those hands would be automatic losers in other games.

Players then look at their cards without revealing them to others at the table. Each person can either fold and lose the ante or call. A call requires an additional bet of twice the ante amount, so a $5 ante would require a $10 call for a total bet of $15. The call bet really functions more like a poker raise as you'll see. When the folding and calling is completed, the dealer reveals her cards. If her hand contains anything less than one pair and it does not contain at least an ace or king then she does not *qualify*; the dealer folds. The ante bets are paid even money and the call bets are pushed (as raises would be in a regular game of poker).

If the dealer qualifies, she turns over all the hands that have called and compares them to her hand. Winners are determined by standard poker hand rankings (see Figure 10.1 and also the section in Chapter 9 that explains how poker hands are ranked). If the dealer's hand beats the player's hand, the ante and call bets are collected. Players who beat the dealer are paid even money for their ante bets and a graduated amount for the call portion of the wager. The scale is listed in Table 10.1.

The ante is always paid 1:1. For example, if the hand is a full house and the ante bet is $5, the payoff would be $70 for the $10 call bet and $5 for the ante, a total of $75. Some casinos pay more on the $1 progressive bet (far right column) for a flush, full house, and four of a kind.

TABLE 10.1: CARIBBEAN STUD POKER PAYOUTS

Ante Wager Payout		
All Hands	1:1	

Hand	Call Wager Payout	$1 Progressive Bet Payout
Pair or less	1:1	$0
Two Pair	2:1	$0
Three of a Kind	3:1	$0
Straight	4:1	$0
Flush	5:1	$50
Full House	7:1	$75
Four of a Kind	20:1	$100
Straight Flush	50:1	10% of Jackpot
Royal Flush	100:1	100% Jackpot

Caribbean Stud Poker also offers the chance to win a progressive jackpot for a $1 side bet. The jackpot amount is displayed on a meter mounted over the table. Drop a coin in the slot between you and the dealer, draw a flush or better, and you'll win the jackpot or a bonus. The progressive bet is valid even if the dealer does not qualify for the hand. It's valid even if the dealer beats your hand. In spite of this, the progressive bet isn't a good wager. We'll tell you why in the next section.

Watch Out!
If you decide to make the $1 progressive bet, be sure the light on the slot is illuminated after you insert the coin. This indicates that the system has received your wager. If there is no light, you have no chance for the jackpot.

Odds and strategy for winning

Are you ready for a shock? Take a shuffled deck of cards and deal ten hands of five cards each. Now turn them over. Only one or two of the hands will fail to qualify by the dealer's standards. Most will have at least a singleton king or ace. There will be a lot of pairs. Do it again. It's always the same. Less than 18 percent of poker hands (about one in five) will be lower than a pair and also won't have an ace or king. That's the subject of a great bar bet, but it's bad news when bluffing Caribbean Stud Poker because the dealer will qualify about 82 percent of time. Remember, the probability of receiving any particular hand is identical for you and for the dealer. About 50 percent of all the hands will be one pair or more and 32 percent of hands that are lower than one pair will have an ace, king, or both. Table 10.2 shows the various probabilities of receiving each hand.

One look at the numbers should tell you that bluffing is absolutely out. If your hand is less than a pair and it doesn't have an ace or king, the dealer has an 82 percent chance of qualifying and beating you. Bluffing is a very bad bet.

Betting with a single ace or king high in your hand isn't much better. You'll win the ante 17 percent of the time. You'll lose the ante and the call bet at least 50 percent of the time, and 32 percent of the time it will be a toss-up; you could win or lose the combined bet. That's still a rotten average.

TABLE 10.2:
FREQUENCY OF CARIBBEAN STUD POKER HANDS

Hand	Number of Occurrences	Percent Probability
Royal Flush	4	0.0002%
Straight Flush	36	0.0014%
Four of a Kind	624	0.02%
Full House	3,744	0.14%
Flush	5,108	0.20%
Straight	10,200	0.39%
Three of a Kind	54,912	2.11%
Two Pair	123,552	4.75%
One Pair	1,098,240	42.26%
Ace or King high	838,440	32.26%
Everything else	464,100	17.86%
Total	2,598,960	

The dealer will qualify 82 percent of the time (100 - 17.86 = 82.14). 50 percent of the time the dealer will have one pair or better.

The numbers become more favorable when you call only with a pair or better. The dealer will fold or lose with less than a pair at least 50 percent of the time. The other 50 percent is a toss-up; the dealer may beat your pair-or-better hand or she may not. Of course, if you're holding a pair of twos, the chance of winning is less than when holding a flush, but we're talking about the chance for any pair-or-better to win.

The big problem with restricting calls to a pair or better is that you'll be throwing away half your hands at a cost of one ante bet per hand. Of course most of those hands would be losers, but some wouldn't lose because the dealer would fold. That's where the house has its edge. The casino always

Unofficially...
The house edge in Caribbean Stud Poker is *not* a result of the rule that requires the dealer to qualify or fold. The order of play is the source of the edge. The casino folds or calls last. The game would have a player edge if the casino went first.

makes you call or fold first. This guarantees them about five percent of every dollar wagered. The figure is a bit higher when a player calls only a pair or better. Calling with an ace and king in your hand reduces the house edge, but it substantially increases the action (total amount of money wagered). If you're willing to put more money into play, this is the best way to go. See the sidebar on this page. But remember, strategy will only reduce the house edge; it won't eliminate it. People who don't play the more aggressive ace/king strategy should fold anything less than a pair and call any pair or higher.

The progressive bet

Caribbean Stud Poker's $1 progressive bet is an exceptionally bad wager. It's worse than the worst slot machine and only marginally better than the lottery. Consider the lowest bonus; a flush pays only $50 and it occurs 0.2 percent of the time. That's once in 500 hands, or $500 wagered to chase a $50 win. The rest of the payoffs are equally anemic. The only situation in which the progressive bet has mathematical reason is when the meter reads more than $263,228. That's when the *total* money required to win the jackpot will probably be less than the payoff. This hypothetically assumes that one person is wagering every dollar. Of course, thousands of people are wagering, and each bet is bucking odds of 1 in 649,740 for the big jackpot. If you play one hand per minute for ten hours a day every day of every year, you can expect to see a royal flush in about three years.

   The whole thing is crazy. Don't bet the progressive unless you have a vision or an out-of-body experience of some sort.

Bright Idea
Here's a strategy to follow if you want more action and you want to lower the house edge a smidge. Call when you're holding an *AKJxx* or higher and call any *AK* hand when you hold a card identical to the dealer's upcard.

Caribbean Stud Poker's price for fun

As we said previously, Caribbean Stud Poker's basic contest has a price for fun that hovers around five percent. The number varies depending on your strategy for calling and folding. The cost will go well above five percent if you bluff rags or you fold on low pairs. Calling with hands that only have an ace and king and no pair will result in the lowest house edge, but will also significantly increase your action. There is no strategy to make Caribbean Stud Poker™ a positive expectation game because players are always required to call or fold first.

The $1 progressive bet has a house edge that varies with the amount in the jackpot. At $100,000 the house edge is about 50 percent. Ouch! Some casinos increase the progressive bet payouts for a flush, full house, and four-of-a-kind to $100, $200, and $500 respectively. That lowers the meter breakeven point to about $110,000. Nice, but it's still a bad bet. Don't make it. Stick to the basic game and resign yourself to losing about $5 for every $100 wagered (plus an amount for bad luck). If that's too much, go play blackjack.

Let It Ride™

If you spend time around card tables in any casino you'll eventually see a Shuffle Master. It's a handy machine that shuffles cards. A few years ago the company that makes the machines introduced Let It Ride a table game that (not surprisingly) uses a Shuffle Master. The contest is based on poker and plays like an ersatz hand of Texas hold 'em.

Let It Ride is popular because it gives people an opportunity to take back a portion of their wager if the hand develops unfavorably. What a concept! Unfortunately, this feature doesn't quite mitigate the house edge.

How to "Let It Ride"

The object of Let It Ride is to use three personal cards and two community cards to build a poker hand that includes a pair of tens or better. There is no opponent. The game is played at a standard casino card table like the one in Figure 10.2. Each player's section of the layout has three circles labeled 1, 2, and $. A bet equal to the table minimum must be placed in each circle, so if the table minimum is $5 the bet will be at least $5 × 3 = $15. A player can optionally withdraw $10 during the course of the hand. Here's how it works.

The Shuffle Master does its thing and the dealer delivers three cards face down to each player and two cards face down in the center of the table. Players should wait until cards are placed directly in front of them before reaching out to review the prospects. Remember, the object of the game is to get a poker hand with a pair of tens or better.

Let's say Barbara's first three cards are two kings and an ace. The hand is already a winner and may improve to two pair, three of a kind, a full house, or

Moneysaver
The first and second bet are not linked. You can withdraw either one or both, so be sure to withdraw the second bet if your hand is not already a winner and it's not clearly improving. The only bet required to ride is the last one.

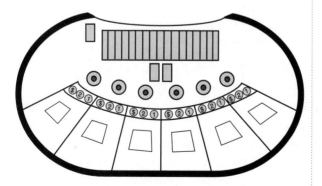

Let It Ride table layout. Note the three circles, one for each bet.

four of a kind as the community cards are revealed. Jim is sitting next to Barbara, and his first two cards are an unsuited seven, six, and two. Jim is holding rags. Everyone has a moment to review cards, and then the dealer offers everyone a chance to withdraw the bet in circle 1 or to "Let It Ride." Barbara obviously should let her bet ride. She does this by slipping the edge of her cards slightly under the chips in the first circle or simply saying, "Let It Ride." Jim (unless he's an optimist) should signal the dealer to return his bet. He does this by scratching the edge of his cards on the table in a motion towards himself; it's similar to calling for a hit in blackjack. A verbal direction is also fine: "Push it back." The dealer will push chips toward players who request them. For security reasons the dealer should do the pushing. Don't do it yourself. Everyone makes a decision about their first bet, then the dealer reveals the first community card.

Let's say it's a seven. Barbara wanted to improve her hand, but she'll win either way. Jim is hopeful but realistic. The dealer gives them both an option to withdraw the second bet. Barbara says, "Let It Ride." Jim scratches and the dealer pushes the second bet toward him. The other players make their choices, and the dealer reveals the last card. It's a seven. Barbara and Jim both win. They're paid on a graduated scale listed in Table 10.3.

Barbara and Jim both bet the minimum $5 per circle, so the payouts would be $15 × 1 = $15 for Barbara, and $5 × 3 = $15 for Jim. Players whose final hands have less than a pair of tens will lose any chips remaining in the three circles.

Watch Out!
Tables have a maximum payout limit. Do the arithmetic and be sure you're not betting more than the table can pay if you win the top prize. For example, a $30,000 limit would mean that $10 would be the maximum you should bet per circle on Let It Ride.

TABLE 10.3: LET IT RIDE PAYOUTS

Hand	Payout
Pair; tens or better	1:1
Two Pair	2:1
Three of a Kind	3:1
Straight	5:1
Flush	8:1
Full House	11:1
Four of a Kind	50:1
Straight Flush	200:1
Royal Flush	1000:1

The payout is calculated on the entire bet, the total amount remaining in all three circles when the last card is revealed.

Odds and strategy for winning

Table 10.4 shows the probability of drawing tens or better. Yes it's true; 76 percent of the hands are losers. 16 percent pay 1:1, and only eight percent pay 2:1 or more.

TABLE 10.4: FREQUENCY OF LET IT RIDE POKER HANDS

Hand	Number of Occurrences	Percent Probability
Royal Flush	4	0.0002%
Straight Flush	36	0.0014%
Four of a Kind	624	0.02%
Full House	3,744	0.14%
Flush	5,108	0.20%
Straight	10,200	0.39%
Three of a Kind	54,912	2.11%
Two Pair	123,552	4.75%
Pair of 10s or better	422,400	16.25%
Pair of 9s or worse	675,840	26.00%
Everything else	1,302,540	50.12%
Total	2,598,960	

Players will lose 76 percent of the hands. 16 percent of the hands will pay even money. Eight percent of the hands will pay 2:1 or better.

These horrible percentages are somewhat improved by the fact that the first three or four cards occasionally show a clear winner, thus allowing the player to bet the maximum. Let It Ride is somewhat like its poker cousin Hold 'Em. You can't play every hand. The best strategy is to wait and lose and lose and lose and lose... and lose some more until the right hand comes along, and then you bet the most.

What is the right hand? The first bet should ride in the following situations:

- A pair of tens or better

- Three consecutive cards to an open-ended straight flush

- Three almost consecutive cards to a straight flush with at least two high cards (Example: 8, 10, jack or 9, jack, queen)

Anything else is not worth riding the first bet. Bring it back. Criteria for the second bet are as follows:

- A pair of tens or better

- Four cards to a flush (including straight and royal flush)

- A hand with a combined ten, jack, queen, and king of any suit

Pull the second bet if the hand has anything less.

Betting the bonus

Some Let It Ride tables offer an additional $1 side bet for a bonus payout. It's not a good wager unless the payouts start with a high pair. This is rare, but it does happen. If the bonus payouts start with two pair, three of a kind, or higher, the wager is usually a sucker bet. Don't spend the money.

Moneysaver
Let's say your first three cards are an unsuited two, six, and nine. What is the probability that the dealer will turn over a high pair? It's 2.5 percent or about one in 40. Those are poor odds considering the payoff would be even money. You should withdraw your bets.

Let It Ride's price for fun

Strictly speaking, Let It Ride has a price for fun of about 3.5 percent, but this includes the value of winning a royal flush. Most people won't play the more than half-million hands normally required to see a royal flush, so their price for fun will be somewhat more than 3.5 percent. Three out of four hands will lose. The fourth will usually win one or two units, occasionally three, so the price for fun will fluctuate. It's about 25 percent of your once-through bankroll unless you're lucky and repeatedly get three-of-a-kind or better. Does that sound expensive? Well it is. Sorry Shuffle Master. The average person has a better chance playing 9/6 video poker.

Pai gow poker

Pai gow (pronounced *pie gow*) is an Asian dominos game. A version of the contest that uses cards instead of dominos has become quite popular in the west and is known as pai gow poker. The game has many charms, two of which are that it moves quite slowly and often ends in a *push* (tie). Smaller

Bright Idea
Don't blow your bankroll learning these games in a casino. Get a pack of cards and play at home. Test your strategies when the cost is zero. The folly of chasing a three-card flush in Let It Ride or calling with a singleton jack in Caribbean Stud Poker will quickly be demonstrated.

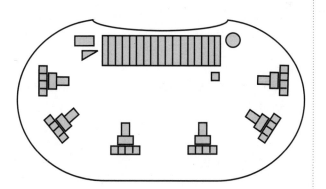

Pai gow poker table layout. The two-card hand is called the high hand or front hand because it is placed closer to the center of the layout.

bankrolls can last quite a bit longer than they would with a game like mini-baccarat or Let It Ride. Also, pai gow poker has no hidden house edge. Casinos and card rooms charge a five percent vig (commission) on winnings or sometimes a flat per-hand fee for each player.

Rules for setting hands

Pai gow poker uses a standard deck of cards and one joker. Two to seven people can play simultaneously. The table layout is shown in Figure 10.3. The object of the game is to beat the banker. Or if you're the banker, the object is to beat the players at the table. We'll cover special rules for banking in a later section.

Each player arranges seven cards into two poker hands. Five cards are in a *low hand* or *back hand;* two cards are in a *high hand* or *front hand.* Both player's hands must beat the banker's hands (front must beat front, back must beat back) for a win. If one hand wins and the other loses then it's a tie. Hands with equal value are called *copies*; the banker wins all copies.

Standard poker rankings are used, but there are a few exceptions. Ace, 2, 3, 4, 5, is the second highest straight. The joker can be used as an ace, or to complete a flush or a straight. In some casinos the joker is wild.

The game begins with bets and a shuffle. The dealer makes seven stacks of seven cards each. The banker then shakes a device called a *teacup* or *dice cup* that holds three dice. The resulting number determines who gets which stack at the table. As you know, from a probability point of view it doesn't matter who gets which stack. From a tradition point-of-view it's critical. The rules for stack distribution are numbingly arcane. The dealer will handle it.

Players look at their cards first and set their hands. The rule is that the five-card hand must have a higher value than the two-card hand. This is in spite of the fact that the larger hand is called the low hand and the smaller one is called the high hand. Confusing? Yes. The nomenclature of high and low has nothing to do with the hand values and everything to do with position when placed on the table. For clarity, we will from this point forward only use the terms *back hand* and *front hand*.

If the two-card front hand is accidentally set higher in value than the five-card back hand, both are called *foul* and will automatically lose. We'll cover how hands should be set in the next section.

Players lay their arranged cards face down in the appropriate spaces. The dealer turns the banker's cards over and arranges them into two hands at the banker's direction. When she's finished, the player's cards are revealed, and the dealer compares them to the banker's cards. Winning combinations are paid even money (minus commission). Losing bets are collected and the hand is over.

Odds and strategy for winning

Pai gow poker odds are nearly even; the bank has a slight edge because it wins copies. The downside to banking is the requirement of risking up to six times a normal bet on one hand. Nevertheless, players have an advantage when they frequently bank. Casinos discourage individuals from hogging the bank with rules that require the bank to rotate among the players, or rules that limit a person to banking every other hand or two out of three hands. It depends on the casino. If nobody wants to bank (which is often the case), the house does the job.

Bright Idea
Don't be alarmed if a stranger approaches you and offers *kum-kum* when you're playing pai gow poker. It's an Asian tradition of wagering on another player. You're not required to accept this arrangement, but most people enjoy the added camaraderie.

TABLE 10.5: PAI GOW POKER STRATEGY

This is an abbreviated pai gow poker strategy. See Appendix C for sources with more detailed strategies.

	Back Hand (Five Cards)	Front Hand (Two Cards)
PAIRS		
No pair	highest card	second and third highest card
One pair	pair	two highest singletons
Two pair when one pair is aces	pair of aces	lower pair
Two pair without an ace singleton	high pair	low pair
Two pair with an ace singleton	both pairs	ace
Three pair	second and third highest pair	highest pair
THREE OF A KIND		
Aces	two aces	one ace and the next highest card
2 through king	three of a kind	two highest cards
Two sets of three	lower three	two from the higher set
STRAIGHTS AND FLUSHES		
With no pair	lowest full hand	two highest cards
With one or two pair	lowest full hand	pair if possible, if not then two highest cards
With three of a kind	full hand	pair
With full house	play full house strategy	
With two sets of three	play two sets of three strategy	
FULL HOUSE	three of a kind	pair
FOUR OF A KIND		
Aces	two of the four	two of the four
8 through king without an ace singleton	two of the four	two of the four
8 through king with an ace singleton	four of a kind	ace
2 through 7	four of a kind	two highest cards
Five aces (one joker)	three aces	two aces

Timesaver
Strategy makes your eyes cross? No sweat. The dealer can set your hand. She uses house rules that are similar to the strategy printed here. This charming custom distinguishes pai gow poker from other table games that prohibit dealer assistance.

The real edge is in the strategy for setting hands. A good pai gow poker player can blow away the competition with brilliant hand selection. It's not as easy as it seems. For example, four queens shouldn't necessarily be loaded in the back hand. The other cards will determine if the quad should be divided. Two queens might go in the front (two-card) hand and the other two might be combined with the remaining cards in the back hand. The reasoning behind this is that both hands must win for the player to win the bet.

High singletons are the deciding factor when considering a split of pairs or quads. The higher your singleton, the more inclined you should be to load the five-card hand. A lone ace or king can often carry the two-card hand.

You see how pai gow poker strategy becomes quite complex. Table 10.5 has an abbreviated version of the strategy that works well in most situations.

Here are a few examples of how the strategy works.

A Q 8 8 8 7 2 would be A Q / 8 8 8 7 2
K Q 8 8 3 2 2 would be 2 2 / 8 8 K Q 3
J 10 9 9 8 7 6 would be J 9 / 10 9 8 7 6
J 10 9 9 9 9 4 would be 9 9 / 9 9 J 10 4
A Q 9 8 5 4 3 would be Q 9 / A 8 5 4 3

Pai gow poker's price for fun

The casino's commission on winnings is five percent, and the probability of winning hovers near 50 percent (depending on how often you bank); that makes pai gow poker's price for fun 2.5 percent of your once-through bankroll. Players who are less experienced and those who deviate from optimal strategy will lose more.

Unofficially...
Pai gow poker is as much a ritual as it is a game. Dedicated players will sometimes bet the minimum on empty seats so that the cards will be distributed as they would be at a full table. This ensures that the order predetermined by fate and the universe is not disturbed.

2.5 percent is certainly higher than the optimum price for blackjack or craps, but remember that pai gow poker is a much slower game. $100 in $10 increments can last an hour (depending on your skill and luck). The same money in blackjack could be gone in ten minutes.

Best and worst of the rest

Casinos offer a cornucopia of other table games begging for your dollars. Here's a quick rundown of a few.

Spanish 21: The handbill shouts "More Ways To Win!" This is blackjack with a few twists. Player blackjack beats dealer blackjack. Player twenty-one beats dealer twenty-one. Surrender is allowed. A double down can be withdrawn. Wow! In very small print the handbill says, "Played with six Spanish packs 2-9, J, Q, K, A." What's a Spanish pack? What happened to the tens? You'll get a better deal with regular blackjack.

War: Yes, the contest you played as a kid is now available in a casino. Tommy didn't take your money as frequently as the casino will.

California blackjack: A hand busts with twenty-two. If your hand goes over twenty-two and the aler's does too, then the hand closer to twenty-two wins. Confused? That's a common reaction. The game is offered in California casinos.. It's not a bad deal, but it requires an entirely new basic strategy. People who play a lot of regular blackjack may find the California version induces headaches. The casino charges a vig.

There are so many more; Vegas Shootout, Red Dog, Super 9s, and Super Pan 9 are just a few. They often come with a slick brochure and a thick house edge. If you find a contest that appeals to you then play it, but don't blow your bankroll trying to understand why a game seems so easy to win yet it continually takes your money.

Just the facts

- Caribbean Stud Poker plays a lot like regular five-card stud poker, but you only need to beat the dealer to win.

- Players can either fold and lose their ante bet or call (actually a raise) with twice the ante. The contest is decided by standard poker rankings. Payoffs are made on a graduated scale.

- Caribbean Stud Poker has a price for fun of about five percent. The price varies depending on the player's strategy. The $1 progressive bet is a bad wager and should be avoided.

- Let It Ride plays a lot like Texas Hold 'Em poker, but there is no opponent. Players must have a pair of tens or better to win.

- Players bet in three equal increments and are given an option to withdraw one or two of their bets as the hand is revealed. The contest is decided by standard poker rankings. Payoffs are made on a graduated scale.

- Let It Ride has a price for fun of 3.5 percent, but that includes the value of the royal flush. The price without the royal flush is higher.

- Pai gow poker players compete with a banker to simultaneously win two poker hands. A player's five-card back hand must always outrank the two-card front hand.

- Pai gow poker has a price for fun of 2.5 percent if a player occasionally banks.

Waiting Games

PART IV

GET THE SCOOP ON...
Keno's long odds ▪ How to win more and
spend less with way tickets ▪ Bets that
cost more but don't win more ▪ Keno betting
system scams ▪ Situations that void
a winning keno ticket

Keno

Do you like playing the lottery? Keno is a lottery-type contest with better odds, more winning numbers, and a game every five minutes. Best of all, you don't have to buy the ticket in a convenience store. No standing in line while people squeeze past to use the ATM. You can play keno while dining, swimming in the hotel pool, or even sitting in bed. Keno comes to you.

What's the catch? Let's call it "perspective." A person must see the truth, accept the odds, and bet appropriately. This is true of every casino game, but it's particularly true of keno. It can be leisurely, entertaining, and inexpensive when played with perspective. A lack of perspective makes keno ruinous. The house edge, usually about 30 percent, will gobble a bankroll with more certainty than any table game or slot machine.

Long odds and high payouts

Keno is simple. Twenty numbers are selected randomly from a field of eighty. The process is similar

Unofficially...
Lotto (the fore-
runner of keno
and bingo) was
played in Italy
during the six-
teenth century. It
was a child's
game in colonial
America. Keno,
bingo and modern
lotteries devel-
oped from lotto
in the mid-nine-
teenth century.

to bingo and state lotteries: Numbered Ping-Pong balls are randomly blown into a tube. Players try to accurately predict one or more of the numbers that will be selected.

A wager can be made on a single number or a combination. If the player's numbers "catch" in the machine, the player wins. As with a lottery, the match doesn't have to be exact, but a closer match wins more.

Table 11.1 shows a portion of a typical keno pay table. We've included payouts for correctly choosing one, five, six, seven, eight, and ten numbers. A full pay table would include all the winning possibilities up to the casino limit (usually fifteen or twenty catches). But it would never include the information in the far right column. Those are the true odds of catching the numbers.

TABLE 11.1: TYPICAL KENO PAYOUTS AND ODDS

These are typical payouts. Actual amounts vary from casino to casino. True odds are rounded to the nearest whole number.

Choose 1				True Odds Against (N:1)
Catch	$1 pays	$3 pays	$5 pays	
1	3	9	15	3
Choose 5				
Catch	$1 pays	$3 pays	$5 pays	
3	1	3	5	11
4	7	21	35	82
5	850	2,550	4,250	1,550
Choose 6				
Catch	$1 pays	$3 pays	$5 pays	
3	1	3	5	7
4	3	9	15	34
5	95	285	474	322
6	1,500	4,500	7,500	7,752

Choose 7				True Odds Against (N:1)
Catch	$1 pays	$3 pays	$5 pays	
4	1	3	5	18
5	15	45	75	115
6	450	1,350	2,250	1,365
7	8,000	24,000	40,000	40,978

Choose 8				
Catch	$1 pays	$3 pays	$5 pays	
5	8	24	40	54
6	100	300	500	422
7	1,500	4,500	7,500	6,231
8	22,000	66,000	100,000	230,114

Choose 10				
Catch	$1 pays	$3 pays	$5 pays	
5	2	6	10	18
6	20	60	100	86
7	140	420	700	620
8	850	2,550	4,250	7,383
9	5,000	15,000	25,000	163,380
10	40,000	80,000	200,000	8,911,700

One glance at this abbreviated pay table quickly shows how keno is different from other casino games. Nearly every winning combination has odds that are greater than 10:1. The odds are mostly in the hundreds, thousands, and millions. On the other hand, a $1 wager can win hundreds, thousands and occasionally hundreds of thousands of dollars. Keno is obviously not the kind of game where the winning and losing alternates while the house edge steadily nibbles at your bankroll. A typical keno session is a lot of losing with an occasional modest win. Every few hundred or few thousand wagers bring a bigger payoff. The biggest payoffs are rare. Most people will never see them.

Moneysaver
Keno odds never
change, but the
amount paid for
a win varies from
casino to casino.
The difference is
sometimes hun-
dreds of thou-
sands of dollars.
Rules, minimums,
and specials also
vary. You should
shop around for
the most favor-
able wagers and
payoffs.

Gamblers who are unwilling to accept this reality sometimes bet large amounts on keno in an attempt to force big wins. That's really dangerous. The approach is not good with any casino game, but it often works with contests that have a narrow house edge, like blackjack or craps. Throw a pile of money at craps and there is nearly a 50 percent chance of seeing big wins. Keep doing it and there will be a lot of winning and surely even more losing. Lots of action. Not with keno. Throw money at keno and it will swallow most of it. Gone. Two weeks later the game will dump the cash on a little old lady who bet a dollar.

Keno can't be rushed. It moves at its own speed. The only way to win is with patience, patience, and more patience. In fact, that is the greatest pleasure of the game. A few dollars can buy hours of unhurried enjoyment.

How to write a keno ticket

Keno can be played anywhere in a casino, but the game is physically located in the keno lounge. It's a bucolic area set apart from the ringing bells, snapping cards, and clattering balls of the main casino. People unfamiliar with keno often find it by accident. They stumble in with hurting feet, tired of wandering the mega-maze of tables and machines. It takes them a few minutes to adjust to the tranquillity, but soon they're ordering free drinks and playing keno specials.

The lounge has tables and chairs or desks (looking very much like the kind you used in high school) arranged in rows and facing a large electronic board. The display shows eighty numbers, and it highlights those that have been selected. Below the board is an area where wagers are made and the game is conducted.

This is a straight keno ticket for one game. Seven spots have been marked and the wager is $1.

Straight tickets

Forms like the one in Figure 11.1 will be everywhere in the lounge. You'll also find a glossy brochure with the various payouts. The basic bet is a *straight* ticket (one set of numbers). Scan the brochure and decide how many numbers you want to play. Let's say seven numbers. The minimum bet on a straight ticket is usually $1. Larger bets win more, but only in direct proportion to the additional amount wagered; $2 doubles the $1 payout. There is no bonus for betting extra money as with slots and video poker.

Use a crayon (also provided by the casino) to mark an X over each of the seven numbers. Write the amount wagered, the number of games, and the number of spots in the appropriate spaces above or to the right of the grid. Then take the ticket to the desk. A keno "writer" will take your money, process the ticket, and return a printed copy.

Watch Out!
Be sure the printed ticket given to you by the keno writer matches the one you wrote. If a mistake is not corrected before the game begins, the casino will consider the printed ticket as the wager. What happens if the original written numbers win? You lose.

Now just grab a seat, order a free drink, and relax. A new keno game begins about every five minutes. The drawing takes approximately thirty seconds. You've seen something like it in bingo halls or during the lottery break on the evening news. Air pushes Ping-Pong balls around in a container. Gradually they are trapped one by one in a device called a *gooseneck* or simply a *goose*. One of the keno writers will call out the numbers printed on the balls. They'll be displayed on the big board and on closed circuit video screens throughout the casino. Some casinos have a newer electronic version without the balls, but most still use the traditional system. Perhaps plastic balls seem more benevolent and trustworthy than computer chips.

Check your ticket. If it's a winner, then one of the most important keno rules becomes urgently significant. In many casinos the ticket must be redeemed before the next game begins. It is otherwise invalid. No exceptions. This rule was once universal, but some casinos have recently extended the time to hours and in some cases days for redeeming single game tickets. Multiple game tickets have other rules and we'll cover them later in the chapter. The important thing to remember here is that you should know exactly how much time is allowed. If you don't know, then assume a ticket must be redeemed before the next game begins.

Does the payoff seem $1 short? Keno keeps your original wager, so a $1 win on a $1 ticket is actually a push. If your ticket isn't a winner but you want to play the numbers again, just hand it back to the writer with more money. You'll get a new ticket and a new chance to win thousands of dollars. Sit down and order another drink.

Way tickets

One of the most irritating aspects of playing a state lottery is when the winning number is composed entirely from three or four of your choices. Experienced lottery players avoid this by *wheeling*. It's a system of betting every possible combination of a particular number set. Unfortunately, a lottery player must write every wager separately.

Keno has a *way* of making that easier. It's appropriately called a way ticket. Figure 11.2 has an example. Four sets of three numbers have been selected.

This is a way ticket for one game. Twelve spots have been marked in four groups of three. Fifteen bets have been placed. The total amount wagered is $15.

The sets are circled and the notation on the right indicates how many bets have been placed. The top figure above each slash is the number of bets; the bottom figure is the number of spots. 4/3 means

Bright Idea
One number grouped by itself on a way ticket is called a *king*. Writing a ticket with seven or eight kings makes it highly likely that the ticket will pay something (if not even money). The probability of catching one, two or three out of seven or eight is actually greater than the probability of catching zero.

three spots four ways. 6/6 means six spots six ways. 4/9 is nine spots four ways, and 1/12 is twelve spots one way. It's one ticket with fifteen bets (6 + 4 + 4 + 1) for $15 total. Fifteen straight tickets could be written for the same wagers, but one way ticket saves time and insures you won't miss a number combination (unless that is what you choose). This ticket also pays for as few as two spots, depending on which numbers are drawn. A straight ticket with twelve numbers wouldn't pay for anything less than six spots.

In Figure 11.3 eight spots are marked and they're separated into groups of two. The bets are 4/2, 6/4, 4/6, and 1/8. The total wager is $7.50. Notice that the price for each bet is only fifty cents. Casinos allow the minimum wager per way to be less than what would be required for the same bet on a straight ticket. The more ways you bet, the lower the price for each way. Some tickets are only ten cents per way. The keno brochure will have the exact price information.

Eight spots have been marked. The total number of bets is fifteen and the wager is $0.50 per way, or $7.50 total.

The payout on each winning combination is reduced proportionately when the bet amount is reduced. If all eight numbers were to catch for this ticket, the top prize would be $11,000 instead of $22,000. The other fourteen wagers would win too, but the total would be only $14,384. Remember, the straight ticket costs $1.00. This way ticket costs $7.50.

What happens if four numbers catch? The $1 straight bet would pay nothing. This way ticket would win $138. A way ticket increases the chances for winning and allows you to spend less per way, but that lowers the total possible payoff.

Combination tickets

Multiple straight bets can be combined onto one ticket even when they're not wagered various ways. This is called a *combination*. Figure 11.4 has an example. Two sets of numbers are divided by a hard line. Both sets are played straight. You can also combine a straight bet and a way bet on one ticket.

This is a combination ticket. The four spots in the upper left are one bet. The six spots in the lower right are a second separate bet.

Watch Out!
A way ticket is a good way to spend less per bet and simultaneously increase the overall chance of a win. But a way ticket doesn't change the odds or the payout ratio. The probability of winning a particular bet (one way) remains the same.

These are two common casino specials. The E in the center of the ticket indicates an edge bet. T/B means top and bottom. Both tickets cost $5.

Casino specials

Casinos usually run keno specials. You can pick x numbers for y dollars (a fixed amount) and the pay-off is made on a scale established just for that special. Patterns are popular specials. Figure 11.5 shows some common examples. Table 11.2 has samples of corresponding pay tables.

TABLE 11.2: EDGE BET AND TOP/BOTTOM PAY TABLES

$5 Edge		$5 Top & Bottom		
Catch		Top Catch	Bottom Catch	
0	25,000	0	20	100,000
1	1,500	1	19	20,000
2	300	2	18	2,500
3	30	3	17	1,150
4	10	4	16	150
5	3	5	15	35
6	1	6	14	10
7	1	7	13	3
8	1	8	12	2
9	1	9	11	1
10	1	10	10	1
11	3	11	9	1
12	10	12	8	2
13	50	13	7	3
14	200	14	6	10
15	1,000	15	5	35
16	5,000	16	4	150
17	25,000	17	3	1,150
18	60,000	18	2	2,500
19	100,000	19	1	20,000
20	250,000	20	0	100,000

These pay tables correspond to the tickets written in figure 11.5. The amounts here are examples; each casino pays differently.

Timesaver
Do you have a
question about
how to write a
particular ticket?
Ask the keno
writer for help.
That's her job.
She will show
you how to draw
the more compli-
cated combina-
tions and explain
any shorthand
unique to
the casino.

Betting the edge is popular. Other favorite combinations include top and bottom, left and right, or
all eighty numbers divided into groups of four. Tickets like this technically can't lose because every combination pays something. Unfortunately, most combinations pay much less than the amount wagered.

Keno to go

Keno is a bit like a faithful and always hungry dog,
or perhaps having gum on your shoe is a more accurate analogy. Once you've learned the game it will
follow you in the casino. Are you dining? Shopping?
Strolling? Sleeping? You can play keno almost anywhere thanks to eager runners who will gladly provide tickets and take wagers to the keno lounge. Tipping is the custom, especially when a runner returns
with a win. $1 or $2 tips are appropriate for wins
between $10 and $40. Five percent is common for
amounts up to $500. Use your judgment for wins
above that. One strategy is to tip generously for the
first ticket whatever the outcome and not again until
you win.

If the constant back-and-forth is too hectic, simply write a *multi-game* or *multi-race* ticket. It's one ticket repeated for as many games as you choose. You
can play dozens, even hundreds of games. The keno
balls will be blowing as you golf, dine with friends, or
lounge by the pool. Some people go directly to the
keno lounge at the beginning of their casino visit,
write a multi-game ticket, and don't return until
hours or days later.

As we said before, the rules for when you must
redeem a ticket were once universal but are now in
a state of flux. Check before playing. Below are the
original rules. Follow them unless you read something different in the keno brochure.

- Redeem single-game tickets before the next game begins.

- Redeem multi-game tickets written for twenty games or less after the last game is called and before the next one begins.

- Redeem multi-game tickets written for more than twenty games up to one year after the last game is called.

Strategies for choosing numbers

The odds for a particular catch can be in the millions. Unfortunately, keno payouts aren't. All regular keno games have a limit. It may be $100,000, $200,000, $350,000, or something else, but there is always an aggregate amount per game beyond which the casino will not pay.

That's why experienced keno players don't usually bet more than eight spots on a straight ticket. The odds against hitting eight of eight are 230,114 to 1. Nine out of nine increases the odds to more than 1.3 million. A straight $10 ticket would hit the payout limit both ways. Why take the extra risk?

A smarter strategy would be to divide the $10 into multiple bets on a way ticket. You can bet fifty cents on the big catch and the rest on smaller sets. If lightning strikes, you'll get a whopper payoff, but you'll also win with the other combinations that are hundreds and thousands of times more likely to appear.

Which numbers should you play? You've probably read Chapter 2 ("Probability and the House Edge") so I won't repeat the information. As you know, each trial is independent and every number has an exactly equal chance. The maxim that's popular for stock market funds also holds true for keno: Past results are not an indication of future performance.

Bright Idea
Video keno is a fun alternative if you like keno but find the big board too slow. The odds are identical to the big version, but the payouts will usually be different. Read and compare pay tables before playing.

Unofficially...
A progressive game is the only situation when keno doesn't have a payoff limit. It's a positive expectation contest if the top prize reaches a certain amount. Unfortunately, the odds are still immense.

Bright Idea
Scratching your head about which numbers to pick? Try keno's quick pick. The numbers are chosen randomly, so they have a slightly better chance of winning. Why? People tend to pick numbers between 1-31. They miss combinations made with higher numbers.

You will read advertisements to the contrary. They will offer systems to track and predict which numbers will appear. They will use patterns and schemes that are "guaranteed" to perform. Some of the ads will require you to sign an agreement to send them money when you win. One inventive approach is to sell the system in a series of payments. The total price is $1,995, but they will send it to you after a first payment of only $49. You must pay the rest out of your winnings. Aren't they generous to give you such a break?

Anyone with a truly winning keno system would lock it up and use it in ultra-secrecy. You wouldn't find it advertised in the back pages of a magazine or on the Internet.

The best way to pick the numbers is to follow your heart and your intuition. Did you wake up this morning with seven numbers dancing in your brain? Then by all means bet them!

Keno's price for fun and money management

Let's say you repeatedly bet $1 on one number. You will lose on average three times and win once. Remember, keno keeps your winning wager. That works out to $4 cost and $3 profit, or 25 percent of your once-through bankroll. Keno's house edge doesn't get much better, and it frequently gets worse. 30 percent is common. That includes the astronomical probability of catching a big combination so the effective edge (without the big win) is even higher. If you're betting straight tickets be prepared to lose it all. Every penny. Yes it's possible to catch three out of three or four out of four, but the odds are against it. Play three spots forty times and you may break even, but you probably won't. The odds against you are 71:1 and the payoff is usually a paltry $42. Take another look at Table 11.1. It's that way for all the bets.

Write a good way ticket and you'll see a steady trickle of money coming back, but it will rarely match what you're spending. The result is similar to roulette. The house edge doesn't change. The more you spread the risk, the less you will potentially win. And there will always be a number combination that will eventually do you in.

So the price for fun is 30 percent. But what is your once-through bankroll?

The answer to that question is the key to playing keno. The house edge is massive, but the price for fun can still be minuscule. Why? Look at it this way. A bad run at $5 per hand blackjack will have you down $25 in about 2.5 minutes. The same $25 can last two hours when playing keno. That's one dollar per ticket every five minutes. How much could you ever win playing blackjack? Compare that to keno. Consider the free drinks, the relaxation factor, and the pleasure of contemplating a big windfall. Put it all together. Many people consider keno a positive expectation experience, if not a positive expectation game.

Obviously, the smart and fun way to play is to bet small and be prepared to lose everything. What is small? That's up to you, but here are some suggestions:

- Keep the total cost for a single game way ticket at $20 or less.

- Always bet the minimum per way.

- Don't bet more than $5 on a straight ticket.

- Don't bet more than $20 on a special ticket.

- Bet as many multiple games as you think are appropriate, but follow the above suggestions and remember to subtract the wagered amount from your bankroll.

Just the facts

- Keno's house edge is about 30 percent, but the price for fun can be quite low. $10 or $20 per hour is not unusual because keno's minimum bet is small and the game moves slowly.

- Large bets do not necessarily translate into large wins when playing keno.

- The best keno odds are 3:1 against on a single number. The rest of the odds are much worse. They're mostly in the thousands or tens of thousands and above. Some are in the millions.

- Straight tickets for catch nine and above are extremely poor bets. Five, six, seven, and eight have better odds.

- A way ticket combines multiple straight bets onto a single ticket. It's a good deal because the casino allows the minimum amount per bet on a way ticket to be lower than a comparable bet on a straight ticket.

- Avoid keno betting systems. They're a waste of time and money.

- Know the rules for when a ticket must be redeemed. Follow the rules or your winning ticket will be worthless.

GET THE SCOOP ON...
Where you can legally bet
on sports ▪ Point spreads and money
lines ▪ How sports books determine
odds ▪ Taking and laying odds

Chapter 12

Sports Betting

Sports and betting; the two go together like peanut butter and jelly. Betting requires a contest. What better contest than real people competing in organized sports? Who hasn't bet an office pool or $10 with a friend on the outcome of Sunday's game? The papers are crammed with statistics and the latest "line." Everyone seems to be betting. You might even know someone who makes a bundle on the games every week. Unless he's in Nevada, it's against the law.

It's true. Betting on sports is against the law in 49 states. Surprised? Of course the attorney general won't break down your door when you and the spouse have a bet on the World Series, but making book (taking wagers from opposite sides for a profit) is thoroughly and completely against the law everywhere in the United States except Nevada. And your state's attorney general does break doors of illegal sports books.

What about sports betting on the Internet? Read Chapter 13 for a full discussion of Internet betting, but let's just say it's a legal gray area at best. That

Unofficially...
Three of the most prestigious and popular sports books in Las Vegas are at Caesars Palace, the Mirage, and the Las Vegas Hilton. Other Las Vegas casinos with sports books include MGM Grand, Binion's Horseshoe, Golden Nugget, Bally's, Palace Station, and Rio.

means you could win the bet and still lose your money. Toll-free numbers and credit card convenience aside, the only lawful place where you can bet on sports (not including horse racing, dog racing, and jai-alai) is in Nevada.

So if you're reading this in Biloxi or Atlantic City, remember that you won't find the sports book conveniently sandwiched between the keno lounge and the coffee shop. You'll have to go to Vegas, Reno, or somewhere else in Nevada to bet Green Bay over San Francisco.

What's my line?

A sports book performs a function similar to a stock broker. The stock broker's goal is to provide a market for buyers and sellers. In the case of a sports book, the market is a particular contest, and the goal is to match bets from both sides. The casino isn't playing against a bettor as in blackjack or craps, and the casino doesn't bank in the traditional sense. The sports book simply charges a *vig* (commission) on the wager and hopes to find someone on the other side to cover the bet. Since there is usually an underdog, there must a *line* established to handicap the favorite and make the contest equal. Without a line, the bettors on one side would outnumber the bettors on the other side and create an inefficient market (and a lot of unpleasant exposure for the casino). Everyone would bet on Dallas or Green Bay and nobody would bet on Tampa Bay. A line makes a bet on Tampa Bay potentially profitable.

Betting the spread

A spread is one way to designate a line. Let's say the Bills are playing the Colts. Experts will analyze the two teams and then set the line as a point spread. If the Bills are favored to win, and the experts (including the public) think it will be by seven points, then the line is Bills -7. It would be displayed in a sports book this way:

0000	Indianapolis Colts	30 o/u
0000	BUFFALO BILLS	-7

Timesaver
The minus sign is sometimes not included in the point spread, but don't let this confuse you. The number always appears next to the team favored to win. When you see the letters *PK* in the line, that means "pick"; the two teams are even. A name next to a baseball team indicates who is pitching for that game.

The home team is always at the bottom. The negative number indicates the spread and is next to the favored team. The larger number is the total points expected in the game. *o/u* means over or under; it's the basis for a bet we'll explain later. *0000* will be a number reference for placing the bet. Sometimes the display is different, but not much. A full display would include the time of the contest, the money line (which we'll cover in the next section), and other pertinent information.

Let's say you bet the Bills. They must win and beat the spread (win by more than seven points) for you to win. What if you bet the Colts? The Colts can win or lose, but a loss must be by less than seven points for you to win the bet. If the Bills spank the Colts with twenty-four unanswered points, you lose (unless you bet the Bills). If the game ends with Buffalo ahead exactly seven points then it's a push and your money is returned.

Where's the vig? This ain't no pai gow poker; they stick it to the losers. You pay $11 to win $10. Bet correctly and you'll receive the full $21. Back a loser and the $11 disappears. The casino has earned $1 on the transaction. You're not required to bet in multiples of $11 (or $5.50) but it makes payments easier and that's how experienced players do it.

Betting the money line

Contests like baseball are often decided by one run, so a spread isn't a very effective way of establishing a line. In baseball and in most sports you can also bet the money line. It's similar to taking or laying odds in craps (see Chapter 7). The wording is the same. Here's a typical money line; Houston is the visiting team and they're favored:

0000	Houston Astros	-140
0000	CHICAGO CUBS	+130

A $10 bet on the Cubs will win $13. The bettor is *taking odds* that the Cubs will win. Someone who prefers Houston would *lay odds* and risk $14 to win $10. The casino profit is the ten-point difference in the two numbers. The wider the difference, the bigger the profit.

Other sports bets

If the spread and the money line aren't enough to excite you, a panoply of other sports wagers is available. They include the following:

Over/Under. This is a bet on the total points scored by both teams. Will the total be over or under the o/u amount?

Propositions. Almost any question can (and has) been the subject of a proposition. Who will score the first touchdown? Who will kick the first field goal? Who will appear in the World Series? Will Elvis be found alive?

Parlays. The bettor is making a wager on the outcome of a combination of contests. All of the bettor's choices must win for the parlay to win. Parlays can be cheap to bet, and they promise big rewards, but they usually lose.

Teasers. This is a parlay with the point spread shifted in the bettor's favor. The downside is a corresponding drop in the payout.

Betting in a sports book

A typical sports book looks like a cross between mission control for the space shuttle and your uncle Al's TV den. It's usually done in dark colors with giant video monitors on the walls. Placing a bet is easy. Simply walk to the desk and hand money to the *writer* with instructions on what to bet. Remember that multiples of $11 (or $5.50) are preferred for bets on the spread. The writer will give you a printed ticket. It's a bearer instrument, so treat it like money until it's paid or the contest is decided against you. Winning tickets are paid at the cashier's cage in the sports book or at the cage in the main casino.

Which team?

A common misconception is that the line represents what the experts consider will be the outcome of the contest. This is not exactly true. Here's why:

Let's say you're making odds on a football game between the Manglers and the Liquidators. You happen to know the Manglers' starting quarterback has girlfriend problems and he'll be a mess this Sunday. Normally the line would be Manglers -7 (Manglers to win by seven), but you know the Liquidators will probably stun them by ten. The quarterback's problems have been everywhere in the newspapers, but nobody except you and a handful of the experts think this will affect the game. How will the public react if you set the line as Liquidators -10? You'll certainly be swamped with bets on the Manglers. Great, but nobody will bet on the Liquidators. Not even Liquidators fans will make such a (they think) stu-

Watch Out!
Don't wait too long to cash your winning ticket. Most are good for 60 days after the contest, but some are void after 30 days. Read the back of the ticket to know exactly how much time you have. Also, be sure to check the front of the ticket for accuracy before leaving the window.

pid bet. The casino will be required to cover all the wagers on the Manglers without any offsetting Liquidators wagers.

The line is accurate (you think), but things will be looking bad. Now what happens if the Manglers fall behind twenty-one points and pull the starting quarterback? The backup does an admirable job. He gets two touchdowns but it's no use. The Liquidators win by seven points. That's fourteen points more than the public expected, but the Liquidators didn't make your spread. The red ink pours from the casino books.

Wouldn't it have been smarter to set the line where the public expected it to be set? Is it the sports book's job to publicize and promote what might (or might not) be the exact situation? Or is a sports book's job simply to make a market for betting? Manglers -7 would have worked for everyone. Or maybe Manglers -3. That would have taken into account the girlfriend problems. On game day there would have been a lot of surprised winners and losers, and your casino would have been one of the winners.

So the line is a combination of the actual factors affecting the game and the psychological effect of those factors on the betting public. The purpose of having the line is not to predict the game, but to evenly divide the bettors. The public isn't stupid, so the line is usually close if not dead-on to the likely outcome, but sometimes it's off. Your goal as a bettor is to know when. The public can be swayed by a flamboyant personality, wishful thinking, or simply a lack of information. The line will shift as the public (including the odds makers) change their perceptions. Is the new information revealing or misleading? Is the public misinformed or are you? That's the critical question.

Sports betting's price for fun and money management

Betting on sports can be a highly positive expectation activity, but only if you consistently pick winners. Average luck won't do it. Here's the arithmetic for twenty games when 50 percent of them win. Each bet is $110.

Wins	10 × $100 =	1,000
Losses	10 × $110 =	1,100
Total		-100

The resulting price for fun is 4.5 percent of your once-through bankroll. To get that price down to zero and begin to turn a profit you must win more than 52.4 percent of your bets (assuming each wager is of equal value).

Unfortunately, there is no basic strategy as in blackjack or video poker to direct your decisions. The only way to consistently win is to know the sport and know the personalities who are playing it. You've got to be smarter and have more information than most of the general public and you must be at least as informed as the people making the odds.

Anything less and you'll be guessing. That's OK, but guessing means it's not a positive expectation contest. Guessing puts sports bets on par with roulette, keno, craps, and all the other guessing casino games. 4.5 percent isn't bad, but you'll do better playing blackjack.

Here's another thing to consider. Most people bet multiple games simultaneously. That's fine, but never bet beyond your bankroll even if you reasonably expect some of the current wagers to pay off. Let's say your bankroll is $1,100 and you bet ten

Moneysaver
Parlays pay well because the bet is low and the payoff is high, but they only make sense if you can pick winners. Average results won't cut it. Regular luck brings the average cost of parlay bets to 12.5 percent of your once-through bankroll. That's nearly three times the cost of betting single contests.

games. That's it. No more bets until something wins. Yes, it is very likely something will pay off, but you should wait until it actually happens before risking more money.

Just the facts

- Betting on sports is legal only in Nevada.

- The two most common methods of betting on a game are betting the spread and laying or taking odds on the money line.

- Bets on the spread should be made in multiples of $11 (or $5.50). Money-line lay bets should be in 1/10 multiples of the line.

- Sports books are in the business of evenly matching groups of bettors, so odds reflect the actual probability of winning, and also the public perception of the contest.

- The price for fun of sports betting is 4.5 percent when your luck is exactly average. You must win more than 52.4 percent of your wagers to make sports betting a positive expectation activity.

Casino Systems
and Secrets

GET THE SCOOP ON...
How a casino works ▪ Gambling and
organized crime ▪ Casino security
▪ The best places to gamble

Chapter 13

Casinos:
An Inside Look

Now that you know the price for each casino game, let's talk about the fun that the money is purchasing.

Blackjack at the Mirage in Las Vegas is quite different from blackjack on a boat on the Ohio River. Craps at Binion's Horseshoe is different from craps at Bally's. Location, ambiance, amenities, even the mathematics for winning and losing can be different. You'll lose more in some casinos and less in others. Rules, payouts, promotions, and comps vary. It's all a reflection of the individual organization. Choosing a venue that offers the best value for your money requires a basic understanding of how a casino works.

The state holds all the cards

Some of the most important aspects of a casino's character are dictated by the state. Casinos and the corporations that own them may seem powerful, but it's the voters and politicians (via state government)

Unofficially...
Any new game or change in an existing game, no matter how minor, must be approved by state regulators. Nevada slots are tested in the lab and then go through field tests of at least 180 days. Slot machines in New Jersey are tested in high-speed simulations to assure their payback percentages will be consistent over a period of at least six years.

who have the ultimate say about what is offered and how it's presented. Why can't you find a roulette game in California? Ask the legislature. Why must Atlantic City slots pay back at least 83 percent? Ask the legislature. Why are all Mississippi casinos on barges? Ask the legislature. Every state has its own ideas about how casinos should operate. The state makes the rules and the casinos follow them. End of discussion.

What happens if a casino breaks the rules? Penalties start with fines and can quickly escalate into a total closure. It happens, but not very often because casino owners are even more concerned about following the rules than the regulators. They want to continue earning money.

So if you don't like the frequency of riverboat cruises, or you can't find your favorite game, don't blame the casino. Write a letter to the local legislator.

Organized crime and casinos

It's a fact that organized crime once dominated the casino business. This is no longer the case. The turnaround is due to a number of factors which can't be easily condensed into a few paragraphs without oversimplification, but with that caveat here is what happened.

Casinos used to be relatively small operations. Basically they were clubs that did business in the major U.S. cities. Their illegal status made them ideal targets for organized crime. Nevada legalized gambling in 1931, and in the following decades "entrepreneurs" with casino experience left their legal hassles in other states and moved to Las Vegas. Bugsy Siegel and the Flamingo are examples of this period in gambling history. The situation persisted until the 1960s, when a change in Nevada law allowed corporations to buy casinos. Organized crime sold out (mostly to Howard Hughes) because they couldn't compete with the infinitely larger bank accounts of organized business. Mobsters and crime syndicates apparently aren't as rich as Hilton and Holiday Inn. Improved state regulations encouraged the mob exodus. In the end it was a combination of a lack of capital and an inhospitable legal environment that drove organized crime out of Las Vegas. These days the regulations are tougher than ever. Business and community leaders are working hard to keep it that way.

New Jersey learned a lesson from Nevada's struggles. The regulatory system that the New Jersey legislature established for Atlantic City has fostered an industry that can only be characterized as squeaky clean. Extensive background checks are required for anyone who works in a casino from a janitor to the president. Gambling regulators are on site at every casino at all times, and New Jersey's game approval process is certainly the nation's toughest. That's why you won't see the big six and big eight on Atlantic City craps tables.

Regulated gambling in other states has developed similarly. Corporations run it, and the state supervises it. Organized crime has no room to operate. Disorganized crime is another issue. Graft and cheating happen, though they are not widespread. We'll cover cheating in the section that deals with casino security.

Who runs a casino?

A casino is created by a person who has a vision. Sometimes it's an individual with a high profile like

Watch Out!
Organized crime has been ejected from regulated gambling, but it still operates in unregulated venues. Avoid games that are not sanctioned by the state. Poker with friends is fine, but stay out of private casinos. The people who run them may not be playing honestly. They're definitely breaking the law.

Unofficially...
Steve Wynn, CEO
of Mirage
Resorts, Inc.,
was a bingo
caller in his
youth. He some-
times jokes
about having
that job to fall
back on if his
current job at
Mirage doesn't
pan out. Right
now Wynn's posi-
tion looks
secure. According
to *Forbes* maga-
zine, his annual
salary is more
than 2.5 million
dollars. Bonuses
add another
1.25 million.

Steve Wynn, Donald Trump, or Merv Griffin, but just as often it's someone like Bob Stupak, Ed Fishman, or Jack Pratt. Who are they? Lesser known casino entrepreneurs but visionaries nonetheless. Famous or otherwise, the person sees slots and tables where there is currently asphalt or an empty field. These individuals become the proverbial bee in the bonnet. Bankers eventually throw up their hands and shout, "OK! OK! You can have the money!" And so the casino is built.

Casino executives and supervisors

The visionary sees a giant tower or a gleaming building of gold, but it's the casino executives who create an organization that functions on a practical level. The casino business has much in common with the hotel industry and also theme parks and entertainment. There is a lot of crossover in personnel and procedures. For example, some casinos call their employees "cast members," refer to customers as "guests" and talk about the guest visit as an "entertainment experience." This practice began in Disneyland during the 1950s. The custom worked its way into the theme park business, then to the hospitality industry, and finally into the casinos. It's all connected. If you understand how theme parks, restaurants, or hotel chains work then you have a head start in understanding the casino mentality.

The casino upper hierarchy is pretty standard. It starts with a president who supervises vice-presidents. Each VP is in charge of operations, marketing, finance, or another vital area. The VP of casino operations will be over a casino manager who in turn will supervise shift managers. The highest person you will likely encounter in normal dealings will be a pit boss or slot supervisor who reports to a shift manager. You'll also deal with casino hosts. We'll cover them in the next chapter.

Pit boss and floor persons

A *pit* is a collection of tables arranged in a loop, and though there may be many people who seem to have authority in the pit there is only one pit boss. That person's responsibility is to ensure that the games are conducted according to casino procedures and that transactions such as refilling a table with chips or providing a marker are properly handled. The pit boss is also the final authority in the pit on the subject of comps.

Floor persons assist the pit boss. They monitor the change and chip requests, handle markers, rate players for comps, and generally supervise the games.

Dealers

Dealers make the games go. They handle the cards, spin the balls, and take the chips. They are trained extensively in security procedures and usually spend weeks (sometimes months) learning how to properly deal each game. Nevertheless, they generally know little or nothing of the mathematics behind the contest. The average blackjack dealer knows that a bet spread between $5 and $100 is the sign of a card counter, but the dealer probably can't tell you why. Dealers are not card sharps. They don't control the game in any way that allows them to determine the outcome. In most cases they prefer that you win because this means that you might give them a tip.

Dealers aren't stupid, but they're often not particularly involved in the game. They're frequently young, part-timers, semi-retired, or bucking for a

Unofficially...
The term *pit boss* is a holdover from the early days of casinos when owners actually worked the floor. The person running the pit really was a boss, a mob boss. As the casinos expanded and the big bosses moved upstairs, the new person in the pit was designated the pit boss.

Moneysaver
Most dealers are good at their jobs, but you may occasionally encounter one who is rude, careless, or inexperienced. Don't stay at a table if the game is poorly handled. Mistakes and misunderstandings will cost you money. Find another table or another casino.

promotion to floor person. The dealer's major concern is less about who is winning or losing and more about following procedures to avoid heat from the pit.

Slot supervisors and slot attendants

Slots have their own hierarchy. A slot attendant is the first person you'll encounter if you have a question or problem with a machine. Slot supervisors (the slot equivalent of a pit boss) are over the attendants. The machines are repaired by slot technicians. None of these people has any control over how often a slot pays. Most attendants don't even know how a slot works. The average slot attendant thinks RNG is the minimum level of vitamins you should have every day.

Their biggest concern is security and hospitality. They rarely have a clue as to where the loose slots are, but they'll be happy to direct you to the last few machines that have paid big. Occasionally, you will meet an attendant or supervisor who is more perceptive. It's a gut thing. A well-timed toke will influence that person to point out a bank of machines that is "usually popular." You'll have to figure out which of the four or five is the loose one.

Security and surveillance

One aspect of the casino business that makes it more like a bank than a theme park is the absolute focus everyone has on money and how it's handled. Dealers and players must follow strict rules for touching cash, chips, and cards. They include the following:

- Players must never hand money or chips directly to a dealer. Money or chips must be placed on the table.

- A bet must never be touched by the player once the deal has started or the dealer has stopped bets. Additional bets (doubling in blackjack is an example) must be placed next to the original bet, never on top of the original chips.

- Cards dealt face up must never be touched.

- Cards dealt face down (that the player may touch) must never be taken from the table or concealed from the dealer.

Always follow these rules and any others you see posted. Always follow the directions given to you by a dealer. Any deviation from approved player conduct will cause the dealer to stop the game. Remember, we're talking here only about the rules for playing the game. Don't follow any directions that perpetuate a mistake against you. Don't allow yourself to be treated rudely or unfairly. We'll discuss those subjects in Chapter 15.

The rules for dealers are considerably more strict. Dealers are discouraged from performing seemingly innocent actions like straightening their ties, tucking in their shirts or pulling on their collars. All those behaviors could be covers for stealing. When dealers leave a table they clap their hands and then turn them palms up. The fingers are spread to show the floor person that no chips are concealed.

Is all this security necessary? Unfortunately, yes. Most dealers and players are honest, but there are always a very few rotten apples who want a personal piece of the casino action. The scams could fill another book but here are a few examples.

Bright Idea
Want to know how paranoid the casino bosses are? Next time you're in a casino look for pockets on a dealer costume. You'll rarely see them. Dealer clothing is designed with no easily concealable spaces. The purpose is to make hiding a chip difficult.

Watch Out!
The craps crew is always on the lookout for a dice mechanic, so don't jinx the table by handling the cubes in a strange way. Just take them and throw them. Don't position them in your hand. Don't toss them short of the wall. Odd behavior or a short toss will be grounds for considering the roll invalid.

Player scams

Switching dice or cards: It only takes a moment for a three to disappear and an ace to take its place.

Marking cards: One popular trick is to use an invisible ink that can be seen only with specially tinted glasses. The marking is done secretly at the table during the game! How's that for bold?

Past Posting: Upping the bet after the contest is decided. Seven chips suddenly become eight.

Bet Claiming: This is a craps scam at a busy table. The thief claims a bet placed by a player who has six or seven bets out. The sucker probably won't miss that one wager. If the thief is challenged, a confederate backs the false claim.

Dice Mechanic: This is a dice thrower who sets the cubes a certain way and then tosses them in what appears to be a fair throw but is actually a controlled spin (or sometimes a slide). Dice mechanics often work with confederates who distract the crew while the mechanic is actually throwing.

Dealer scams

Overpaying: This is done with one or a series of player confederates at an otherwise empty table. The dealer busts? The player wins. The player busts? The player wins. The player stands on nine? The player wins.

Palming Chips: Chips go into shoes, into shirts, under belts, in the mouth. It might be uncomfortable but at $100 a pop it's a lucrative scam.

Relay: The dealer conceals a chip and a confederate floor person moves it out. The dealer appears clean. You'll notice that none of these dealer scams involve cheating the player. The casino is a much richer and bigger target.

What about a casino using an organized system to cheat you? Reputable casinos in regulated jurisdictions have absolutely no incentive to steal from players. Why should they do something that would put their multi-million-dollar investments in jeopardy when the game is already legally rigged? The house has an edge.

Eye in the sky

In early casino days the ceilings were constructed with catwalks and two way mirrors. People would patrol the catwalks looking for cheaters on the tables below. The surveillance system was nicknamed the "eye in the sky." Decades later the mirrors are still there, but now video cameras record the action. The information they gather is amazingly detailed. The number of chips in a stack can be counted. The smallest move to conceal a card or a chip will be recorded, played back, and analyzed by security experts. Suspicious actions are watched from every angle. If something is obviously not right, a large-chested man with thick arms and a badge will introduce himself to the suspect. Borderline cases result in an ejection. An arrest will be made in any situation where there is clear evidence of cheating.

Do the casinos ever take cheaters "for a ride?"

Bodily harm inflicted upon casino thieves is a thing of the past, but these days casinos do something almost as damaging. They take the thief's picture, collect as much identifying information as they can about that person, and then share the informa-

Unofficially...
Slot claim-jumping is one particularly nasty player scam that has become obsolete due to the advent of video cameras. Two or three confederates would wait for someone to win a large jackpot. One of the scammers would push the player aside and claim the pot. The others would corroborate the thief's lie.

Unofficially...
About 30 million people visit Las Vegas every year. The average stay is four days. The average bankroll is about $600. Most people play slots. Their annual combined losses at all the games totals more than $6 billion.

tion with other casinos via Griffin Investigations, Inc., a company that provides an international subscription service. A person listed in the Griffin book can never work in a casino or gamble in a normal way again. That person can never again check into a casino hotel, join a slot club, or receive a comp using his or her real name.

Tough stuff, but it's done to ensure the integrity of the game. State regulators, casino staff, surveillance, security and outside companies are all working together (and watching each other) so that everyone stays honest. You can have confidence that the contest is legitimate.

Where should you gamble?

Nevada held the gambling monopoly in the United States for nearly half a century until Atlantic City came along in 1978. For another decade it was only Nevada or Atlantic City, but a boom in legalized gambling swept the nation in the 1990s and now almost every state either has casinos or is adjacent to a state that does. You can choose a riverboat, a Native American reservation, a barge, the Boardwalk, or the Strip. If you're connected to the Internet you can gamble in a virtual casino and never leave home.

Where is the best gaming? Every venue has obvious advantages and most have some not-so-obvious disadvantages.

Las Vegas

It's the big enchilada, the granddaddy, the city where gambling was defined. People come from all over the world to take their shot in this desert town. The overall quality of the games and the gaming venues is unparalleled, but you must choose carefully. Las Vegas is also filled with a lot of bad deals and unfavorable contests. Stiff competition results in bait-and-switch situations; a casino will advertise one special and then sock you on everything else, or they might advertise something that sounds great but isn't. Does the video poker pay well? Don't automatically assume the other games are as liberal. Single deck blackjack doesn't necessarily mean a lower house edge. Crapless craps, Double Exposure blackjack (all cards dealt face up), and Spanish 21 aren't as favorable to the player as the traditional contests no matter what the advertising suggests.

On the other hand, some casinos offer baccarat with a four percent banker vig and video poker machines that pay back more than 100 percent. The loosest slots in the world can be found in Las Vegas. You can play world-class hold 'em at Binion's Horseshoe or make world-class sports bets at the Mirage. Craps at Caesars Palace is a truly regal experience, and the keno there tops out at $300,000.

Wherever you play there is a feeling, an edge, that permeates the games. It's an inexplicable sensation of danger combined with exhilaration. The feeling (usually) has nothing to do with a lack of physical safety but has everything to do with an atmosphere that encourages pushing the limits and taking emotional risks. People who like that feeling love Las Vegas.

Fold the glitter and icky stuff together and you have the ultimate gambling destination. Las Vegas absolutely beats every other place on earth.

Atlantic City

Remember the edge I mentioned in the previous section? Atlantic City doesn't have it. Why? Perhaps

Bright Idea
Planning a trip to Las Vegas? Macmillan's *Unofficial Guide to Las Vegas* is a must. Every major casino, hotel, show and restaurant is thoroughly reviewed. Author Bob Sehlinger gives you inside tips for wrangling seats, rooms, and other perks. Buy a fanny pack because you'll want to carry the book around town.

Unofficially...
Atlantic City had 34 million visitors in 1997. Most were day-trippers. Their annual combined losses totaled 2.7 billion dollars.

it's because the games and everything surrounding them are so heavily regulated. Perhaps it's because a large percentage of the people who visit Atlantic City are retired. They're day-trippers who arrive on countless buses from every imaginable burg within a few hundred miles. It's hard to feel an edge when everyone is so gosh-darned down to earth.

Residents will cheerfully remind you that gambling didn't build Atlantic City. It was Atlantic City that built gambling. Just a few steps away from the ringing bells and dropping coins are the sounds of crashing waves and the sight of tourists strolling the Boardwalk. Atlantic City had tourists before Las Vegas had inside plumbing. This is the town that inspired the board game Monopoly. All those names you remember from childhood, like Baltic Avenue and Marvin Gardens, are real streets in Atlantic City.

The Boardwalk is romantic. The White House subs are delicious. The taffy is legendary. The gambling is just OK. Weekends can be a zoo when everyone from New York and Philadelphia squeezes into this little island. $5 blackjack? Get real. The few seats available will be at $25 tables.

Did I mention the taffy?

Mississippi

It's the third largest gambling market in the United States. Are you surprised? People from all over the country are finding southern hospitality and gambling an intoxicating mix. Tunica and Biloxi have most of the action, and it's flavored with mint julep. The people are friendly, games are well-run, and $10 bets are appreciated in a way that would be impossible in Las Vegas or Atlantic City.

Casinos in the Magnolia State have done their homework. Slot clubs, slot tournaments, poker rooms, entertainment headliners—it's everything you would expect. One caveat: The charm only works if you mentally let go of Las Vegas. Mississippi has it's own unique ambiance. Try the gumbo.

Gambling towns

You will pass through a gambling town on your way to a natural wonder or a national monument. Perhaps the town will be close to where you live, or you'll be on a trip and the highway will just go there. That will be your reason for visiting places like Reno, Lake Tahoe, Mesquite, Deadwood, Cripple Creek, and other gambling towns. The casinos there can be fun and occasionally (particularly in Lake Tahoe) world-class, but mostly they're just small and quaint. Sometimes you will find a good game. Sometimes you won't. When it's the latter, don't be disappointed. Remember, you didn't go there just for the gambling.

Riverboats

They're smaller than land-based casinos. The slots are generally tighter. The limits are lower and they're jammed on the weekends. If you live in the Midwest, it's easier to get to a riverboat than to Las Vegas, but it's a trade-off. When you're losing at a casino in Las Vegas you can cash out and walk across the street. Try that on a riverboat.

On the other hand, if you've had your fill of big city attitude (or never had a taste for it), then a riverboat may be the gambling venue for you. Midwest sensibility permeates riverboat employees and players alike. The buffet has biscuits. People make eye contact. Table limits are usually $500. Who in his right mind would bet more?

And of course when those tight slots have gobbled the last quarter you can always grab a beer, go outside, and watch the sunset.

Unofficially...
Deadwood in South Dakota is where Wild Bill Hickok lost his life playing poker. The hand was two pairs, aces and eights. If Wild Bill were playing today he would probably fold and save himself the trouble. Deadwood table limits are $5.

Watch Out!
Riverboat deck space is a precious commodity because the boat is the only place where gambling is allowed. Space-consuming restaurants, gift shops, and other amenities will be on the mainland. Don't board if you're hungry or you want to shop. The boat will have drinks and snacks, but that's about it.

Native American reservations

The legal issues surrounding gambling on reservations are numbingly complex, but they boil down to one fact. The United States recognizes Native American reservations as sovereign lands. Activities conducted on a reservation are subject to different rules than activities conducted elsewhere.

The practical result is Native American casinos. In 1997 these casinos generated $27 billion in revenue. Some places like Foxwoods and Mohegan Sun in Connecticut are comparable to properties in Atlantic City and Las Vegas. Others are medium-sized casinos, and some are little more than bingo halls.

The best ones follow standard industry rules and procedures. They can be good places to gamble, but you shouldn't automatically assume the word casino means roulette, craps, and all the other traditional games. It does in Connecticut; it doesn't in California. Call before taking the long drive. The only consistent drawback to Native American casinos is that they're nearly always out of the way, an unfortunate result of policies pursued by previous generations.

Cruise ships

Cruise ships are not riverboats. The games are not regulated by the state or the federal government. They're conducted in international waters and the only authority is the cruise ship company. The rules and payouts are whatever the company decides they will be. The dealer wins a push? Too bad. You can't double down except on ten or eleven? Too bad. The slots are tight? Too bad.

Not all cruise ships have unfavorable rules, but many do. A lack of competition and a captive audience is hardly incentive to offer contests with a low house edge. Most people who cruise don't even realize they're getting a bad game. Most are just thrilled to be gambling.

If your choice is the cruise or nothing, then take the cruise. You might be lucky and find a contest with good rules. If not, skip the casino and enjoy the buffet and the fresh sea breezes.

Betting on the Internet

There is no state in the United States that expressly allows betting on the Internet. It is definitely illegal in Minnesota, Missouri, Maryland, and Wisconsin. A host of other states including California and Connecticut are also moving to ban the business. Congress may beat them to the punch. Legislation has been introduced to make betting on the Internet a federal crime. The Justice Department believes that accepting bets via the Internet is already a federal crime. They have repeatedly closed businesses and arrested operators for violating existing gambling laws. By the time you read these words more federal and state action will surely have occurred.

You wouldn't know any of this by reading the Web pages. The online casinos make it so easy; just give them your credit card number and play via modem. It's all approved and perfectly legitimate... in the Caribbean or somewhere else. But not in the United States.

What does that mean for you? Gambling on the net is a double risk. You can lose in the normal way and you can also lose your entire bankroll when the U.S. assets of the corporation are seized. Are you already gambling on the Net? Don't panic. The Feds won't be knocking on your door just yet. Give them some time to finish writing the new laws. Meanwhile, don't expect a dispute with an online casino to be resolved by your state's attorney general.

Timesaver
Don't miss the boat. Gambling cruises depart on a strict schedule. Late arrivals will be cooling their heels at an empty dock. Don't expect to immediately gamble once you're onboard. The boat must cruise to international waters before the games begin.

66
The time has come to send a message to Internet betting operators everywhere: You can't hide online and you can't hide offshore.
—Janet Reno, U.S. Attorney General
99

International gambling

Gambling rules and regulation in the Caribbean, United Kingdom, Europe, and the rest of the world can vary considerably. Some places are fair and friendly, some are simply nasty. You might win a ton of money and then realize that it's not allowed out of the country. It happens. All these factors mean you should gamble with care in other countries. Don't blow your bankroll. Be mindful of exchange rates and rules for exporting currency. Treat an international casino like a cruise ship. Look for a favorable game, and if you can't find one then walk.

Just the facts

- The state is the ultimate authority regarding how a casino operates.

- Organized crime is not involved in regulated gambling conducted in the United States. The same can't be said for unregulated gambling. You should avoid gambling businesses that are unregulated.

- Dealers cannot cause you to win or lose. Dealers, floor persons, and the pit boss aren't even particularly concerned if you win or lose. Their primary interest is the integrity of the game.

- You should always follow the casino's rules for handling cards and chips. Any deviation will cause the dealer to stop the game.

- All casino games are monitored by remote video cameras. Casinos are very vigilant about catching and prosecuting cheaters.

- Internet gambling is illegal in the United States. People who gamble on the Internet risk losing in the traditional way and also losing their bankroll when the Internet casino is prosecuted by the government.

- Gambling on cruise ships and gambling off-shore (outside the United States.) is subject to different rules than United States regulated games. You should avoid playing if the rules are unfavorable.

GET THE SCOOP ON...
Casino markers ▪ How casinos rate
players ▪ What it takes to get a
comp ▪ Comps you should avoid

Cash, Credit, and Comps

Chapter 14

What is your gambling style? Most people fit on a spectrum between the following extremes:

Hit-and-run: This person likes to wander around a casino and change tables or machines often. Three or four consecutive losses is a signal to move on down the road. Casino hopping is also popular with this kind of gambler. It's MGM in the morning, Bally's in the afternoon, and Caesars at night.

Long-haul: Gamblers of this variety sit down at a table or machine and don't move for hours. They only stop when they've reached a win limit or loss limit.

Casinos prefer long-haul customers because they tend to lose more (they won't stop during a losing streak) and they stay at one venue. All casino financial and marketing systems are designed to encourage long-haul players. They're referred to in the industry as being "casino-oriented." Long-haul customers get the perks and complimentary rewards (called comps). Hit-and-run players get a friendly smile and the bill for dinner. Red carpet treatment is offered only when a player demonstrates that he or she is casino-oriented. All customers, including high rollers, are held to this standard. Comps are not an enticement. They are a compensation for allowing the casino a shot at your money.

Should you encourage this relationship? How will it affect your approach to the games? Financial and practical issues like using credit and the length of your session can get all wrapped up with casino marketing issues. Sorting it out and explaining how the casino comp system works is what this chapter is about.

Red chips, green chips, and black chips

A relationship with a casino starts the moment you make a bet. Slots take coins, but they also take bills and give you credits. Table games require chips. See how trustworthy the casino is? You give them money and they'll hold it while you play with something that reflects their debt.

Timesaver
Do you have too many small chips? Ask the dealer to "color up." It's a casino term that means exchanging chips of a lower denomination for fewer chips with a higher value. Just push the chips forward and say, "Color these up."

Chips come in denominations that range from one dollar to thousands of dollars, and they're formally referred to as checks (or cheques) because that's the way they function. They're a promise of payment.

The colors are somewhat standard in the industry, but there is no rule (except in Atlantic City) that requires chips to be a particular color. The following table lists the colors and their usual denominations.

$1	White/Light Blue
$5	Red
$25	Green
$100	Black
$500	Purple
$1,000	Orange
$5,000	Gray

Some casinos have chips of other denominations, including $20 and $0.50.

Remember that chips represent money, but they're only pieces of plastic. The real money, your money, is in the cashier's cage. Don't keep chips at the end of a session. Cash out. It's an important psychological break and it has practical value, too. You can't take chips across the street and spend them in another casino.

Cash is king, credit is costly

Everyone has a unique way of handling money. Some people can walk into a casino with three credit cards and $5,000, yet stick to a session bankroll of $200. Other people leave credit cards at home and give the cash to their spouses with strict instructions regarding how to dole it out. Whatever works for you is fine, but here are some things to consider when you decide to get into the action.

The easiest and cheapest way to gamble is with cash. It's uncomplicated, universally recognized, and accounting is effortless. When it's gone, it's gone.

The next step down from folding money is an ATM card. Some people will tell you to leave cards in the hotel safe or at home. If that's what you need to do, then do it. But if you have the willpower and don't feel like carrying large amounts of cash around, use the ATM. The only drawback is the fee the casino machine will charge per withdrawal. Expect about double the cost you would pay at home.

Watch Out!
It's OK to take a few chips home with you as souvenirs, but don't expect them to have value when you return. Chips aren't currency and the casino can change the design at any time. The old ones become worthless. Always convert your chips to cash after every session.

A credit card is absolutely the worst way to bankroll your session. The fees are exorbitant, commonly about five percent to 10 percent of the amount advanced. The exact fee depends on the credit system and how much you request. Of course, you'll be paying interest on the money, and the credit card company may charge a cash advance fee, too. The only advantage to using a credit card is the convenience of having a much higher limit. Most ATMs top out at $300. Credit cards can go into the thousands. But a higher limit isn't much of an advantage when you consider the astounding cost.

Casino credit: a no-cost alternative

Casino credit is a smarter alternative. It combines the high limit of a credit card with the convenience of an ATM. It's also one more step down that enticing road to a casino relationship. Here's how it works.

You apply for casino credit as you would for credit at a department store or a bank. The casino will check your regular credit history and will also review your gambling history through a company that specializes in gambling credit information. If you already have a big line at another casino, that may help or hurt. It depends on your income. With good credit and money in the bank you'll get at least $1,000 and often more on a casino line.

The process takes a few hours, sometimes a few days, so you might want to send an application before your next visit. When the credit has been approved, and you've signed the appropriate forms, then you're ready to go. Just sit down at a table (or machine) and ask for a "marker." A floor person will give you a piece of paper that will look very much like the document Robert Redford signed in Indecent Proposal. The only difference is that it probably won't be for one million dollars.

How to use a marker

A *marker* is basically a check written on your bank account. Sign it and a floor person will bring you chips. The casino will hold the marker until the end of your visit, and usually for a few days after that. You can buy the marker back with cash, chips, or a regular check. Markers that aren't redeemed are eventually deposited, but most casinos prefer that you settle up before then because the money is interest-free. A floor person may ask you to buy the marker if you're winning. The cashier will probably ask you to settle the marker when you cash chips at the cage. Some casinos require you to sign an agreement that you won't leave with chips when you owe them on a marker. The exact arrangement between you and the casino regarding how the marker will be repayed can vary, but the basic system is designed to make playing convenient, and at the same time make it difficult to move the borrowed money out of the house. Casino A doesn't want to finance action at Casino B.

Besides being convenient, markers can also be useful as a method of regulating your bankroll. Some people use markers as their sole source of funds when gambling. The big drawback to this strategy is that the credit line only works in one casino. And of course that is exactly what the casino wants.

Comps and the casino system

About the time you will be signing your first marker, or maybe when you buy in for $500 or $1,000, a friendly gentleman or lady in a stylish suit will come to say hello. That person will be a "casino host." Hosts work in a department called "player development." They're looking for casino-oriented players.

Bright Idea
Some people bypass time-consuming credit applications and the issue of settling markers by depositing cash in the cage. The player draws markers from the cash and the account is automatically settled. The cage is also a good place to put money when you have too much to safely carry.

Moneysaver
A good way to demonstrate your level of play is to cash out after every session and then buy in with a marker or cash at the beginning of the next session. Another advantage of cashing out is that you finish with real money in your pocket instead of chips. That helps you quit when you've reached a limit.

The host holds the casino cookie jar. Your goal is to snatch a few sweets without getting your hand stuck. The two of you will play a friendly game of cat and mouse. Sometimes you will be the cat; occasionally you will be the mouse. Or maybe it will be the other way around. It depends on the host.

Casino hosts and player ratings

A casino host can handle your room, show, and dining reservations. You can get the best seats, the best suite, the most expensive meal. The host can comp the entire package and top it off with a basket of fruit or champagne when you arrive. The only thing you must do is play at a certain level for a specified length of time. $500 per hand, six hours per day for three days would be nice. A floor person will monitor your action.

If you play for lower stakes, let's say $25 per hand and only four hours per day, the comps will have less value. $5 per hand for exactly one hour probably won't get you a trip to the buffet. The casino wants a shot at your money and they will comp you to get it. Here's a simplified comp formula.

Average Bet × Hours Played × Bets Per Hour = Total Amount Wagered
Total Amount Wagered × House Edge = Expected Total House Win

Let's say your game is blackjack and you intend to bet $25 per hand at least six hours every day for three days. The host doesn't know that you read this book, so she thinks you'll lose two percent of your total wagers. Her formula would look like this.

$25 × 18 × 60 = $27,000
$27,000 × 2% = $540

$540 is how much the casino thinks it will probably win from you over the weekend. Anything could happen, but this is the average. You'll be comped a portion of $540, usually about 30 percent. If this seems meager for $27,000 worth of action, take comfort in the fact that high rollers fare worse. The percent goes down as the numbers grow, so high rollers actually get less per dollar. The casino couldn't and wouldn't comp $900,000 to possibly win $3 million.

The actual formula used by a host to rate players is more complex and includes other factors. How much did you win/lose during your last visit? What is your style of play? To what degree are you casino-oriented?

Negotiating for comps

The host puts it all together and then makes a gut decision. Occasionally she will be swayed by some horse trading on your part, but 30 percent of $540 is only $162. You might push it to $200 and get a fruit basket, but that's it. Remember, the host doesn't owe you a thing. If it seems that you're shopping for comps and aren't particularly casino-oriented, you'll get a free buffet, maybe.

A casino-oriented player would probably be offered a free room for three nights. What happens if you ask for a gourmet meal, too? The host might respond with a meal and the rooms at the "casino rate," which is a discount off the published rate, or she might just ask you to gamble more and "then we'll talk."

You see where this is going. Now you "owe" them some play. You're committed to one casino for most of the weekend, and your game will be monitored. If it's not up to standard, you won't be comped at the same level again. Have a nice day!

Watch Out!
Acting too savvy will get you rated as a more experienced player. That's bad. Don't talk about the house edge or reveal that you understand how the games work. Act surprised when you win. Be yourself. Be friendly. But be discreet.

Moneysaver
The next level up from RFB (room, food, and beverages) includes limousine service and travel expense reimbursement. Don't hesitate to ask for both if your play warrants it.

Comps from the pit

Pit bosses and slot supervisors also issue comps. They use the same formula as a host does to evaluate your level of play. Let's say you have an urge to play Caribbean Stud Poker and you want a comp for dinner afterwards. Go to the casino, sit at a table, and tell a floor person you'd like to be "rated." That's a request to have your play monitored and appraised. If you buy in for $500 or $1,000, a floor person will probably approach you first. Simply ask how much play will be required for the comp you want. The floor person will send the pit boss over and the two of you can work it out. He'll ask for your VIP card or club card (see the next section), or if it's your first visit to the casino, the pit boss will ask for some information. This will include your name and whatever else the casino policy requires. The rating and comp will go into the pit's computer. All comps and player ratings are reviewed by casino management. Every employee must account for the comps he or she writes.

The important thing is to be rated at the beginning of your session. Playing unrated for three hours and then asking for a comp won't work because people in the pit won't know when you sat down.

Casino players club

If negotiating for comps makes you queasy, there is an alternative that isn't quite as lucrative, but it's certainly easier and more predictable. Every major casino has a comp system that uses a card to track your play. These systems were originally created for slot players, but some casinos are now integrating table play into the card rating system.

It's really easy. You fill out a form and the casino gives you a card. Insert the card into the slot machine every time you play and the wagers will be recorded. Hand the card to a floor person and your table play will be rated. Points accrue for dollars wagered. The clubs offer comps and cash back for points. They also offer promotions and discounts for simply being a club member.

Of course this is a casino, so it's not quite as uncomplicated as a grocery discount. The first mystery is how many dollars equal a point. Some club brochures clearly tell you. Some have fuzzy information and you have to ask. Occasionally you'll find clubs that treat the question as if you were asking to audit their books.

The second mystery is what you can get for the points. Most clubs have printed brochures that state clearly how many points it takes for a comp room or comp meal, but none of them tell you that a casino host or pit boss has the option to give you more. Another thing to consider is that table play is usually rated and comped separately from slot play. So you're back to horse trading.

Don't play for comps

Later in this chapter we'll give you some practical suggestions for getting comps, but before we do that it's important to review the cost of comps and how they figure into your price for fun.

Qualifying for comps can be a bottomless pit. It's certainly OK to accept them, and negotiating for them is fine, but never let your betting patterns be dictated by what the casino is giving you for "free." It's not free if you wager more to get it. Comps earned by betting are at least three to four times

Moneysaver
You've heard the adage "two can live as cheaply as one." It works in reverse for casino comps. Two people earn points twice as fast, so make sure your spouse is also rated and is a member of the casino club. The two of you together will qualify for more comps.

Watch Out!
Meal and show comps usually include a line pass. Comped guests go ahead of the people who are not comped. It's fun to be served first and it certainly makes you feel special, but don't let the perk make you lose sight of the comp's actual value.

more expensive than paying cash. Were you planning to sit at that table for X hours over the next X days? If yes, then take the comp. But don't play longer or bet more just for a room or meal.

Table 14.1 shows how playing for comps can affect your price for fun. Both examples are based on the host formula we showed you previously. The game is blackjack. Let's say the actual house edge is only one percent because the players are using basic strategy. The host thinks the players have average skill so she's comping them at an expected loss rate of two percent. Both players have a total bankroll of $3,000. Both have a modest unlucky streak followed by an equally modest lucky streak at the end of Day 2. The first streak is forty losses out of sixty hands; the second is the other way around. The overall house edge remains one percent. Unfortunately, the $50 bettor never sees the lucky streak because he busts out. His bankroll isn't big enough to sustain his level of betting.

The $3,000 bankroll is divided into three $1,000 sessions. The streak on Day 2 is a run of forty losses in sixty hands followed by forty wins in sixty hands.

TABLE 14.1

	$25 Player	$50 Player
Day 1 $1,000	-90	-180
Day 2 $1,000	-90	-1,000
Day 3 $1,000	-90	-180
Total loss	-270	-1,360
Amount comped	200	400
Price for fun	70	960

Mr. 50 wasn't satisfied with a free room. He wanted meal comps, too. The host told him what level of play was required. He played to that level and it cost him. Ms. 25 paid $70 for her fun and had plenty of money left for gourmet meals and gifts for friends. She spent less and enjoyed more.

But what if the players had won? Mr. 50 would have been ahead. Yes, but that's a big "if." This is gambling. Anything can happen, but the casino has the edge. It's nice to hope for a lucky run; counting on luck is simply foolish. Remember that Ms. 25 and Mr. 50 weren't lucky or unlucky. Their luck was exactly average over the long run. In fact, for the sake of simplicity, it was too average. A more detailed scenario might have Mr. 50 busting out on two or all three days.

Here is the bottom line: Don't play for comps.

Perception is everything in the world of comps

Once you've decided not to spend money chasing comps, you'll be in the proper frame of mind to actually get them. Large bets automatically bring attention from the pit or a casino host, but if you're only betting $5 or $10 per hand you'll probably have to start the discussion. Don't be embarrassed. Just wave a floor person over and ask an open-ended question. Something like this:

"I was hoping for a comped bistro dinner this evening. Is that something you can arrange?"

Or maybe this:

"I wanted to spend the night here and try my luck again tomorrow. Could you arrange a room comp?"

Don't phrase the request as a demand. Leave the door open for an alternate offer because your level of play may not warrant the full comp. It's also not a bad idea to finger the stacks of your bankroll (preferably green or black chips) as you pose the question.

Whatever you do, don't let the person get away with a flat "no." Begin a negotiation. Nobody is making promises, and you never know what might come up in the conversation.

Bright Idea
The first and most basic comp is free drinks. It's a courtesy extended to every player. Being rated or being a member of the casino club is not required. Anyone at the tables or the slots is eligible. Just flag down a cocktail person and place your order. Be sure to tip.

Tips for getting comps

Here are some thing you can do to put the pit in more of a "yes" mood.

- Buy in big. Let's say your session bankroll is $750. Buy in for the full amount rather than for a portion. That will get the pit's attention.

- Play at a low limit table. Your $25 bets will look bigger when the minimum is $5.

- Comps of all types are easier to get during mid-week and off-season. Busy periods, especially conventions, are the worst times.

- A room comp is sometimes easier to get than a restaurant meal. That's because the room is charged at a fixed rate but the meal is open-ended. It depends on the restaurant and your relationship with the casino. Can you be trusted in the gourmet bistro?

- Rooms at a discount and buffet meals are the easiest comps. Go for those when all else fails.

Swimming with the whales

A "whale" is casino slang for a high-roller. Gambling around whales can be fun, but don't expect $25 bets to generate comps at Caesars Palace and Bellagio, as they would at some other properties. Competition also plays a big part in the availability of comps. A Davenport riverboat will be jammed on a Saturday in June. Not so for a Strip casino on a Tuesday in August.

What if you prefer swimming with the whales? What if you prefer the riverboat? Play where you want. Don't pick a casino strictly for the comps. On the other hand, don't ignore their value. Figure the comps in when you calculate the overall price for fun. Look at the big picture and decide how much fun the comps contribute.

Comps and casino thinking

The casino understands probability, so don't feel bad about asking for comps when you're winning. You're doing your part; they're getting a shot at your bankroll. It's not your fault that luck is temporarily against them. The casino will be happy to comp you because they want another chance at your money.

Conversely, losing is not automatic criteria for getting a comp. So you lost. So what? It's gambling. Losing a bundle (thousands) may get you a meal or a room for the night, but don't expect much unless the casino has some expectation of more action from you tomorrow or on your next trip. The type of gambler least likely to get a comp is the one who loses $200 and expects to get $150 of it back in a meal and a free room. Not a chance.

Another situation that tends to close the comp spigot is giving a host the impression that your shopping. It's fine to compare programs at various casinos, but don't act like you're squeezing melons (even if you are). The host wants customers who are casino-oriented, people interested in a long-term relationship. If the host gets the impression that you'll cut and run for a few show tickets, then you'll see less effort to develop your business.

It's all about relationships and verifying your play. Use your club card, get rated, use markers to demonstrate that you're a player. Remember, markers cost nothing. Everything helps when the time comes to negotiate comps.

And, of course, be realistic. Use the comp formula in this chapter and ask for what is reasonable. Hosts, supervisors, and pit bosses want to say yes. Make it easy for them.

Timesaver
One advantage of being a casino club member is getting rooms when the hotel is officially booked. It's not a guarantee, but club members usually have a better chance than someone off the street. This applies to shows and dinner reservations, too. The exact policy depends on the casino.

Watch Out!
If you like get-
ting comps, don't
abuse them.
Don't order the
most expensive
meal in the
restaurant. Do
remember to tip
at least 20 per-
cent on what
the bill would
have been.

The comp alternative

Do you see where the subject of comps has led us?
The entire system is focused on involving you exclusively with one casino. Comps require you to constantly prove what a wonderful customer you are.
Are you? Then be sure to get what you deserve. If
you prefer to hit and run, accept the fact that most
comps are not for you. That's OK. Join a few clubs at
your favorite casinos and maintain the level of relationship you feel is appropriate.

Focus on your game, not the comps, because the
best comp is purchased with money you've won.

Just the facts

- A casino's financial and comp systems are
  designed to encourage customer loyalty to that
  particular casino. You should be aware of this
  when making choices influenced by comps and
  credit.

- Cash is the least expensive and most convenient
  way of funding your bankroll. Credit from a
  credit card is the most expensive way. The cost
  for a credit card cash advance in a casino can be
  five percent to 10 percent of the amount
  advanced.

- An alternative to cash and credit cards is casino
  credit (commonly known as a *marker*). You can
  apply for casino credit as you would any credit.
  There is no charge for the service.

- Comps are based on the level of your play. You
  must be "rated" or a member of the casino players club to receive comps. There aren't many
  absolute rules as to how comps are awarded, so
  you usually must negotiate for them with a casino host, pit boss or slot supervisor.

- Accepting comps is fine, but playing for them is strictly for suckers. The average player will lose at least three to four times more than the value of the comp.

- Join the players club at your favorite casino. It costs nothing. Even if your level of play is minimal you will probably get some advantage from membership, including a special rate at the hotel.

GET THE SCOOP ON...
What the IRS requires from
gamblers ▪ Avoiding rip-offs ▪ Keeping your
cool in the casino ▪ Tipping the dealer

IRS and Other Matters

T he material in this chapter is not as much fun as learning about blackjack or video poker, but it's important. We'll keep it short and sweet.

Uncle Sam's house edge

The IRS expects you to pay taxes on your gambling income. Casinos are required by law to file a form W2-G when they pay you $1,200 or more on a machine win, $1,500 in keno, or when you cash in $5,000 or more in chips. You should have your Social Security number handy or the casino will automatically withhold 30 percent.

Gambling losses are only deductible to the extent that they offset wins. Let's say you win $4,000 and lose $10,000. You can only deduct $4,000. The income must still be reported and the loss must be documented. Your records must be detailed and they should show when you bet and how much you lost. Table 15.1 is an example of a typical gambling record.

Feel free to use this as a general guide for your own record-keeping, but be sure to review it with your tax advisor.

TABLE 15.1: GAMBLING EXPENSE RECORD

Date	Casino	Time	Machine/Table #	Buy-In	Extra	Total	Left With	Won	Lost	Session Balance
25-Jun	Strat	7pm-10pm	vp6587	50	60	110	30		80	
		10pm-1am	bj #7	100		100	150	50		-30
28-Jun	Trop	6pm-9pm	bj #2	150		150	160	10		
		9pm-1am	vp3865	80	80	160	40		120	-110

One advantage of keeping records is that it helps you remember where the money went. This player is doing better at blackjack than video poker. If the trend continues, she should switch exclusively to blackjack or practice her video poker strategy.

So even if a big win doesn't come your way this year, it's always helpful to keep records as if it will. You never know.

Personal security

In the last chapter we told you that cash is king in the casino. Unfortunately, carrying large amounts of cash is risky. Having a casino line of credit (see Chapter 14) is one way to avoid carrying cash. Another way is to deposit money in the cage. The casino will gladly hold the funds, and even allow you to draw markers against it.

Here are some more tips for protecting yourself.

- Watch your chips in the slot machine tray and on the rail at the craps table. A loud noise or a nearby disturbance should be a cue for you to look down and check your bankroll. Thieves use distractions to quickly grab unattended chips.

- If someone falls or trips near you, don't immediately abandon your chips to rush over and help the person. It sounds cruel, but you should first gather and secure your belongings (including your money) before moving to help. If someone falls against you, immediately check your pockets and then your bankroll.

- It's tough and mostly pointless to avoid showing your money at the tables. After all, it's a casino. But be aware of the people around you. Don't walk upstairs with forty black chips stuffing your pocket. Cash out and leave most of it in the cage.

Timesaver
Deducting a gambling loss isn't easy. You must file a Schedule A and itemize. Consult with your tax advisor before doing that. You may be better off taking the standard deduction.

- Be wary of friendly strangers, especially if you're alone. It's nice to be popular. Having coffee at the bar or a sandwich in the restaurant with a new friend is fine, but don't give anyone your room number. Be particularly careful if your new friend suddenly appeared after you won money.

- Don't drink too much. The liquor may be free, but it will cost you at the table when your judgment is impaired.

- Avoid carrying a purse or handbag. If you must carry one, put it between your legs wherever you sit.

You and the casino

A casino operates in two modes. The first mode is the one you see most frequently. It's smiling faces and people eager to please. Everyone wants you to play, relax, and spend money. Occasionally, you may glimpse the second mode. It's a few tense faces in the pit or a gaggle of serious looking men in suits striding purposefully on their way somewhere. That second mode is all about security and keeping the peace. The people who do it for the casino are professionals. Sometimes they deal with crooks. Sometimes they deal with people who are angry or dangerous. A casino attracts all types. A security person must deal with all types.

Now imagine what might go through that security person's mind if he sees a player having a heated disagreement with a dealer.

You don't want to be that player, even if you're right.

Of course you're not a hothead, but the security person doesn't know that. That's why you should be extra careful in a casino when you have a dispute with a dealer or another player. Never respond to provocation. Never allow a situation to escalate. That's tough advice to follow when a dealer has mistakenly scooped up your winning hand and a $200 bet. It's even tougher when he says your five-card twenty-one was twenty-two. Complain to the pit, and to the shift supervisor if necessary, but don't lose your head.

That's all that needs to be said about that.

How to toke (tip)

A *toke* is casino jargon for a tip. Toking isn't a bad thing, and I thought it would be nice to close the chapter on an upbeat note. There are two ways to tip a dealer: You can simply push him the chip and say, "This is for the dealer." Or you can bet it for him. It adds a bit of excitement when the two of you are hoping for the same outcome.

Just the facts

- Income from gambling is taxable. Losses are deductible only to the extent that they offset winnings. You should keep records of your wins and losses

- Be careful with your money in and near a casino. Be aware of who is around you. Don't carry a lot of cash out to your car without an escort.

- Never respond to provocation in a casino. Never challenge casino security.

- Toke your dealer.

> " Don't let a winning streak lure you into a sense of invulnerability. Remember that a Smith & Wesson beats every hand including a royal flush.
> —A. James Lee, security consultant "

Glossary

action Refers to the relative amount of money wagered in a game. More money is synonymous with more action.

ante In poker, a minimum bet placed into the pot that allows a player to be dealt into the hand. In Caribbean Stud Poker, the initial bet that allows a player to receive cards.

baccarat pit An area in a casino that is set aside for one or more baccarat tables.

bank craps The version of craps played in casinos. The house banks the action in bank craps. Street or "G.I." craps is played in private venues and is banked by players.

banker The person or entity who provides financial backing for a game. The banker pays winning wagers and receives bets that lose. Most casino games are banked by the casino, but some games (such as pai gow poker) can be banked by players.

bankroll An amount of money set aside specifically for the purpose of gambling.

bar the 12 A craps term that indicates which number is a push for a don't better on a come-out roll. Some casinos bar the 2 instead of the 12.

basic strategy A set of optimum choices for various playing situations. The term is most commonly used in blackjack, but any game strategy that is optimum and has been reduced to a series of if-then decisions can be considered a basic strategy.

betting progression A betting system that uses previous wins or losses to determine the level of subsequent bets. Negative progressions increase bets after a loss. Positive progressions increase bets after a win. The best progressions are generally ineffective, and the worst ones will quickly decimate a bankroll. Negative progressions are particularly virulent. See *chasing losses*.

bias Refers to a roulette wheel that is not perfectly balanced and consequently favors certain numbers over others.

big eight/big six Two sucker bets in craps that are identical in risk to place six or place eight, but only pay even money. Big six and big eight are not allowed in Atlantic City casinos.

blind bet A poker bet made before the hand is dealt, similar to an ante. Not all players are required to make a blind bet. In hold 'em the two players to the left of the designated dealer put up a "big blind" and a "little blind".

bluffing Playing aggressively with a weak poker hand in the hope of misleading other players and causing them to fold.

board Community cards that are dealt face-up in the center of a poker table.

box The center section of the craps table where proposition bets are placed.

boxcars Slang term for a roll of two sixes in a craps game.

boxman (boxperson) The person who supervises a craps game.

break See *bust*.

break-even To win an amount equal to the amount lost. The break-even point is the demarcation between a positive and a negative expectation game.

bring-in A mandatory first round opening bet in seven card stud. The bring-in is made by the player with the lowest upcard.

buck See *button*.

burn To remove a card from the top of the deck without putting it into play. Burning one or more cards is a procedure to discourage cheating.

bust To go over twenty-one in blackjack. A bust is an automatic loss for the player.

button Also known as a *puck* or a *buck*. A button is a marker that designates the dealer position in hold 'em. The button moves one player to the left after each hand. The purpose of designating a dealer has nothing to do with who actually handles the cards and everything to do with who is required to bet blind. See also *blind bet* and *designated dealer*.

buy A craps bet on a particular number. The buy bet wins if the number is rolled before seven. Buy bets are paid at true odds but the casino charges a 5% vig on the amount wagered.

buy in To exchange money and receive chips for the purpose of playing.

cage The area in the casino where the real money is stored. The cage is where players exchange chips for cash, redeem markers, temporarily deposit money and perform other casino financial transactions.

call In poker, betting an amount equal to the previous player's bet for the purpose of remaining in the hand. In Caribbean Stud Poker, betting an additional amount that is double the ante amount for the purpose of remaining in the hand.

card counting Observing the cards that have been played in blackjack and using that information to predict what cards will subsequently be played. Card counting is legal but very unwelcome in most casinos. People who count cards are frequently ejected and/or barred from further play.

card sharp A person who is an expert card player, also frequently used to describe someone who artfully cheats at cards.

carousel A group of slot machines positioned in a circle or ring.

casino players club A comp system that uses a card to track wagers. The casino rewards players on a scale proportionate to their level of action.

casino rate Reduced-rate hotel rooms offered to casino players club members and other regular casino customers.

casino-oriented Casino industry term for a person who tends to play in one casino for extended periods of time. Casino-oriented players are the most desired customers.

catch To select a winning keno number.

center bets See *proposition bets*.

chasing losses Betting an increased amount in an attempt to recoup a previous loss. Chasing losses usually results in greater losses.

check (1) An alternate term for a chip.

check (2) Remaining in a poker hand but offering no bet. A player who checks must call or raise if another player bets in that round.

chip A money token used in a casino in lieu of cash.

chip tray The tray that sits in front of a dealer and holds the chips that are used by the dealer to pay bets.

cold Describes a table or machine that takes money without producing a win. Also describes a person unable to win.

color up Exchanging chips of a lower denomination for fewer chips with a higher value.

combination ticket A single keno ticket written for more than one wager.

come-out roll The first roll for a do or don't bet in craps.

comps Complimentary rewards such as free meals, free rooms, free shows, and travel reimbursements. A casino give comps to players who are perceived to be casino-oriented.

copy A player hand that is identical to a banker hand in pai gow poker.

craps (crapping out) Rolling two, three or twelve on a come-out in craps.

croupier European term for a dealer.

dealer signature Refers to an unconscious habit exhibited by some roulette dealers of spinning the ball in a predictably consistent way.

designated dealer A rotating designation used mostly to determine blind bets and the order of betting in poker.

dice mechanic Someone who cheats at craps by throwing dice in a way that limits their random movement. This makes the numbers somewhat more predictable.

discard tray A tray holding cards that have been burned, mucked, or otherwise taken out of play.

do Slang for a pass line bet or a come bet in craps.

don't Slang for a don't pass bet or a don't come bet in craps.

double down A blackjack bet which requires the player to wager an additional amount equal to the original bet and to receive exactly one more card to complete the hand. Usually restricted to hands that have two cards.

draw A poker term commonly used in video poker. To "draw" is to throw away cards and receive replacements in the hopes of improving a hand.

drop box A fortified box placed under a table that is connected to a slot in the table surface. Dealers put cash (and sometimes chips) into the drop box. The box is periodically replaced and moved to the cage where the contents are removed.

drop percentage The money actually spent by players in a casino. Drop percentage is a ratio of the original buy in (drop). The house edge may be three percent, but the drop percentage may be 20 percent because players repeatedly risk the same money.

en prison A roulette rule option offered in some casinos. In the U.S. (where the rule is known as surrender) even money wagers that lose to zero or double-zero are only half-lost. In Europe an even money wager that loses to zero or double-zero must remain on the table for an additional spin of the wheel. Losing wagers are taken and winning wagers are returned.

even money Winning an additional amount equal to the original wager.

eye in the sky Slang for casino surveillance systems.

field bet A craps bet that the next number rolled will *not* be 5, 6, 7 or 8.

first base The player seat to the blackjack dealer's far left. This position receives cards first and is first to hit or stand.

flat top A slot machine with a top prize that is a fixed non-progressive amount. See *progressive.*

flop The second round of betting in hold 'em when three community cards are dealt face-up in the center of the table.

fold In poker, declining to bet and giving up any claim to the pot. In Caribbean Stud Poker, declining to call and forfeiting the ante.

give odds See *lay odds.*

hard hand Any blackjack hand that does not contain an ace valued at eleven.

hardway A 4, 6, 8 or 10 rolled with both dice showing identical numbers. It's more difficult to roll a *hard* four than it is to roll a four the easy way.

high-roller Someone who consistently bets large amounts of money in one or more casinos.

hit To request a card in blackjack.

hole card(s) The dealer's face-down card in blackjack. The face-down cards in hold 'em.

hop Any craps bet determined by the next roll of the dice. See *proposition.*

hot Describes a table or machine that frequently produces wins. Also used to describe a person who frequently wins.

house edge The financial advantage a casino has in a wager. House edge is usually expressed as a percentage. The term is synonymous with price for fun. It is the price a casino charges for gambling entertainment. Not to be confused with *drop percentage.*

house odds The amount a casino will pay for a winning bet. Not to be confused with *true odds.* House odds are expressed as an amount that will be paid for an amount wagered.

inside bets Roulette bets placed on the inside of the layout on a particular number or group of numbers.

insurance A side bet in blackjack that pays 2:1 when the dealer has a natural. Insurance is offered when the dealer's upcard is an ace.

jackpot A top prize, usually associated with slot

machines, but generally synonymous with any large game prize in a casino.

keno board A large electronic display posted in the keno lounge and duplicated on video screens throughout the casino. The keno board shows the numbers that catch for each game.

keno lounge The physical location of a casino's keno game.

keno runner A casino employee who picks up keno bets from players throughout the casino, shuttles the bets to the keno lounge and (hopefully) returns with winning tickets.

kicker An unsuited card held in draw poker, usually as a bluff. Kickers should never be held in video poker.

lay A craps bet against a particular number. The lay bet wins if seven is rolled before the number. Lay bets are paid at true odds but the casino charges a 5% vig on the winning amount.

lay odds (laying odds) Also known as giving odds. This is a a money line sports bet on the team favored to win. Having the advantage requires the bettor to risk more to win less. Laying odds has a similar meaning in craps where it is used to describe a side-bet on a don't wager after the come-out. The odds favor the bet so the payoff is less than the amount risked.

limit See *table limits*.

line A sports betting handicap (often a point spread) used by a sports book to divide bettors into two equal groups.

load To play maximum coins in a slot machine.

loose (1) Refers to a slot machine that often pays.

loose (2) Refers to a player more likely to take risks.

loss-limit A fixed amount of allowable loss. A disciplined player stops gambling when losses reach the loss-limit. See *bankroll.*

marker A promise of payment to a casino. A marker is the legal equivalent of a counter check. It can be drawn against a player's checking account.

Martingale A dangerous negative betting progression in which bets are doubled after a loss.

mini-baccarat A less ostentatious lower-limit version of American baccarat.

money line A sports book's line expressed as an amount required to lay odds or a payout for taking odds. A bet on the favored team requires the bettor to lay odds (risk more to win less). A bet on the underdog allows bettors to take odds (risk less to win more).

muck To throw away cards, usually in poker.

natural A two-card hard valued at twenty-one in blackjack, a two-card hand of eight or nine in baccarat, a dice roll of seven or eleven on the come-out in craps,

negative expectation Refers to a game that takes more in the long run than it pays. Negative expectation games have a house edge.

no roll An invalid dice roll in craps. Also sometimes referred to as "no dice."

off A craps bet that is on the table but is not "working". The dealers and player understand that the money is not at risk.

on A craps bet that is "working." The money is at risk.

on tilt Playing badly or erratically. The term is usually used to describe a flustered poker player.

open The first bet in a round of poker.

outside bet Roulette bets made on groups of numbers on the outside of the layout.

over/under A sports bet that the combined total of points scored by both teams will be over (or under) a specific total.

parlay (1) One sports bet on the outcome of a combination of games. All the chosen teams must win for the parlay bet to win.

parlay (2) To increasing winnings by making multiple winning bets.

pass To roll a natural in craps, or to roll a point before rolling seven.

past posting Making or increasing a bet after the results are known. Past posting is a form of cheating.

pat A blackjack hand of hard seventeen or more. Pat hands should never be hit.

pay table The schedule posted on a slot machine that shows how much is paid for each winning combination.

payline The line on a slot machine where the symbols must appear to signify a win. Most slot machines have multiple paylines.

payoff The money returned on a winning bet.

pit The inside section formed by a circle of gaming tables. Casino personnel who work in the pit are supervised by a pit boss.

place A craps wager similar to a buy bet except that the casino takes vig as a lowered payout rather than as a percentage of the wager.

point In craps, a number that must be rolled for a player to pass. Rolling the point causes pass line bets to win and causes don't pass bets to lose.

point-spread One form of a betting line (a sports betting handicap) used by a sports book to divide bettors into two equal groups.

positive expectation Refers to a game that pays more in the long run than it takes. Positive expectation games have a player edge.

pot The pile of chips that accumulates in a poker game as each player antes, calls or raises. The pot goes to the winner of the hand.

pressing bets To wager the same money twice or more times. Winnings are generally included when pressing bets.

price for fun Synonymous with the house edge. It's the financial advantage a casino has in a wager. Price for fun is what the casino charges for gambling entertainment.

probability The likelihood of an event happening. Probability is expressed as a number between 0 and 1. An impossible event is 0 and an event that is certain to occur would be 1.

progression See *betting progression.*

progressive A slot machine jackpot (or other jackpot system) that increases in proportion to each bet that is made. A winning combination wins the entire progressive jackpot.

proposition (1) Craps bets in the center of the layout.

proposition (2) Any single decision with two possibilities that is the subject of a wager.

puck (1) In craps, a disk (white on one side and black on the other) that is used to indicate the current point.

puck (2) See *button*.

push A tie in the outcome of a contest. The player doesn't win or lose.

quad Poker slang for four-of-a-kind.

rags A worthless poker hand. A combination of cards that are unlikely to improve.

rail (1) The top edge of craps table.

rail (2) The boundary of the spectators' area in a poker game.

raise Matching a previous bet and then betting more in a poker game. A raise requires all the other players in the hand to either call, raise or fold.

rake The money taken by a casino or card room for providing services to a poker game. A rake is usually collected as a percentage of the pot or as a flat fee.

random number generator (RNG) The heart of a slot machine. The RNG randomly generates numbers that determine the winning combinations.

reel One of three or more wheels inside a slot machine that are visible through a window at the front of the device. The various winning symbols are printed on each reel.

RFB An abbreviation for "room, food, and beverages". Used primarily by casino personnel when discussing player comps.

right Slang for betting the do or come in a craps game.

river The final round of betting in hold 'em or seven card stud.

runner See *keno runner.*

scared money Money at risk that is not discretionary. Scared money includes funds for rent, food, and other necessities. Gambling with scared money is a sickness.

sequence bets Craps bets that require multiple rolls of the dice to win.

session A period of time designated for gambling.

set The act of arranging cards in pai gow poker.

seven-out Rolling a seven while attempting to roll a point in craps. A seven-out causes pass line bets to lose and causes don't pass bets to win.

seventh street The final round of betting in seven card stud.

shoe A box that holds multiple decks of cards.

shooter The person throwing dice in craps.

showdown The end of the last round in a poker hand when all remaining players reveal their cards.

singleton A card that is unsuited in a poker hand. A card that does not belong to a winning combination or a possible winning combination.

slot club See *casino players club*.

snake eyes A roll of two in craps.

soft hand Any blackjack hand that contains an ace counted as eleven.

splitting Dividing a blackjack hand that has two cards of equal value into two hands. Each hand is played independently. Splitting requires an additional wager.

spot One number on a keno ticket.

stand To refuse additional cards in blackjack. Stand is the opposite of hit.

stiff A blackjack hand greater than eleven and less than seventeen that doesn't contain an ace valued as eleven.

straight ticket A keno ticket written for one bet and one combination of numbers.

straight up A roulette bet on one number.

street bet A roulette bet on three adjacent numbers. The wager is placed at the end of the row.

surrender (1) To retrieve half the bet and forfeit the hand when playing blackjack.

surrender (2) See *en prison*.

table limit The betting limits established by a casino for a particular table game. Table limits include the minimum and maximum amounts that can be wagered on one bet. They also frequently include the maximum payout allowed for one hand.

table stakes A poker rule that requires players to limit wagers to the chips on the table at the beginning of the hand.

take a bet down Removing a bet from the craps layout.

take odds (taking odds) This is a a money line sports bet on the team expected to lose. Wagering on the underdog allows the bettor to risk less and possibly win more. Taking odds has a similar meaning in craps where it is used to describe a side-bet on a pass line wager after the come-out. The odds are against the bet so the payoff is greater than the amount risked.

teaser A sports parlay with a point spread adjusted to be more favorable to the player. This results in a lower potential payoff

tell Unconscious movements or body positions that indicate what a player or dealer has "in the hole." Tells are used primarily in poker and blackjack. See also *hole card*.

third base The player seat to a blackjack dealer's far right. This position receives cards last and is last to hit or stand.

tight (1) Refers to a slot machine that rarely pays. The opposite of loose.

tight (2) Describes a player averse to taking risks.

toke Casino slang for a tip.

trips Poker slang for three-of-a-kind.

true odds The true probability of an event occurring. Not to be confused with house odds

under See *over/under.*

upcard A blackjack dealer's exposed card.

vigorish (vig) Strictly speaking, vigorish is synonymous with any casino house edge. All games have vigorish, but the word is mostly used in situations that involve a betting fee or commission charged by the casino.

VIP See *high-roller.*

way ticket A keno ticket that combines groups of numbers into multiple bets.

whale See *high-roller.*

win-limit A fixed amount of profit that signals an end to a session. A disciplined player stops gambling upon reaching the win-limit, or resets the loss-limit to insure that most of the money won will not be put at risk. See also *loss-limit.*

working A craps bet that is at risk. The bet can win or lose on the next roll of the dice.

wrong Craps slang for betting the don't.

Resource Directory

Bookstores, magazines and publishers

Casino Player Magazine
Casino Journal Publishing Group
8025 Black Horse Pike, Suite. 470
West Atlantic City, NJ 08232
(800) 969-0711
www.casinocenter.com

Casino Player is perhaps best known for its monthly slot charts. They show which casino machines are paying the most. Sorry no floor plans. The machines are grouped by individual casino and denomination.

Gambler's Books Club
630 South 11th Street
Las Vegas, NV 89101
(800) 522-1777 or (702) 382-7555
www.gamblersbook.com

GBC is ground-zero when it comes to published information about gambling. Their Web site contains the entire store catalog.

Las Vegas Advisor/Huntington Press
3687 S. Procyon Avenue, Suite. A
Las Vegas, NV 89101
(800) 244-2224 or (702) 252-0655

The coupons alone make it worth the price.

Web sites
LasVegas.com
www.lasvegas.com

This comprehensive site is sponsored by the Las Vegas Review-Journal and other Las Vegas businesses. It contains numerous resources and links for gambling and entertainment in the neon oasis.

Atlantic City Convention & Visitors Authority
(888) 222-3683 or (609) 449-7101
www.atlanticcitynj.com

The source for information about Atlantic City.

Casino City
www.casinocity.com

An online directory of every casino in North America. Extensive gaming links and a good search engine.

BJ21
www.bj21.com

Author Stanford Wong's online forum. A good resource for people interested in the professional side of playing blackjack. Use with caution (see listing below).

Blackjack Forum
www.rge21.com

Blackjack Forum is an online version of Arnold Snyder's popular magazine. These people are serious card counters. They all use aliases because the public portion of the site is monitored by casino security experts. Be careful what you post.

Research Services Unlimited
www.smartgaming.com

Author Henry Tamburin's Web site. Excellent links and good information.

Gambling problems
Gamblers Anonymous
P.O. Box 17173
Los Angeles, CA 90017
(702)385-7732 Las Vegas, (323)386-8789 Los Angeles
www.gamblersanonymous.org

Further Reading

Most of these titles are gambling classics, but I've also included a few lesser known works that offer interesting perspectives on the games or the business.

Authors like Stanford Wong, Henry Tamburin, Frank Scoblete and John Gollehon are prolific, so consider this list as a starting point.

American Casino Guide, Steve Bourie (Dania, FL: Casino Vacations, 1998). Do you want to travel and visit casinos? This is the book for you. ACG is updated annually.

Basic Blackjack, Stanford Wong (La Jolla, CA: Pi Yee Press, 1995). Includes strategies for dozens of rule variations.

Beat The Dealer, Edward O. Thorp (New York, NY: Random House, 1966). This is the book that started the revolution in blackjack card counting. After three decades it's a little long in the tooth, but it's still an interesting read.

Big Deal: A Year As A Professional Poker Player, Anthony Holden (New York, NY: Penguin Books, 1990). A fascinating first-hand look at the world of professional poker.

Break The One-Armed Bandits, Frank Scoblete (Chicago, IL: Bonus Books, 1994). A must-buy for any serious slot player.

Casino Games II, John Gollehon (Grand Rapids, MI: Gollehon Books, 1997). Gollehon has a no-nonsense approach. Three out of four hands lose? Leave the table.

Comp City, Max Rubin (Las Vegas, NV: Huntington Press, 1994). The title says it all.

Conquering Casino Craps, John Gollehon (Grand Rapids, MI: Gollehon Books, 1997). This has betting strategies from *Casino Games II* applied to craps.

Henry Tamburin on Casino Gambling, Henry Tamburin (Greensboro, NC: Research Services Unlimited, 1998). A collection of informative articles written about various casino games.

How To Be Treated Like A High Roller, Robert Renneisen (New York, NY: Carol Publishing Group, 1996). Robert Renneisen is President of Claridge in Atlantic City. His book is short and to the point about who gets comps and why.

Professional Blackjack, Stanford Wong (La Jolla, CA: Pi Yee Press, 1994). Advanced blackjack strategies for the most dedicated professional players. Includes card counting. Don't say we didn't warn you.

Super/System, Doyle Brunson (Las Vegas, NV: B&G Publishing, 1978). Considered by most players to be the definitive book about poker.

The Complete Idiot's Guide to Gambling Like a Pro, Stanford Wong and Susan Spector (New York, NY: Macmillan, 1996). Contrary to the title, this book is ideal for smart people, particularly anyone who is in a hurry. The chapters are short and to the point.

The Encyclopedia of Gambling, Carl Sifakis (New York, NY: Facts On File, 1990). Like most encyclopedias, this one includes a lot of history. You're unlikely to encounter faro or whist in a casino, but it's nice to know the rules.

The Frugal Gambler, Jean Scott (Las Vegas, NV: Huntington Press, 1998). Jean Scott was dubbed the "queen of casino comps" by CBS *48 Hours.* She delivers on the title.

The Las Vegas Advisor Guide to Slot Clubs, Jeff Compton (Las Vegas, NV: Huntington Press, 1998). Another must-buy for a serious slot player.

The Theory of Blackjack, Peter Griffin (Las Vegas, NV: Huntington Press, 1996). Pull out your calculator. People who are mathematically inclined will find this fascinating.

The Unofficial Guide to Las Vegas, Bob Sehlinger (New York, NY: Macmillan, 1998). This book is a necessity for anyone visiting Las Vegas.

Winning Strategies for Video Poker, Lenny Frome (Las Vegas, NV: Compu-Flyers, 1997). Not a lot of prose, just sixty detailed strategies for sixty different versions of video poker.

House Edge— Price For Fun

Table D.1 shows the average hourly price of the games we've covered in this book (excluding poker and sports betting). Keep in mind that these numbers are subject to the following variables:

- Decisions per hour vary depending on the speed of play.

- Prices are calculated on the usual house edge. This assumes the bettor is not playing optimally or recklessly. An actual house edge could be anywhere in the listed range.

- Bet per hand varies with the game. Slots and video poker are calculated as quarter machines that are loaded. Also note that Caribbean Stud Poker's ante is not separated from the call bet in this chart, so the average of all the bets is $15.

- Luck plays a significant roll in the short run. Any of these games can produce wins that make the price $0 and put money in your pocket. The opposite can happen too. Bad luck can double the price or make it ten times higher.

TABLE D.1

	House Edge Range	Usual House Edge	Decisions Per Hour	Bet Per Hand	Price Per Hour
Slots NV	1% to 25%	5%	400	1.25	25.00
Slots AC	1% to 17%	9%	400	1.25	45.00
Video Poker	-2% to 10%	4.5%	400	1.25	22.50
Blackjack w/o counting	0% to 4%	2%	60	5.00	6.00
Roulette	5.26% to 7.89%	5.26%	50	5.00	13.15
Craps	0% to 16.7%	1.5%	30	5.00	2.25
Baccarat	0.6% to 14.36%	1.24%	80	5.00	4.96
Caribbean Stud Poker	5%	5%	40	15.00	30.00
Let It Ride	3.5%	3.5%	40	5.00	7.00
Pai Gow Poker	2.5%	2.5%	10	10.00	2.50
Keno	25% to 50%	30%	10	5.00	15.00

A

Action, definition of, 281
All-day bets in craps, 149
"All-in" in poker, 188
Ante, definition of, 281
Atlantic City, casinos in, 252
Atlantic City Convention &
    Visitors Authority, 300

B

Baccarat, 161–71
    average price-for-fun for-
        mula, 9
    big versus mini, 168–69
    card counting in, 169–70
    European-style, 161, 162,
        166
    on grand scale, 164–67
    house edge in, 164, 308
    mini-, 167–68
    money management in,
        170–71
    roots and rules of, 162–64
    rules for drawing, 163,
        164
    shuffle for, 165
    strategies in, 169–70
    versus blackjack, 91
Baccarat pit, definition of,
    164, 281
Bank craps, definition of,
    281
Banker, definition of, 281
Bankroll
    deciding how much to, 17
    definition of, 15, 281

discretionary money for,
    16
price-for-fun formula and,
    18–19
session, 17
size of your, 15–19
versus winnings, 15
win limit, 36–37
worksheet to calculate,
    15–16
Bar the 12, definition of,
    282
Basic strategy, definition of,
    282
Beat the Dealer, 103
Bet claiming, as scam, 248
Bets, increasing to cover
    losses, 13
Better, version of video
    poker, 63, 64–66, 70,
    71, 72, 75
    pay table for, 64–66
    strategy, 72
Betting progression, defini-
    tion of, 25, 31, 282
Betting systems
    dangerous, 25–31
    for sale in Internet or
        magazines, 30–31
Bias, definition of, 282
Big eight/big six, definition
    of, 148, 282
Bingo, 216
Binions's Horseshoe, Las
    Vegas, 174
BJ21, 300
Blackjack, 25, 35, 85–110,
    136
    average price-for-fun for-
        mula, 9, 10
    basics of, 86–92
    basic strategy in, 92–99

L

M

The *Unofficial Guide*™ Reader Questionnaire

If you would like to express your opinion about casino gambling or this guide, please complete this questionnaire and mail it to:

The Unofficial Guide™ Reader Questionnaire
John Wiley & Sons, Inc.
111 River Street
Hoboken, N.J. 07030

Gender: ___ M ___ F

Age: ___ Under 30 ___ 31–40
      ___ 41–50 ___ Over 50

Education: ___ High school ___ College
            ___ Graduate/Professional

What is your occupation?

_____

How did you hear about this guide?
___ Friend or relative
___ Newspaper, magazine, or Internet
___ Radio or TV
___ Recommended at bookstore
___ Recommended by librarian
___ Picked it up on my own
___ Familiar with the *Unofficial Guide*™ travel series

Did you go to the bookstore specifically for a book on casino gambling? Yes ___ No ___

Have you used any other *Unofficial Guides*™?
Yes ___ No ___

If "Yes," which ones?

_____
_____
_____

What other book(s) on casino gambling have you purchased?

_____

_____

_____

Was this book:
___ more helpful than other(s)
___ less helpful than other(s)

Do you think this book was worth its price?
Yes ___   No ___

Did this book cover all topics related to casino gambling adequately?   Yes ___   No ___

Please explain your answer:

_____

_____

_____

Were there any specific sections in this book that were of particular help to you?   Yes ___   No ___

Please explain your answer:

_____

_____

_____

On a scale of 1 to 10, with 10 being the best rating, how would you rate this guide? ___

What other titles would you like to see published in the *Unofficial Guide*™ series?

_____

_____

_____

Are *Unofficial Guides*™ readily available in your area?   Yes ___   No ___

Other comments:

_____

_____

_____

Get the inside scoop...
with the *Unofficial Guides*™!

Health and Fitness

The Unofficial Guide to Alternative Medicine
ISBN: 0-02-862526-9

The Unofficial Guide to Coping with Menopause
ISBN: 0-02-862694-X

The Unofficial Guide to Dieting Safely
ISBN: 0-02-862521-8

The Unofficial Guide to Having a Baby
ISBN: 0-02-862695-8

The Unofficial Guide to Living with Diabetes
ISBN: 0-02-862919-1

The Unofficial Guide to Smart Nutrition
ISBN: 0-02-863589-2

The Unofficial Guide to Surviving Breast Cancer
ISBN: 0-02-863491-8

Career Planning

The Unofficial Guide to Acing the Interview
ISBN: 0-02-862924-8

The Unofficial Guide to Earning What You Deserve
ISBN: 0-02-862716-4

The Unofficial Guide to Hiring and Firing People
ISBN: 0-02-862523-4

Business and Personal Finance

The Unofficial Guide to Beating Debt
ISBN: 0-02-863337-7

The Unofficial Guide to Investing
ISBN: 0-02-862458-0

The Unofficial Guide to Investing in Mutual Funds
ISBN: 0-02-862920-5

The Unofficial Guide to Managing Your Personal Finances
ISBN: 0-02-862921-3

The Unofficial Guide to Marketing Your Business Online
ISBN: 0-7645-6268-1

About the Author

Basil Nestor leads a double-life as an author and television producer.

He began his career as a journalist for affiliates of CBS and NBC. Freelance assignments for CNN, PBS, and other networks soon followed. As an independent producer, Basil made the award-winning documentary *Casinos in the Community,* a history of gaming in Atlantic City. He also produced *Riverboat,* a powerful chronicle that examines how gaming is changing the Midwest.

Basil's inside knowledge about casinos comes from television projects with companies like Players Casinos, Resorts and The Griffin Group. Audiences across the country have enjoyed his whimsical commercials featuring Merv Griffin.

Meanwhile, in his other life, Basil writes for magazines and authors books. His career includes stints as a contributing writer to *Video Review, Video Magazine, Video Pro* and other publications. Basil's most recent book, *Judy Garland—A Life in Pictures,* is a revealing account of the mercurial life of Hollywood's beloved singer and actress.

This book for the *Unofficial Guides* is allowing Basil to finally "get his life together." Gaming and writing are in one project.